nil me poenitet

DUGDALL

ODNB

ex libris

Jan Broadway Ph. D

OXFORD ENGLISH MONOGRAPHS

The Antiquary

John Aubrey's Historical Scholarship

KELSEY JACKSON WILLIAMS

OXFORD
UNIVERSITY PRESS

OXFORD
UNIVERSITY PRESS

Great Clarendon Street, Oxford, OX2 6DP,
United Kingdom

Oxford University Press is a department of the University of Oxford.
It furthers the University's objective of excellence in research, scholarship,
and education by publishing worldwide. Oxford is a registered trade mark of
Oxford University Press in the UK and in certain other countries

© Kelsey Jackson Williams 2016

The moral rights of the author have been asserted

First Edition published in 2016

Impression: 1

Published in the United States of America by Oxford University Press
198 Madison Avenue, New York, NY 10016, United States of America

British Library Cataloguing in Publication Data
Data available

Library of Congress Control Number: 2015959812

ISBN 978–0–19–878429–6

Printed in Great Britain by
Clays Ltd, St Ives plc

Acknowledgements

Aubrey took great pleasure in acknowledging the many debts he owed to others, with phrases such as 'this I had from' this or that friend often recurring in his manuscripts. In the same spirit, I take real satisfaction in being able to acknowledge here the many helps and kindnesses I have met with in the six years of this book's gestation.

When the ideas for this project first began to germinate during an MSt at the University of Oxford, I was fortunate to be supported by the Clarendon Fund. Subsequently a studentship from the Mellon Foundation through the Cultures of Knowledge project allowed me to continue forward to the DPhil and a thesis addressing Aubrey and his antiquarianism. Finally, the British Academy generously awarded me a Postdoctoral Fellowship at the University of St Andrews as this book was being finished.

Throughout the course of this project I have been met with unfailing kindness, courtesy, and assistance far beyond the line of duty from the staff of the Bodleian Library, British Library, All Souls, Balliol, and Worcester College libraries, and Wiltshire Archaeological and Natural History Society Library. The Bodleian Libraries, University of Oxford, also kindly allowed the reproduction of several images from Aubrey's manuscripts. I am especially grateful to Colin Harris, Russell Edwards, and all those who worked in Duke Humfrey's Library and the interim special collections reading room in the Radcliffe Science Library for making my research in Oxford always a pleasure and often a joy.

This book began life as a doctoral thesis and I am indebted to my supervisor, Rhodri Lewis, for his support, his generosity, and his composition of far too many letters of reference, as well as for his incisive commentary and sound advice throughout the doctorate. My examiners, Noel Malcolm and Nigel Smith, were meticulous, thoughtful, and polymathic; I hope their wise suggestions for the evolution of this project from thesis to book are reflected in the following pages. During the writing of the thesis and beyond, William Poole was an invaluable mentor and friend, sharing his immense erudition and boundless enthusiasm for the continent of early modern learning with a younger scholar only beginning to explore its foreshores.

Mordechai Feingold, Anthony Ossa-Richardson, and Thomas Roebuck all read and commented upon portions of this work at various stages, while

Kate Bennett, William Poole, and Amy Wallace read the final manuscript with wonderful attention to detail. I am immensely grateful to all of them for spotting errors, correcting typos, challenging my thinking, and improving this book. Conversations with Michael Hunter and Peter Davidson changed my thinking about Aubrey at crucial stages. For support during and beyond the thesis I am deeply indebted to Paulina Kewes, who has also looked on with a friendly eagle eye as it progressed from idea to reality. The final few months of the book's composition were made far easier and more rewarding by the supportive and collegial environment provided by my new colleagues in the School of History at St Andrews.

I am very grateful to the Oxford English Monographs Committee for recommending a long and inward-looking thesis for publication and to the two anonymous reviewers commissioned by Oxford University Press whose advice was invaluable in turning that thesis into a rather shorter and more accessible book. Rachel Platt guided the book through the initial stages of the editorial process and Eleanor Collins saw it through to its end. I am grateful to both for their hard work and support.

My parents, Kenneth and Gloria Williams, have provided constant love and support throughout the years in which I was engaged with Aubrey. Their presence has always made it easier. In the latter part of the project, my parents-in-law, Vic and Sue Hollis, offered laughter, companionship, and a home away from home with unstinting generosity. Finally, these pages could never have been written without Dawn Hollis. At every turn she provided proofreading, thoughtful and challenging commentary, and fresh ideas, while always being there on the other side of our respective projects at the end of a long day. She has read these pages more times than anyone should have to endure, but most of all I am grateful to her for her love, which has made all the difference.

Crail, Fife
October 2015

Table of Contents

List of Figures

Abbreviations

For ease of reference, the following abbreviations and short titles are used throughout.

Aubrey, 'Hobbes'	John Aubrey. 'The Life of Mr. Thomas Hobbes, of Malmesburie', in *'Brief Lives', Chiefly of Contemporaries, Set Down by John Aubrey, Between the Years 1669 & 1696*, 2 vols., ed. Andrew Clark. Oxford: Clarendon Press, 1898. i. 321–403.
Aubrey, *Lives*	John Aubrey. *Brief Lives with an Apparatus for the Lives of our English Mathematical Writers*, 2 vols., ed. Kate Bennett. Oxford: Oxford University Press, 2015.
Aubrey, *Monumenta*	John Aubrey. *Monumenta Britannica, or, a Miscellany of British Antiquities*, 2 vols., ed. John Fowles and Rodney Legg. Sherborne, Dorset: Dorset Publishing Co., 1980–2.
Aubrey, *Remaines*	John Aubrey. *Remaines of Gentilisme and Judaisme*, ed. James Britten. London: Published for the Folk-Lore Society by W. Satchell, Peyton, and Co., 1881.
Aubrey, *Three Prose Works*	John Aubrey. *Three Prose Works: Miscellanies, Remaines of Gentilisme and Judaisme, Observations*, ed. John Buchanan-Brown. Fontwell, Sussex: Centaur Press, 1972.
BL	British Library, London.
Bodleian	Bodleian Library, Oxford.
Hunter, *Aubrey*	Michael Hunter. *John Aubrey and the Realm of Learning*. London: Duckworth, 1975.
ODNB	*Oxford Dictionary of National Biography*, 60 vols., ed. H. C. G. Matthew and Brian Harrison. Oxford: Oxford University Press, 2004.
OED	*Oxford English Dictionary*, 2nd edn., 20 vols., ed. J. A. Simpson and E. S. C. Weiner. Oxford: Clarendon Press, 1989.
Poole, *Aubrey*	William Poole. *John Aubrey and the Advancement of Learning*. Oxford: Bodleian Library, 2010.
Powell, *Aubrey*	Anthony Powell. *John Aubrey and His Friends*, new and rev. edn. London: Heinemann, 1963.

Transcription and Dating Conventions

Aubrey's manuscripts present certain challenges for the would-be transcriber. He regularly abbreviated, underlined, bracketed, deleted, inserted, and hesitated between words. I have attempted to render this as readable as possible without compromising the meaning of the original. Thus, deletions and insertions are not noticed except where they significantly alter the meaning of the text, contractions have been expanded, and superscript material has been brought into the line without comment except where Aubrey has hesitated between two words (there the word above the line is given \thus/). All underlining is Aubrey's. In addition, Aubrey habitually used square brackets where we would prefer parentheses. To avoid confusion and to distinguish Aubrey's parenthetical comments from editorial insertions, his square brackets have been represented by parentheses; the square brackets which remain are editorial.

All dates are given in the Julian Calendar, as they appear in the original sources. However, where a date falls after the New Style new year (1 January) but before the Old Style (25 March) I have given the year as it would appear in the New Style. For example, 20 February 1692/93 would be given as 20 February 1693, not 1692.

Introduction

The winter of 1648 was cold. After a long, wet summer—the worst in forty years—famine had spread across Scotland and Ireland. Once again the Thames froze as far as London Bridge.[1] Amidst the ice and snow, the Royalist newsbook *Mercurius Pragmaticus* lamented that Christmas had been 'turn'd into good Friday' and Britain enjoyed an uneasy pause between Pride's Purge in November and the trial of Charles I at the end of January.[2] Francis Seymour, Baron Seymour of Trowbridge, kept a quiet Christmas at home that year. A moderate Royalist, he had spent much of the decade writing private meditations on the merits of patience and celebrated Christmas 1648 at his country home in Marlborough, Wiltshire.[3] In the shadow of 'the Mount', Marlborough's ruined Norman castle, Seymour's house was a modest Jacobean building which he had built only two decades earlier; an appropriately inconspicuous dwelling place for a man living away from the public eye.[4] With him that Christmas was his son, the Honourable Charles Seymour, then aged twenty-seven. Charles had attended one meeting of the Royalist Sequestration Committee in 1642, but never supplied the royal cause with money or took arms against Parliament. In 1648 he, like his father, was lying low and waiting for the storm to pass.[5]

---

[1] Geoffrey Parker, *Global Crisis: War, Climate Change and Catastrophe in the Seventeenth Century* (New Haven, CT, 2013), 5–6.

[2] *Mercurius Pragmaticus* 39 (19–26 December 1648): sig. Eeer, and for the quotation's context see Bernard Capp, *England's Culture Wars: Puritan Reformation and its Enemies in the Interregnum, 1649–1660* (Oxford, 2012), 20.

[3] Andrew Thrush, ed., *The History of Parliament: The House of Commons, 1604–1629*, 6 vols. (Cambridge, 2010), vi. 283–92; *ODNB, s.n.*; George E. Cokayne, *The Complete Peerage of England, Scotland, Ireland, Great Britain and the United Kingdom*, 13 vols. in 14, ed. Vicary Gibbs et al. (London, 1910–98), xi. 640–1.

[4] D. A. Crowley, ed., *Victoria County History of Wiltshire*, vol. 12: *Ramsbury Hundred, Selkley Hundred, Borough of Marlborough* (Oxford, 1983), 160–84.

[5] Basil Duke Henning, *The History of Parliament: The House of Commons, 1660–1690*, 3 vols. (London, 1983), iii. 411; Cokayne, *Complete Peerage*, xi. 641–2.

Subdued though it may have been, Christmas in Marlborough was more than just a family affair. Charles had invited his close friend, a young north Wiltshire squire named John Aubrey, to join them.[6] Aubrey was a few years younger than Charles, not quite twenty-three, and was fleeing difficult times at home. His education had already been interrupted once by the course of the Civil Wars and, after returning to Trinity College, Oxford, in November 1646 he had 'enjoyed the greatest felicity' of his life there for only two years before being called home on Christmas Eve to the bedside of his dying father.[7] Relations between the young man and his family had always been strained and it is unclear what their reaction was to the prospective heir leaving Richard Aubrey's deathbed for a house party only a few days after his return home.

The day after Twelfth Night, Charles Seymour met another neighbouring landowner, Sir William Button, to hunt. Button had supported the king, had been raided by parliamentary troops twice, and was, at the time, suffering under a crippling fine as a delinquent, but evidently still lived in sufficient style to keep a pack of hounds. They met at the Grey Wethers on Fyfield Down that 6 January 1649.[8] The young Aubrey joined them and, writing decades later, still vividly remembered the scene. 'These Downes', he wrote, 'looke as if they were sowen with great Stones, very thick, and in a dusky evening, they looke like a flock of Sheep: from whence it takes it's [*sic*] name, one might fancy it to have been the Scene, where the Giants fought with huge stones against the Gods.'[9]

The unfortunate fox was flushed and the course of the chase led men and dogs west for two miles until they came to the hamlet of Avebury. Seymour and Button, familiar with the local landscape, took no notice of its unusual situation. Aubrey's mind, however, was already turning on problems of natural history and natural philosophy and he could not help but be 'wonderfully surprized at the sight of those vast stones: of which I had never heard before': the Stone Age megaliths which dominated, and continue to dominate, the village. 'I left my Company a while', he recalled, 'entertaining my selfe with a more delightfull indagation' of the site.[10] There he saw 'in the Inclosures some segments of rude circles made with these stones, whence I concluded they had been in the old time complete'.[11] His mental reconstruction of Avebury's appearance echoed

---

[6] The circumstantial details of this Christmas gathering are derived from Aubrey's later account at Aubrey, *Monumenta*, i. 17–19.

[7] Aubrey, *Lives*, i. 433

[8] Thrush, *History of Parliament, 1604–1629*, iii. 372–3.

[9] Aubrey, *Monumenta*, i. 18.

[10] 'Indagation', a searching out or investigation (*OED, s.v.*).

[11] Aubrey, *Monumenta*, i. 18.

an observation by the philosopher Meric Casaubon which Aubrey would later copy into his notebooks. For Casaubon, one of the remarkable powers of antiquaries was the way in which 'visible superviving evidences of antiquitie represent unto their minds former times, with as strong an impression, as if they were actually present, and in sight'.[12] It was Aubrey's first foray into what was to become a familiar way of seeing.

Before Aubrey had time to completely lose himself in the stones, he was 'cheered by the cry of the Hounds' and, like any good huntsman, 'over-tooke the company, and went with them to Kynnet, where was a good Hunting dinner provided'.[13] It would be another five years before he began noting down, during another country house visit, 'philosophicall and antiquarian remarques' in a pocket notebook he had bought for that purpose, but already—in his fascination with the stones and in his attempt to reason out their original appearance—the young John Aubrey was engaging in an act of antiquarianism, the early modern study of, amongst many other things, the ancient physical past.[14]

Antiquarianism has traditionally been understood to be one of the central disciplines of early modern historical enquiry.[15] But 'antiquarianism' was

[12] Aubrey, *Monumenta*, i. 259, quoting Meric Casaubon, *A Treatise of Use and Custome* (London, 1638), 97–8. Casaubon and perhaps Aubrey were echoing a much earlier description of the power of the historical imagination in Cicero's *De Finibus* (V.i.2) where Marcus Piso is made to say that 'one's emotions are more strongly aroused by seeing the places that tradition records to have been the favourite resort of men of note in former days . . . even the site of our senate-house at home . . . used to call up to me thoughts of Scipio, Cato, Laelius, and chief of all, my grandfather, such powers of suggestion do places possess'.

[13] Aubrey, *Monumenta*, i. 19.

[14] Aubrey, *Lives*, i. 434. This was in 1654 at Llantrithyd, Glamorganshire, the home of his cousin Sir John Aubrey, for whom see George E. Cokayne, *Complete Baronetage*, 6 vols. (Exeter, 1900–9), iii. 93–4.

[15] The modern study of antiquarianism was inaugurated by Arnaldo Momigliano, 'Ancient History and the Antiquarian', *Journal of the Warburg and Courtauld Institutes* 13 (1950): 285–315. The narrative he developed there was elaborated in 'Gibbon's Contribution to Historical Method', *Historia* 2 (1954): 450–63, and 'The Rise of Antiquarian Research', in *Classical Foundations of Modern Historiography* (Berkeley, CA, 1990), 54–79. Momigliano's holistic approach to antiquarianism has been continued and developed by Peter N. Miller, first in *Peiresc's Europe: Learning and Virtue in the Seventeenth Century* (New Haven, CT, and London, 2000) and subsequently in the edited volumes *Momigliano and Antiquarianism: Foundations of the Modern Cultural Sciences* (Toronto, 2007) and *Antiquarianism and Intellectual Life in Europe and China, 1500–1800*, ed. Miller and François Louis (Ann Arbor, MI, 2012). Major contributions from an art historical angle include the two monographs by Ingo Herklotz, *Cassiano Dal Pozzo und die Archäologie des 17. Jahrhunderts* (Munich, 1999) and *La Roma degli antiquari: cultura e erudizione tra Cinquecento e Settecento* (Rome, 2012), while its archaeological aspects have received attention in Alain Schnapp, *The Discovery of the Past*, trans. Ian Kinnes and Gillian Varndell (London, 1996). Parallel to this tradition there have been a series of works focusing on antiquarianism and its cognate disciplines in the English-speaking world, beginning with D. C. Douglas, *English Scholars*, 2nd edn. (London, 1951) and Stuart

not a concept familiar to early modern scholars. The term is first recorded in English in 1761 and there are no earlier equivalents in any other European language.[16] Instead, the category with which the early moderns were familiar was not the discipline *antiquarianism* but the person *antiquary*. 'Antiquary', however, was a fluid signifier which changed dramatically over the course of the early modern period. To understand why Aubrey's fascination with Avebury could define him as an antiquary, it is necessary to go back two centuries earlier and follow the evolution of the word through the thorny paths of humanist erudition.

Antiquary, *antiquario*, *antiquaire*, and similar cognates all stemmed from the Latin *antiquarius*. This was an unusual word, present in only a handful of classical texts, and had originally had connotations of one who intentionally used or misused archaic words and language. At the outset of its journey through the early modern world, *antiquarius* had no association with the types of non-textual physical artefacts—coins, monuments, archaeological sites—whose study is usually understood to characterize the antiquary. Many early definitions of *antiquarius* or its vernacular equivalents reflect this sense. Antonio de Nebrija in 1513 glossed *antiquarius* as a 'lover of antiquities', while Robert Estienne in 1531 described an antiquary as one 'who loves to use antiquated words', and Andrea Alciati in 1523 noted that '*antiquarius* means one who expounds on ancient words'.[17] The opponent of Erasmus, Étienne Dolet, elaborated on this

---

Piggott's *Ruins in a Landscape: Essays in Antiquarianism* (Edinburgh, 1976) and *Ancient Britons and the Antiquarian Imagination: Ideas from the Renaissance to the Regency* (London, 1989). More recent contributions to this school of thought include Stanley G. Mendyk, *'Speculum Britanniae': Regional Study, Antiquarianism, and Science in Britain to 1700* (Toronto and London, 1989); Graham Parry, *The Trophies of Time: English Antiquarians in the Seventeenth Century* (Oxford, 1995); Rosemary Sweet, *Antiquaries: The Discovery of the Past in Eighteenth-Century Britain* (London, 2004); Jan Broadway, *'No Historie so meete': Gentry Culture and the Development of Local History in Elizabethan and Early Stuart England* (Manchester, 2006); Angus Vine, *In Defiance of Time: Antiquarian Writing in Early Modern England* (Oxford, 2010). Antiquarianism as one possible form of historical erudition has also been discussed by Anthony Grafton in *What Was History? The Art of History in Early Modern Europe* (Cambridge, 2007) and *The Footnote: A Curious History* (Cambridge, MA, 1999), 148–89, and by Daniel Woolf in *The Social Circulation of the Past: English Historical Culture, 1500–1730* (Oxford, 2003).

[16] Its first known usage in English is in a letter from William Warburton to Richard Hurd dated March 1761: '[a]ntiquarianism is, indeed, to true letters what specious funguses are to the oak; which never shoot out and flourish, till all the vigour and virtue of that monarch of the grove be effete and near exhausted' (William Warburton, *Letters from a Late Eminent Prelate to One of His Friends* [Kidderminster, 1793?], 264–5).

[17] Antonio de Nebrija, *Relectio nona de accentu latino aut latinitate donato quam habuit Salma[n]tice* (Seville, 1513), fol. XII ('el amador de las antiguedades'); Robert Estienne, *Dictionarium, seu Latinae linguae thesaurus* (Paris, 1531), not paginated ('qui est curieux de user de mots anciens'); Andrea Alciati, *Paradoxorum ad Pratum libri VI* (Basel, 1523), 217 ('antiquarius enim significat eum qui antiqua verba interpretatur').

definition in his compendious *Commentarii linguae Latinae* of 1536.[18] Recent examples of *antiquarii*, he wrote, were Filippo Beroaldo, Giovan Battista Pio, Caelius Rhodiginus, and Raffaello Maffei, scholars active at the turn of the sixteenth century who would all now be considered more philologists than antiquaries.[19] Sallust among the ancients and Guillaume Budé amongst the moderns were other examples.[20]

Alongside the definition mapped by Dolet, however, another meaning had been growing. As early as 1464 the Italian humanist Felice Feliciano (1433–1479) could describe himself as an *antiquarius* when writing of his studies of Roman monuments and inscriptions.[21] This meaning came from a redefinition of *antiquarius* as a student of *antiquitates*, echoing works of classical antiquarianism, particularly Varro's monumental *Antiquitates rerum humanarum et divinarum libri XLI*. Building upon seminal archaeological and philological studies by early figures including Petrarch, Cyriac of Ancona, and Poggio Bracciolini, Italian scholars of the fifteenth century such as Flavio Biondo and Angelo Poliziano developed the study of *antiquitates* into a scholarly province in its own right, although the term *antiquarius* was not yet systematically applied to its practitioners.[22] By Dolet's generation, John Leland in England could style himself '*antiquarius*' on the basis of his chorographical peregrination of England—a method of scholarly research he had borrowed from Biondo—without fear of misinterpretation.[23] In the 1578 *Thesaurus linguae Romanae et Britannicae* the two definitions co-existed, with *antiquarius* glossed as both 'men curious in using olde and auncient words' and 'a searcher of antiquities, or reader of olde workes'.[24] By 1583 the publisher of Johannes Rosinus's *Romanarum antiquitatum libri decem* could express the hope

---

[18] Étienne Dolet, *Commentariorum linguae Latinae tomus primus* (Lyons, 1536), col. 1342.

[19] Maffei's *Commentariorum rerum urbanorum libri XXXVIII* (Rome, 1506) is a recognizably antiquarian work, however.

[20] Budé, like the other scholars cited by Dolet, was primarily interested in the study and interpretation of texts, but his *De asse et partibus* (Paris, 1516) was a pioneering study of ancient numismatics. It is unclear, however, whether Dolet intended to highlight this aspect of his work.

[21] Momigliano, *Foundations*, 71. For an example of 'Felicianus Antiquarius' see Paul Oskar Kristeller, ed., *Iter Italicum: A Finding List of Uncatalogued or Incompletely Catalogued Humanistic Manuscripts of the Renaissance in Italian and Other Libraries*, 6 vols. (London, 1963–96), i/1. 34.

[22] Peter N. Miller, 'Major Trends in European Antiquarianism, Petrarch to Peiresc', in *The Oxford History of Historical Writing*, vol. 3: *1400–1800*, ed. Jose Rabasa et al. (Oxford, 2012).

[23] John Leland, *The Laboryouse Journey [and] Serche of Johan Leylande, for Englandes Antiquitees* (London, 1549), sig. Fv.

[24] *Thesaurus linguae Romanae & Britannicae tam accurate congestus* (London, 1578), not paginated.

that the study of antiquity would become an *ars* in its own right, reifying as a discipline the practices of the *antiquarii*.[25]

In the early seventeenth century, scholars including Pirro Ligorio, Onufrio Panvinio, Cassiano dal Pozzo, and Nicolas-Claude Fabri de Peiresc came to focus on non-textual images and objects as sources in and of themselves.[26] The aftermath of this increasing privileging of visual as well as textual evidence saw the sixteenth century's secondary definition of 'antiquary'—a person 'studious to know ancient things, one that searcheth out antiquities, as of Coins, Monuments, Evidences, or old words' in the 1664 definition of Francis Gouldman—become the dominant one.[27] The 'old words' remained, however, as did an uncertainty concerning the relationship of the antiquary's ambiguously defined scholarship to its sibling disciplines of history and philology. Francis Bacon and Gerardus Joannes Vossius both distinguished between 'Perfect Histories' or *historia justa* and the study of antiquities, which they saw as 'history defaced or some remnants of history which have casually escaped the shipwreck of time'.[28] Concerns about the antiquary's relationship to philology were articulated in a less confrontational manner and instead revealed themselves in ambiguities of terminology: even the Greek and Middle English philologist Thomas Gale could be described as a 'great antiquary'.[29] Throughout much of the seventeenth century, distinctions between the antiquary, the historian, and the philologist remained porous and uncertain, a by-product of the inherent ambiguity of the antiquary's discipline and scope.

By the end of the century, however, the province of the antiquary was subjected to increasing definition and circumscription as both practitioners and onlookers carved out a tract of learning which stood midway between history and philology. The physical objects of the antiquary's study were demarcated by scholars such as Jacques Spon, who, in 1685, distinguished the appropriate objects of the antiquary's investigation as coins, inscriptions, architecture, statues, gems, bas reliefs, manuscripts, and technology.[30] For antiquaries studying the classical world, at least, a recognizable discipline with clear-cut boundaries was coming into being, a

---

[25] Miller, 'Major Trends', 255, referring to Johannes Rosinus, *Romanarum antiquitatum libri decem* (Lyons, 1585), sig.)(5r.

[26] Miller, 'Major Trends', 256.

[27] Francis Gouldman, *A Copious Dictionary in Three Parts* (London, 1664), *s.v.*

[28] Momigliano, 'Ancient History', 292; *Foundations*, 71. See also Grafton, *What Was History?*, 231–6.

[29] Francis Drake, *Eboracum, or, the History and Antiquities of the City of York* (London, 1736), 25.

[30] Jacques Spon, *Miscellanea eruditae antiquitatis* (Lyons, 1685), sig. ã3r–v.

discipline which would ultimately contribute to Wolfian *Altertumswissenschaft* at the end of the following century.[31]

At the same time that classical antiquaries were defining their subjects of study with ever greater precision, antiquarian techniques were being deployed to reshape understandings of the ancient and medieval history of northern Europe. Scholars as diverse as George Hickes in England, Jean-Jacques Chifflet in France, Ole Worm in Denmark, and Olof Rudbeck in Sweden used the tools forged by earlier generations of predominantly classically focused antiquaries to construct interpretations of the histories of non-classical civilizations.[32] These scholars, like their predecessors, engaged with the full range of antiquarian subjects, from manuscripts, at the philological end of the spectrum, through the mixed media of coins and inscriptions, to a variety of artefacts, ruins, and sites at the archaeological end of antiquarian research. While engaged in an ongoing dialogue with antiquaries studying the classical world, these scholars built a more methodologically expansive toolbox in their pursuit of the non-classical past, liberally helping themselves to the practices not only of historians and philologists, but of natural philosophers and physicians.[33] In Aubrey's lifetime, a scholar could be described as an antiquary as a result of activities as diverse as editing saints' lives and excavating prehistoric burial mounds, and could explain his findings with theoretical tools drawn from areas as widely separated as geology and comparative religion.

Is it possible to define an antiquarian text, given the ambiguity and expansiveness of this field of study? Arnaldo Momigliano's classic 1950 definition stressed the systematic, as opposed to chronological, nature of the antiquarian work; he imagined a classic antiquarian text as being akin to a catalogue of coins, systematic and comprehensive, and contrasted that with the chronological progression of a Livy or a Tacitus. Narrative history, which Momigliano implicitly defined as the normative state of historical scholarship, relied upon this chronological succession of events

[31] For these later developments see Friedrich August Wolf, *Prolegomena to Homer*, trans. and ed. Anthony Grafton, Glenn W. Most, and James E. G. Zetzel (Princeton, NJ, 1985); Anthony Grafton, 'Prolegomena to Friedrich August Wolf', *Journal of the Warburg and Courtauld Institutes* 44 (1981): 101–29 (reprinted in *Defenders of the Text: The Traditions of Scholarship in an Age of Science* [Cambridge, MA, 1991], 214–46); Suzanne Marchand, *Down from Olympus: Archaeology and Philhellenism in Germany, 1750–1970* (Princeton, NJ, 1996), chs. 1–2.

[32] Peter Burke, 'Images as Evidence in Seventeenth-Century Europe', *Journal of the History of Ideas* 64 (2003): 273–96; Schnapp, *Discovery*, ch. 3.

[33] Examples of antiquaries drawing upon the disciplinary tools of science and medicine can be found in Gunnar Eriksson, *The Atlantic Vision: Olaus Rudbeck and Baroque Science* (Canton, MA, 1994) and Craig Ashley Hansson, *The English Virtuoso: Art, Medicine and Antiquarianism in the Age of Empiricism* (Chicago and London, 2009).

to shape its structure, while antiquarian writing was 'static' by virtue of its systematic nature. A corollary of this was that antiquarian writing was descriptive rather than explanatory.[34] This interpretation has informed much modern scholarship on antiquarianism but is limited in its explanatory power. Many antiquarian works, including whole subgenres such as *historia literaria*, were chronological in structure, classic examples being Jean Foy-Vaillant's 1681 reconstruction of the history of the Seleucid Empire upon numismatic and epigraphic evidence and Anthony Wood's 1691 biobibliography of Oxford-educated writers and bishops.[35] Likewise, while many antiquarian texts were primarily descriptive insofar as they represented catalogues or collections of previously inaccessible data, whether in the form of coins, charters, genealogies, or inscriptions, other antiquarian works focused on the resolution of a particular historical question, for example the contested meaning of an inscription and its larger significance, as in the case of late seventeenth-century Scottish controversies over the so-called 'Macduff's Cross'; such texts were inevitably explanatory.[36] Rather than seeking to define antiquarianism by these limiting, if not actively pejorative, comparisons with 'proper' history, it would be more accurate to define it as the whole length and breadth of historical scholarship, as understood today, which fell outside the rubric of classical narrative history, together with vast tracts which would later be claimed by philology, languages, and the social sciences.[37] Antiquaries were scholars of the past in the broadest possible sense and brought with them an impressive range of interests and techniques, some recovered from the scholarly traditions of the ancient world, others invented by its early modern successors.

In England this tradition flourished in the century following the first publication of William Camden's paradigmatic *Britannia* (1586), a

---

[34] Momigliano, 'Ancient History', 285–6; *Foundations*, 61.

[35] Jean Foy-Vaillant, *Seleucidarum imperium, sive historia regum Syriae* (Paris, 1681); Anthony Wood, *Athenae Oxonienses*, 2 vols. (London, 1691–2). For the wider contexts of *historia literaria* see Kelsey Jackson Williams, 'Canon before Canon, Literature before Literature: Thomas Pope Blount and the Scope of Early Modern Learning', *Huntington Library Quarterly* 77 (2014): 177–99. Blount, in his *Censura celebriorum authorum*, explicitly rejected a systematic structure in favour of a chronological one as the latter would better help the reader observe the 'flowing to and fro of learning' (Thomas Pope Blount, *Censura celebriorum authorum* [London, 1690], sig. av, and cf. Jackson Williams, 'Canon before Canon', 184).

[36] See, for example, James Cunningham, *An Essay upon the Inscription of Macduff's Cross in Fyfe* (Edinburgh, 1678).

[37] For a comparable 'wide view' of antiquarianism see Peter Miller's definition of it as the study of 'the entire lived culture of a people or a period' ('Major Trends', 244). Antiquarianism, Miller stresses, 'intersects with natural history, medicine, and astronomy, as well as oriental languages and literature' ('Major Trends', 245).

chorography of the British Isles.[38] Imitators of Camden's particular brand of scholarship produced dozens of chorographically structured county and local antiquarian studies, some of the best known of which, including William Dugdale's *Antiquities of Warwickshire* (1656) and *Monasticon Anglicanum* (1655–73), would define the shape of much British antiquarian scholarship throughout the seventeenth and eighteenth centuries.[39] The *Monasticon* was also one of the more spectacular representatives of a post-Reformation tradition of ecclesiastical antiquarianism which mapped the remnants of England's monasteries and other religious centres, at times with a polemical edge.[40] Meanwhile, the Laudian Church's promotion of oriental studies led to numerous antiquarian works explicating aspects of the Hebrew and Arabic worlds, often following in the footsteps of the Huguenot scholar Samuel Bochart, whose *Geographia sacra* (1646) informed many syncretist attempts at reconciling ancient Britain with a postdiluvian, Biblical worldview.[41] Nor did the megalithic structures strewn across the British landscape escape attention. As early as 1624 Edmund Bolton had questioned the traditional medieval legends explaining Stonehenge, and by the middle of the century a vigorous scholarly debate had arisen which attempted to site Britain's prehistoric monuments within a larger European ancient history.[42]

John Aubrey's first fascination with Avebury belongs to this tradition and he himself was a characteristic practitioner of it. Like many English antiquaries, he came from minor gentry stock, having been born in 1626 at Easton Pierse (now Easton Piercy), a small estate in north Wiltshire. After an isolated, rural childhood, beset with frequent illness, he was sent to the public school at Blandford St Mary, Dorset, though he later credited a neighbouring clergyman, Theophilus Wodenote, with more influence on his education than that provided by any formal schooling. In

[38] For Camden and his legacy see especially Wyman H. Herendeen, *William Camden: A Life in Context* (Woodbridge, 2007); F. J. Levy, 'The Making of Camden's *Britannia*', *Bibliothèque d'Humanisme et Renaissance* 26 (1964): 70–97; Mendyk, *Speculum*, 49–55; Parry, *Trophies of Time*, 1–48; William Rockett, 'Historical Topography and British History in Camden's *Britannia*', *Renaissance and Reformation*, N.S. 14 (1990): 71–80; Vine, *In Defiance of Time*, 80–108.

[39] Jan Broadway, *William Dugdale and the Significance of County History in Early Stuart England* (Stratford-upon-Avon, 1999) and *'No Historie so meete'* as well as Mendyk, *Speculum, passim*, Parry, *Trophies of Time*, 217–48, and Woolf, *Social Circulation*, ch. 5.

[40] See Alexandra Walsham, *The Reformation of the Landscape* (Oxford, 2011), esp. ch. 7, and Margaret Aston, 'English Ruins and English History: The Dissolution and the Sense of the Past', *Journal of the Warburg and Courtauld Institutes* 36 (1973): 231–55.

[41] G. J. Toomer, *Eastern Wisedome and Learning: The Study of Arabic in Seventeenth-Century England* (Oxford, 1996); Zur Shalev, *Sacred Words and Worlds: Geography, Religion, and Scholarship, 1550–1700* (Leiden, 2011); Parry, *Trophies of Time*, 308–30.

[42] See Chapter 1.

1641 he matriculated at Trinity College, Oxford, but the growing unrest across England meant that his university education was both patchy and of brief duration. 'With much adoe' he convinced his father to let him enter the Middle Temple in London in April 1646 and, although he never made any formal progress towards a legal career, he maintained an association with that society for at least the next ten years. That same summer he became acquainted with 'many of the kings party' and subsequently returned to Trinity, before being summoned home, as we have seen at the beginning of this Introduction, by his dying father at the end of 1648.[43]

This unsettled youth gave way to an early manhood of diverse and vigorous scholarship. Aubrey's father died in 1652, leaving him what would have been a comfortable estate had it not come already burdened with debt, and the newly independent Aubrey divided his time between Oxford and London, corresponding with university friends like the natural philosophers John Lydall and Francis Potter, making the acquaintance of Samuel Hartlib the intelligencer, and leading expeditions, together with his friends John Hoskins and Stafford Tyndale, to see such novelties as an engine for weaving stockings.[44] It was in the vibrant scientific atmosphere of Commonwealth London that Aubrey also began his first major work, a *Naturall Historie of Wiltshire*, for which he began to collect materials as early as 1656.[45] Towards the end of the decade he fell in with the radical political theorist James Harrington, buying a copy of his *Oceana* in 1658, and attending the meetings of his 'Rota Club' in 1659–60, but, as Aubrey later regretfully noted, 'upon generall Monke's comeing-in'—that is, the appearance of George Monck, later 1st Duke of Albemarle, and his army in London in February 1660, a turning point which led on to the restoration of Charles II later that year—'all these aierie models vanished'.[46]

In the winter of 1662–3 Aubrey, still only a marginal figure in London learned circles, was proposed and admitted to the Royal Society.[47] Thereafter he occupied a distinctive role in the nascent organization, participating in meetings, preserving and encouraging ideas, seeking out the papers of deceased members before they were 'used to line pies', and orchestrating the group that attempted to revive and develop John Wilkins's scheme for

---

[43] For Aubrey's career to 1663 see Kelsey Jackson Williams, 'Training the Virtuoso: John Aubrey's Education and Early Life', *The Seventeenth Century* 27 (2012): 157–82.

[44] Jackson Williams, 'Training the Virtuoso', 161–8.

[45] Hunter, *Aubrey*, 99–103.

[46] Jackson Williams, 'Training the Virtuoso', 169–70.

[47] Thomas Birch, *The History of the Royal Society of London for Improving of Natural Knowledge* ..., 4 vols. (London, 1756–7), i. 166, 172, 179.

a universal language.[48] At the same time, he became increasingly interested in antiquarian subjects. Together with several other members of the Wiltshire landed gentry, he developed a plan for a history of the county in 1660 and in the summer of 1667, on a visit to Oxford, he made the acquaintance of his future collaborator Anthony Wood.[49] Wood, writing much later, recalled with characteristic acerbity how Aubrey, 'then in a sparkish garb ... flung out ... all reckonings', spending lavishly at the pub and generally behaving like a high-living Restoration squire, a portrait which accords well with the image Aubrey projected during this period of being both a gentleman scholar and a patron of the scholarship of others.

This was a front only. His estates continued to be embroiled in lawsuits and the untimely death of his heiress fiancée, Katherine Ryves, in 1657 further complicated his financial situation.[50] By 1661–2 Aubrey was forced to sell his outlying lands in Herefordshire, while a breach of promise suit filed by his second fiancée, Joan Sumner, ultimately led to his complete insolvency in 1671.[51] The house and lands at Easton Pierse were sold and he was left with only crippling debt and a farm at Broad Chalke in southern Wiltshire, apparently the residence of his much younger brother William, with whom he was on increasingly bad terms.[52]

Despite this complete reversal of fortune, which led him in the dark months of 1671–2 to assume a false name and give out misleading accounts of his whereabouts to throw bailiffs off the scent, Aubrey later came to feel that he had 'never quiett, nor anything of happinesse till divested of all' and had been lucky to escape the cares of lawsuits and land

[48] Kate Bennett, 'John Aubrey, Hint-Keeper: Life-Writing and the Encouragement of Natural Philosophy in the pre-Newtonian Seventeenth Century', *The Seventeenth Century* 22 (2007): 358–80; Rhodri Lewis, 'The Efforts of the Aubrey Correspondence Group to Revise John Wilkins's *Essay* (1668) and their Context', *Historiographia Linguistica* 28 (2001): 333–66, and *Language, Mind and Nature: Artificial Languages in England from Bacon to Locke* (Cambridge, 2007), 188–221.

[49] Aubrey described the inception of the Wiltshire project at 'a meeting of Gentlemen at the Devises for choosing of knights of the Shire' in Bodleian MS Aubrey 3, fol. 10r. Wood, with the benefit of hindsight, recalled his first meeting with Aubrey on 31 August 1667 in Anthony Wood, *The Life and Times of Anthony Wood, Antiquary, of Oxford, 1632–1695, Described by Himself*, 5 vols., ed. Andrew Clark (Oxford, 1891–1900), ii. 116–17.

[50] Powell, *Aubrey*, 83–5. She was evidently related to the learned Ryves family of Blandford Forum, Dorset, but the exact connection is unclear. See William Poole, 'An Early-Modern New College Dynasty: George, Thomas, and Bruno Ryves', *New College Notes* and 'Property of a Late Warden, 1613 with Some More on the Ryves Family', *New College Notes*, online at <https://www.new.ox.ac.uk/sites/default/files/4NCN1%20Ryves'% 20notes.pdf> and <https://www.new.ox.ac.uk/sites/default/files/5NCN7%20Poole%20on% 20Ryves%20addenda.pdf> (accessed 28 January 2015).

[51] Powell, *Aubrey*, 115–26.

[52] For his relationship with William see Powell, *Aubrey*, 212–15.

management.[53] His friends and vast extended family rallied round with considerable forbearance during his 'happy delitescency' (i.e., conceal-ment or seclusion), suggesting occupations—particularly the church, which did not appeal to the anticlerical Aubrey—and offering numerous grants of land in the New World over the ensuing decades.[54] Aubrey, however, preferred to continue his scholarly activities in the south of England, making ends meet by staying at the houses of his well-wishers and, once his financial situation had somewhat recovered, lodging in London, notably with Robert Hooke in Gresham College. The 1670s and 1680s were decades of almost feverish composition for him as he prepared most of his major works: county histories of Wiltshire and Surrey, tracts on architecture and palaeography, biographies, and numer-ous texts on archaeological and philological subjects.

As he grew older, Aubrey became increasingly worried that his manu-scripts would find their way to the tender mercies of the bookbinder and the pie-man. One consequence of this concern was the friendship he formed in the final decade of his life with the assistant keeper (subse-quently keeper) of Oxford's Ashmolean Museum, Edward Lhuyd. Lhuyd convinced Aubrey to deposit some of his papers, supplemented by various artefacts, coins, and paintings, in the newly founded Ashmolean, corres-ponded with him on a variety of antiquarian topics until his death in 1697, and ensured that most of the rest of his manuscripts found their way into the same repository afterwards.[55] Although some members of the younger generation found 'old Hermetic Aubrey' eccentric, to say the least, his reputation as a true polymath in the Restoration mould lasted throughout his life and found enduring form in engagement with his theories of British prehistory by the 1695 edition of Camden's *Britannia* (whose editors included his friends Lhuyd and Thomas Tanner).[56]

Aubrey was in many ways characteristic of his generation. He combined deep interests in mathematics and experimental science with a programme of antiquarian study and moved between a variety of intellectual and social spheres in London, Oxford, and Wiltshire. His scholarly achievements, however, used the learning of his time in new and sometimes remarkable

[53] Aubrey, *Lives*, i. 435. For Aubrey's ongoing attempts to convince the authorities that he was abroad see, for example, Bodleian MS Wood F 39, fol. 141r.

[54] These included six hundred acres in Pennsylvania, offered by William Penn himself, and unspecified prospects in Jamaica, held out by Governor John Vaughan (Powell, *Aubrey*, 154, 192–3).

[55] See Chapter 6 and Kate Bennett, 'John Aubrey's Collections and the Early-Modern Museum', *Bodleian Library Record* 17 (2001): 213–45.

[56] For 'old Hermetic Aubrey' see the letter from Robert Salusbury to Edward Lhuyd, probably from January 1697, Bodleian MS Ashmole 1817a, fol. 422r. See Chapter 2 for the use of Aubrey's ideas in the 1695 *Britannia*.

ways. In this volume I have taken a fresh view of his antiquarian scholarship, setting it within its European contexts, and exploring the ways in which its methodologies and content were determined by larger themes in Aubrey's life and work. His antiquarianism, I propose, can be seen through multiple lenses. Pride in his Welsh heritage predisposed him to a historical narrative which prioritized a Celtic British past, but his conviction that ancient Europe could be understood within a post-Babelic, diffusionist cultural narrative led him to interpret Celtic and Germanic cultures in the light of the Greco-Roman world. He used physical artefacts and sites to argue for new understandings of the ancient world, but later in life came to attach increasing importance to philological and linguistic interpretations of the past. Throughout his career he positioned himself as a node within the larger Republic of Letters, memorializing one province of that Republic in his famous *Lives*, but in many ways he remained on its margins, limited to Anglophone contacts on the western periphery of Europe and gaining access to Scandinavian scholarship, which he would fruitfully use and transform in his own work, almost by chance. This work has been structured around these tensions and the avenues they offer into understanding Aubrey's development as an original and notable practitioner of seventeenth-century antiquarian scholarship.

The archive upon which this study is based is Aubrey's, as it survives in the Bodleian Library, together with a few stray items elsewhere. The Aubrey shelfmarks in the Bodleian include autograph manuscripts of most of his major works, as well as two volumes of correspondence, and some other manuscripts owned but not composed by him.[57] When first deposited with Edward Lhuyd the principal manuscripts were bound in dirty vellum covers while the letters and other miscellaneous material appear to have been loose, but all are now bound in uniform late Victorian half-leather. At various points in his life Aubrey also either donated or left in Lhuyd's keeping a considerable number of books, the rump of his substantial library. These are also preserved in the Bodleian, but not under a single shelfmark.[58] However, both books and manuscripts were first housed not in the Bodleian, but in the Ashmolean Museum, where Lhuyd was keeper. They are listed in its early catalogues and were only transferred to the Bodleian, along with the Ashmolean's other printed collections, in 1860.[59] Two important strays are the manuscripts of the *Monumenta Britannica* and the *Remaines of*

---

[57] Falconer Madan, Richard William Hunt, H. H. E. Craster, and P. D. Record, *A Summary Catalogue of Western Manuscripts in the Bodleian Library at Oxford*, 7 vols. in 8 (Oxford, 1895–1953), v. 103–8.
[58] See the catalogues assembled in Robert T. Gunther, 'The Library of John Aubrey', *Bodleian Quarterly Record* 6 (1931): 230–6; Powell, *Aubrey*, 295–303.
[59] Madan et al., *Summary Catalogue*, v. 81.

Gentilisme. The *Monumenta* was in the hands of Aubrey's potential publisher, Awnsham Churchill, at the former's death and remained in the
possession of Churchill's descendants until donated to the Bodleian in
1836.[60] The *Remaines* was in the possession of White Kennett when
Aubrey died. Subsequently it was acquired by the antiquary James West,
whose collection was purchased by William Petty, 1st Marquis of Lansdowne, and thus came to rest amongst the other Lansdowne Manuscripts in
the British Library when they were purchased in 1807.[61]

Even the most polished of Aubrey's manuscripts are not finished in any
conventional sense. Collectively, they represent the sum of his life's work
which he hoped to preserve for posterity but none of his projects—other
than a small octavo of *Miscellanies* (1696)—were ever finalized through
publication. Even his fair copies came in time to be filled with additions,
corrections, cancellations, and tipped in leaves until they appear just as
disordered as the roughest of notebook jottings. This presents a problem
for any potential interpreter. While I have attempted to recover the
development of Aubrey's thought, it is important to bear in mind that
this is not straightforwardly reflected in his manuscripts, which are more
chaotic than any study of them might suggest. Likewise, their unfinished
status means that assigning a single date to a manuscript is rarely possible;
instead, many of the major texts contain materials which span Aubrey's
entire scholarly career.

Finally, it must be kept in mind that we only have what Aubrey wanted
us to have. We know from a passing reference in the *Lives* that he carried
on a much greater correspondence than survives in the collection which he
donated to the Ashmolean.[62] Similarly, Michael Hunter identified a
number of manuscripts referenced elsewhere which do not appear to
survive.[63] Aubrey's *Hypothesis ethicorum et scala religionis* would likely
have shed light on his treatment of religion in the *Remaines*, while his
Description of the Prospects from Easton-Piers would have complemented
the architectural drawings which survive. Most lamentable, from the point
of view of the present work, is the loss of 'Liber B', apparently a companion volume to his surviving *Description of Wiltshire*, but more geographically wide-ranging in its antiquarian materials.[64]

---

[60] Madan et al., *Summary Catalogue*, v. 449–50.

[61] Aubrey, *Three Prose Works*, 406–7.

[62] Writing of his friend the inventor Francis Potter, Aubrey noted that 'I have all his
letters by me, which are very good, and I believe neer 200' (Aubrey, *Lives*, i. 188). Seventeen
survive in Bodleian MSS Aubrey 12–13.

[63] Hunter, *Aubrey*, 239–42.

[64] Hunter, *Aubrey*, 241–2. Its presumed connection to the Wiltshire manuscript comes
from a letter of Aubrey's to Anthony Wood, dated 17 August 1685, in which he mentions

As well as recovering the specificities of Aubrey's antiquarian scholarship, this work will trace the contours of larger themes in the antiquarian tradition across Europe during this period. The seventeenth century was a golden age of antiquarian research—'the Age of the Antiquaries' in Momigliano's phrase—but it remains poorly understood and a closer study of Aubrey and his work can help us to begin recovering the issues, debates, and approaches that defined a much wider field of scholarship.[65] In doing so, it also presents a way of re-evaluating the relationships between antiquarianism, history, and philology, discussed earlier in this Introduction. By paying close attention to the interactions between disciplines in the work of Aubrey and his contemporaries we can reach a better understanding of the development of historical and philological methods and appreciate the polymathic and now surprisingly alien understandings of the past which defined the pre-modern historical disciplines. Aubrey's work is a microcosm which contains within it these larger, pan-European themes, and a clearer understanding of it can allow us a window onto this still-occluded landscape.

Nonetheless, this volume is also inevitably partial in its focus. I have not attempted to address Aubrey's mathematical, scientific, or occult interests, nor to engage in a new reconstruction of his biography. These aspects of his life and work have already been well and amply treated elsewhere. Anthony Powell's 1948 *John Aubrey and His Friends* is a luminous and meticulously researched biography, while Michael Hunter's 1975 landmark *John Aubrey and the Realm of Learning* remains the standard study of Aubrey's scholarship as a whole. Hunter's work covered the entirety of Aubrey's scholarly interests, devoting its third chapter to 'the study of antiquities'. This was the first comprehensive examination of Aubrey's antiquarian manuscripts and remains extremely valuable. In it, Hunter identified issues which will be returned to in the present work: Aubrey's interest in change, his comparative methodologies, the vividness of his writing, and his emphasis on material 'collected in the field', whether records of sites or actual artefacts. He also went beyond the remit of this volume, considering the relationship of Aubrey's antiquarianism to his study of natural history and the subsequent reception of his works in the eighteenth and nineteenth centuries. *John Aubrey and the Realm of Learning*, however, was an overarching survey and Aubrey's individual works are each given relatively short shrift. In some instances this resulted in Hunter accusing Aubrey of inconsistency, an uncritical attitude, or

that he has sent to Wood 'my two Volumes of Antiquities of Wilts A. & B.' (Bodleian MS Wood F 39, fol. 375r).

[65] Momigliano, 'Ancient History', 285.

oversimplification when a closer study of the text in question would have revealed a different story.[66] Likewise, while recognizing the key position Roman culture held in Aubrey's understanding of world history, Hunter dismissed the parallels Aubrey drew between the ancient and modern worlds as an oversimplification of the past or a 'fusing almost all history together in a single "old time"'.[67] These statements were undoubtedly due at least in part to the understanding of English antiquarianism current when the work was published—Hunter built upon the tradition exemplified by D. C. Douglas, J. G. A. Pocock, and others, which privileged politically engaged antiquarian activity at the expense of more culturally focused approaches like Aubrey's. However, the considerable growth in the study of antiquarianism over the past forty years now encourages a more nuanced interrogation of Aubrey's works.[68] While Hunter's monograph was a pioneering contribution to the field, there is much more to be said and ample material to be re-examined and reassessed.

Since the publication of Hunter's monograph there have been four other major contributions to the study of Aubrey's antiquarianism. First was the chapter in Graham Parry's 1995 *Trophies of Time*, an important reinterpretation of the place of antiquarianism in seventeenth-century English scholarship.[69] Parry saw Aubrey as occupying a critical place in the larger evolution of English antiquarianism, moving away 'from documentary evidences to an emphasis on fieldwork'. He also developed Hunter's theories on Aubrey's 'sense of history', suggesting that he understood it as a series of settled ages punctuated by catastrophic change while also being alert to change within those periods.[70] Some of Parry's conclusions, however, such as his conviction that Dugdale's *Antiquities of Warwickshire* was a 'formative influence' on Aubrey, derived from his attempt to place Aubrey in a scholarly tradition to which he did not entirely belong, that of Camdenian regional and county history.[71]

Next, a short but incisive discussion of Aubrey appeared in Alain Schnapp's 1993 *Le conquête du passé* (translated into English in 1996 as *The Discovery of the Past*).[72] Schnapp placed Aubrey within a larger narrative of the evolution of archaeology and thus emphasized different aspects of his work from those focused on by Parry. For Schnapp, Aubrey was a theorizer and systematizer par excellence. Aubrey, he proposed, 'wished to establish rules of interpretation to govern observation' and invented a new and powerful tool in his recourse to comparatism in

---

[66] See, e.g. Hunter, *Aubrey*, 186, 189.   [67] Hunter, *Aubrey*, 186.
[68] For Hunter's debt to Douglas, Pocock, and others see *Aubrey*, 148–9.
[69] Parry, *Trophies of Time*, 275–307.   [70] Parry, *Trophies of Time*, 277, 296–7.
[71] Parry, *Trophies of Time*, 277.   [72] Schnapp, *Discovery*, 188–96.

antiquarian investigation.[73] In effect, Aubrey was the first theoretical archaeologist.[74] Despite the anachronism of some of these claims, Schnapp's interpretation placed Aubrey solidly within a pan-European context and drew out some of the more novel aspects of his work which had not been previously explored.

William Poole's *John Aubrey and the Advancement of Learning*, published in conjunction with the 2010 Bodleian Library exhibition '"My wit was always working": John Aubrey and the Development of Experimental Science', addressed Aubrey's studies of megaliths and his methodologies.[75] Poole contextualized Aubrey's study of Stonehenge within contemporary controversies over its purpose and origin and discussed the aftermath of his interpretations in the work of the eighteenth-century antiquary William Stukeley. He also emphasized the importance of Aubrey's *Chronologiae*, relating the *Chronologia Graphica* in particular to contemporary continental developments in the study of diplomatic.[76]

Most recently, Kate Bennett's magisterial edition of the *Brief Lives* has set a new standard for the editing and interpretation of Aubrey.[77] It is now the definitive guide to the composition of the *Lives*, but builds upon Bennett's other work on Aubrey, including articles which have addressed his role in the Royal Society, his bibliographical work, his scholarly practices, and his donations to the Ashmolean Museum, amongst others.[78] Bennett has focused in particular on Aubrey's habits of collection, composition, and sociability, greatly expanding our understanding of how he went about his work and significantly reinterpreting his relationship with Anthony Wood.

It is hoped, then, that the present work fills a gap in the literature on Aubrey's antiquarianism. While still attempting a relatively broad survey of his antiquarian writings, it also aims to go deeper and to address in detail several texts—the *Monumenta Britannica*, the *Lives*, and the *Remaines of Gentilisme*—which have been increasingly recognized as central both to the study of Aubrey and to the study of seventeenth-century antiquarianism.[79] By limiting this work to one thread in a rich and

---

[73] Schnapp, *Discovery*, 191.   [74] Schnapp, *Discovery*, 194.

[75] William Poole, *John Aubrey and the Advancement of Learning* (Oxford, 2010), 64–76 (megaliths) and 86–9 (historical methods).

[76] Poole, *Aubrey*, 88–90.   [77] Aubrey, *Lives*.

[78] Bennett, 'John Aubrey's Collections'; 'John Aubrey, Hint-Keeper'; 'John Aubrey and the Printed Book', *Huntington Library Quarterly* 76 (2013): 393–411; 'John Aubrey and the Rhapsodic Book', *Renaissance Studies* 28 (2014): 317–32.

[79] It does not, however, claim to address all of Aubrey's antiquarian texts in detail, in particular leaving aside his county histories of Wiltshire and Surrey and several of his *Miscelany Tractates*. The *Description of the North Division of Wiltshire* is now Bodleian MS Aubrey 3, the *Perambulation of Surrey* is Bodleian MS Aubrey 4, and the *Stromata, or*

polymathic career—the thread which can ultimately be traced back to Aubrey's unexpected encounter with the prehistoric past that cold January morning at Avebury—it unpacks the methodologies, contexts, and assumptions of his antiquarian thought.

The first half of the book follows this encounter through to its eventual outcome in Aubrey's composition of his *Monumenta Britannica*, the first survey of ancient monuments across Britain. Chapter 1 focuses on his study of megaliths and the theories he developed to explain their presence in the landscape, teasing out Aubrey's reactions to contemporary debates over the origins of Stonehenge as well as the parallels between English and Swedish understandings of prehistoric sites. Chapter 2 considers the remainder of the *Monumenta*, including his investigations of ancient fortifications and other physical relics and the ways in which these altered his understanding of the Roman occupation of Britain. It concludes with a discussion of his unsuccessful attempts to publish his magnum opus and its place in subsequent antiquarian scholarship. Chapter 3 concludes this section by exploring Aubrey's complex engagement with architecture and architectural theory, from planning a neo-classical country house to creating methodologies for dating medieval buildings to searching for the origins of all subsequent architectures in Babel and its aftermath. Here Aubrey appears at his most characteristically baroque, engaging in innovative but deeply strange comparative strategies to make sense of a global culture he believed to be only a few thousand years old.

While the first half of the work deals with artefacts and sites, the second half deals with texts. Chapter 4 sites Aubrey's best-known writings, the *Brief Lives*, within antiquarian traditions of *historia literaria* and scholarly memorialization, exploring the ways in which they developed from his collaborations with Anthony Wood and Richard Blackburne. The *Lives* are less *sui generis* than sometimes presented, but instead grew out of a rich humanist tradition of biographical writing which Aubrey infused with an antiquarian awareness of specificity and detail. Chapter 5 returns to the ancient past, but from a new angle, looking at Aubrey's use of folk custom in his *Remaines of Gentilisme*. Folklore and folk practices, Aubrey believed, provided evidence which linked early modern British culture with that of the Greco-Roman world, but they were vanishing as rapidly as the men and women he had attempted to memorialize in the *Lives*. Aubrey's syncretist understanding of culture and his reaction to the trauma of the Civil Wars are identified as the twin motivations of this rich and compli-cated work. Chapter 6 concludes by recovering his studies of linguistics

---

Certain Miscelany Tractates is Bodleian MS Top. Gen. c. 25, fols. 150r–242v. See Hunter, *Aubrey, passim*, and Parry, *Trophies of Time*, 277–80.

and toponyms towards the end of his life and drawing out the relationships between his work in those fields and better-known texts by his younger contemporaries Thomas Gale and Edward Lhuyd. Not traditionally known for his skills as a philologist, Aubrey occupied a central position in a tradition of British philology which was to become an increasingly important way of engaging with the ancient past in the eighteenth century.

Taken as a whole, this volume charts the course of Aubrey's antiquarian thought throughout his scholarly career, addressing his major works in turn, and reading them as part of a larger fascination with the ancient world and the elusive textures of the past. It identifies his sources, untangles the evolution of his ideas, and sets him within a larger European context of scholarly enquiry which sought to make sense of the world, both ancient and modern, in terms both tantalizingly familiar and dazzlingly strange.

1

Stonehenge and the Druids

Antiquarian Controversy in Restoration England

Fifteen years after Aubrey's first encounter with Avebury, megaliths were at the centre of English scholarly debate. A series of publications—by the architect Inigo Jones, his assistant John Webb, and the physician and Fellow of the Royal Society Walter Charleton—had made the origins of Stonehenge a high-profile and controversial subject. The young John Dryden wrote a poem on the topic and the excitement generated by scholarly controversy reached as far as the court itself. There, one morning in 1663, Charles II had a long conversation with the courtier and president of the Royal Society, Viscount Brouncker, and one of the leading figures in the debate, Walter Charleton himself. They began by discussing Stonehenge, but someone, probably Charleton, mentioned in passing Aubrey's anecdotes about Avebury. 'His Majestie admired that none of our Chorographers had taken notice of it: and commanded Dr Charlton to bring' Aubrey to him.[1]

Aubrey showed Avebury to the King during the latter's progress to Bath and was commanded by him 'to write a Description of it, and present [it] to him' (the Duke of York made a similar request that Aubrey should 'give an account of the old Camps and Barrows on the Plaines').[2] The Royal Society seconded the royal command at a meeting on 8 July 1663 when Charleton presented them with a plan of Avebury (it seems to have been the same 'draught of it donne by memorie only' which Aubrey had shown the King) and recommended 'that it was worth the while to dig there under a certain triangular stone, where he conceived would be found a monument of some Danish king'. Aubrey and his Wiltshire neighbour and fellow antiquary Colonel James Long were 'desired to make further

---

[1] Aubrey, *Monumenta*, 21. For the study of Avebury see Peter J. Ucko, Michael Hunter, Alan J. Clark, and Andrew David, *Avebury Reconsidered: From the 1660s to the 1900s* (London, 1991).

[2] Aubrey, *Monumenta*, 21.

inquiry'.[3] Aubrey surveyed both Avebury and Stonehenge in September of the same year (see Figure 1.1) and soon afterwards composed a short manuscript treatise entitled *Templa Druidum*, outlining his results and their implications, which he presented to the King.[4] In it he identified these and other megalithic sites in Britain as temples of the Druids, dating to a period before the Roman invasion. This claim was to be his seminal contribution to the study of British prehistory.

Aubrey's treatise later grew to mammoth proportions, becoming the *Monumenta Britannica*, his attempt at a systematic survey of all prehistoric and Roman sites and artefacts across Britain.[5] Its origins, however, lay within the controversies of the 1650s and 1660s when English scholars tried to fit the inconveniently square blocks of Britain's megaliths into the round holes of biblically informed ancient history. This chapter interrogates Aubrey's deceptively straightforward interpretations of these and other prehistoric sites by first examining this moment of intellectual ferment and its relationship to Aubrey's first drafts of the *Templa*. Then it moves outwards to understand how this debate paralleled another scholarly controversy which occupied scholars in later seventeenth-century Sweden—the origins of a mysterious ancient temple near Uppsala—which sheds light on the methodologies and motivations of Aubrey and his contemporaries. Aubrey's Druidic theories emerge as a product of their time: brilliant and polymathic in their use of widely divergent sources and methodologies, but uncomfortably predetermined in their content and nationalistic in their conclusions.

THE BATTLE FOR STONEHENGE

Stonehenge had been the subject of myth-making and speculation long before Aubrey's time.[6] The predominant popular explanation for its

---

[3] Thomas Birch, *The History of the Royal Society of London for Improving of Natural Knowledge*, 4 vols. (London, 1756–7), i. 272. Sir James Long of Draycot Cerne, Wiltshire (1617–1692), elected to the Royal Society in 1663, was a numismatist and wrote a short account of his family's history, but did not contribute further to the Stonehenge debate (cf. *ODNB*, *s.n.*, and his letters to Aubrey on numismatics at Aubrey, *Monumenta*, 963–70).

[4] Aubrey, *Monumenta*, 22.

[5] Aubrey's final revision of the *Monumenta Britannica* survives as Bodleian MS Top. Gen. *c.* 24–5. It has never been edited, but a partial facsimile has been published as Aubrey, *Monumenta*, and has been cited in the present work in an effort to make references to the original manuscript more accessible.

[6] For another complementary analysis of early modern antiquaries' engagement with Stonehenge see Angus Vine, *In Defiance of Time: Antiquarian Writing in Early Modern England* (Oxford, 2010), ch. 4.

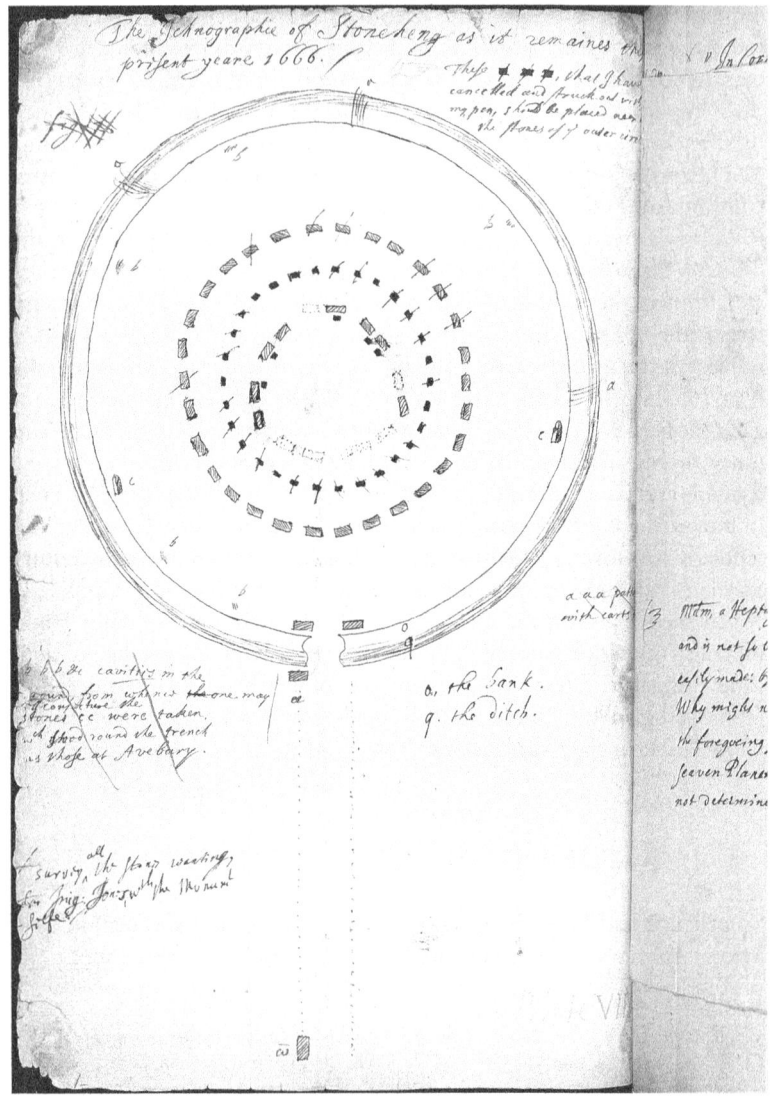

Figure 1.1 Aubrey's ichnography or ground plan of Stonehenge 'as it remaines this present yeare 1666' (Bodleian MS Top. Gen. c. 24, fol. 64v).

presence on Salisbury Plain had been laid out by Geoffrey of Monmouth, who recounted its construction by Merlin, with the help of certain giants, as a memorial to Britons slain in battle by the Saxons, and its subsequent role as a burial place for several legendary British kings.[7] Elizabethan antiquaries, however, paid little attention to prehistoric sites, preferring to concentrate on Roman and post-Roman antiquities which could be more easily understood within the context of surviving classical texts. When William Camden discussed Stonehenge in his *Britannia*, he could only repeat Geoffrey's account and throw up his hands at the impossibility of explaining the origins of such an 'insana substructio'.[8] In 1624 Edmund Bolton had proposed that Stonehenge was the tomb of Boudica, but after that there was a lull in interest until the posthumous publication of Inigo Jones's *Stone-Heng Restored* in 1655.[9] Despite Jones's name appearing prominently on the title page, the work's preface elaborated that it consisted of 'some few indigested notes of the late judicious . . . *Inigo Jones*' which had been polished and set in order by his former assistant, John Webb.[10] In fact, it seems to have been a collaboration between Jones and his assistant, with Jones providing the ideas and Webb posthumously rounding out his master's text with appropriate classical citations.[11]

Stone-Heng Restored systematically explicated the classical sources relating to Britain and the Druids, concluding that as the ancient writers clearly proved the Britons of that time had been 'destitute of the

---

[7] Geoffrey of Monmouth, *Historia Regum Britanniae: The First Variant Version: A Critical Edition*, ed. Neil Wright (Woodbridge, 1988), 175. See also Laura Hibbard Loomis, 'Geoffrey of Monmouth and Stonehenge', *Proceedings of the Modern Language Association* 45 (1930): 400–15.

[8] William Camden, *Britannia* (London, 1607), 182–4. Camden's tag for Stonehenge is derived ultimately from the 'substructionum insanis' of Cicero's *Pro Milone* (31.85). There is, however, also an echo of the description of the Egyptian pyramids ('vastae fuerunt & insanae substructionum moles') given by Hadrianus Junius, *Emblemata* (Antwerp, 1565), 90. Two early drawings of Stonehenge are discussed by Alain Schnapp, *The Discovery of the Past*, trans. Ian Kinnes and Gillian Varndell (New York, 1997), 148–51.

[9] Edmund Bolton, *Nero Caesar, or Monarchie Depraved* (London, 1624), 181–4; Inigo Jones, *The Most Notable Antiquity of Great Britain, Vulgarly Called Stone-Heng on Salisbury Plain Restored* (London, 1655). Bolton's theory was entirely conjectural, but he anticipated later antiquaries in his comparative archaeology: '[t]he dumbnesse of it (unlesse the letters bee worne quite away) speakes; that it was not any worke of the Romans. For they were want to make stones vocall by inscriptions . . . [t]hat Stonage was a worke of the Britanns, the rudenesse it selfe perswades' (Bolton, *Nero Caesar*, 181–2).

[10] Jones, *Stone-Heng Restored*, sig. A4ʳ. The preface states that Jones, like Aubrey, first undertook his study of Stonehenge upon a royal request, in his case that of James I in 1620 (Jones, *Stone-Heng Restored*, 1–2).

[11] Rumiko Handa, 'Authorship of *The Most Notable Antiquity* (1655): Inigo Jones and Early Printed Books', *Papers of the Bibliographical Society of America* 100 (2006): 357–77; John Bold, *John Webb: Architectural Theory and Practice in the Seventeenth Century* (Oxford, 1989); A. A. Tait, 'Inigo Jones's "Stone-Heng"', *Burlington Magazine* 120 (1978): 155–9.

knowledge, even to clothe themselves', then it stood to reason that they surely lacked the skills necessary 'to erect stately structures, or such remarkable works as *Stoneheng*'.[12] It then refuted Geoffrey of Monmouth and his followers, 'who, when they could not search out the truth in deed, laboured to bring forth narrations invented by themselves, without or reason, or authority', and criticized both Camden and Bolton for their failure to reach Jones and Webb's own conclusions.[13]

For a work written by an architect and claiming to found its hypothesis on a survey of the site, *Stone-Heng Restored* relied overwhelmingly on textual evidence. Although Jones surveyed and drew the site during the course of his study, the core of his and Webb's architectural argument rested on readings of Vitruvius and Palladio rather than first-hand observation.[14] Having established the inferiority of the Britons and their architecture, it concluded that Stonehenge was a Roman temple dedicated to the deity Caelus or Coelus. The Britons lived, Jones wrote, a life 'without *Art*, without *Order*, without any whatever means tending to perpetuity' and their buildings 'were not stately, nor sumptuous; neither had they any thing of *Order*, or *Symmetry*, much lesse, of gracefulnesse, and *Decorum* in them'.[15] It then became syllogistically clear that attributing Stonehenge to the Britons was impossible, for, if they were rude and barbaric and it was an 'admired and magnificent' monument, then they could not possibly have been its authors. '[W]ho more magnificent than the *Romans*', however?[16]

At this point, the open-roofed temple to Coelus which the text attempted to find described in Vitruvius and fulfilled in Stonehenge might seem almost superfluous to the main thrust of Jones's argument, but this misses the other goal of the text. Jones and Webb's work was not only antiquarian, but also served, as Rumiko Handa has noted, a very present political purpose. Jones had already used Coelus, the presumptive dedicatee of Stonehenge, as a symbol for James I in his *Coelum Britannicum* (1634) and elsewhere. The god's reappearance here was an attempt to yoke the Stuart monarchy to the Romano-British past, with Vitruvius's architectural theories serving as a convenient rope to tie the two together.[17]

---

[12] Jones, *Stone-Heng Restored*, 7.

[13] Jones, *Stone-Heng Restored*, 16 (medieval historians), 32–40 (Camden), 44–55 (Bolton).

[14] Jones, *Stone-Heng Restored*, 31. For Jones's surveying see Poole, *Aubrey*, 66–7.

[15] Jones, *Stone-Heng Restored*, 4, 11.   [16] Jones, *Stone-Heng Restored*, 66.

[17] Handa, 'Authorship of *The Most Notable Antiquity*', 377. Cf. Thomas Carew and Inigo Jones, *Coelum Britanicum: A Masque at White-Hall in the Banquetting-House, on Shrove-Tuesday-Night, the 18. of February, 1633* (London, 1634); Stephen Orgel and Roy Strong, *Inigo Jones: The Theater of the Stuart Court* (Berkeley, CA, 1973), *passim*, and Rumiko Handa, 'Coelum Britannicum: Inigo Jones and Symbolic Geometry', in *Nexus IV*, ed. José Francisco Rodrigues and Kim Williams (Turin, 2002), 109–26.

The publication of *Stone-Heng Restored* in the midst of the Commonwealth was, perhaps, a not-so-subtle piece of Royalist propaganda.

Jones and Webb's overly deft deployment of textual evidence at the expense of less predetermined observation of the site itself did not sit well with some antiquaries, Aubrey included. In his preface to the *Templa Druidum*, Aubrey recalled that 'having compared [Jones's] Scheme with the Monument it self':

> I found he had not dealt fairly: but had made a Lesbians rule, which is conformed to the stone: that is, he framed the measurement to his own Hypothesis, which is much differing from the Thing itself. This gave me an edge to make more researches . . . [18]

It was not, however, Aubrey who launched the first attack on *Stone-Heng Restored*, but Walter Charleton, the physician who had proposed Aubrey to the Royal Society only months before and who had introduced him to the King.[19] Charleton's *Chorea Gigantum*—Latin for 'giant's dance', a name given to Stonehenge as early as the time of Geoffrey of Monmouth—published in 1663, claimed to take a dramatically different comparative approach, advertising that it 'diligently compared *STONE-HENG* with other Antiquities of the same Kind, at this day, standing in *Denmark*', but, in reality, it was not so very far removed from the antiquarian politics of *Stone-Heng Restored*.[20] Analogous politics did not necessarily lead to analogous scholarly theories.

Charleton demonstrated the falseness of the Jones–Webb reading of Vitruvius and observed, in addition, that Roman sites nearby bore no architectural similarity to Stonehenge.[21] Having deconstructed the existing theory to his satisfaction, he proceeded to erect his own: Stonehenge had been built by the Danes as a site for the election of their kings. His argument for a Danish origin rested on a perceived architectural resemblance between Stonehenge and similar sites in Denmark, though he admitted that

---

[18] Aubrey, *Monumenta*, 19–20. The Lesbian rule, which could be bent to fit any angle, is derived from Aristotle, *Nicomachean Ethics*, v.x.7.

[19] Aubrey had been proposed by Charleton on 24 December 1662 and admitted 21 January 1663 (Birch, *History of the Royal Society*, i. 166, 179). He would have been a Fellow of less than six months' standing when the Society, at Charleton's instigation, requested him to study Avebury.

[20] Walter Charleton, *Chorea Gigantum, or, The Most Famous Antiquity of Great-Britan, Vulgarly Called Stone-Heng, Standing on Salisbury Plain, Restored to the Danes* (London, 1663), sig. ar.

[21] Charleton, *Chorea Gigantum*, 18–28. Charleton engages in a classic scholarly offensive measure when he impugns the accuracy of the Vitruvian quotation as given in *Stone-Heng Restored*, 23–5.

the concordances were by no means exact.[22] As supplementary arguments he adduced the Danes' skill in mechanics, the possibility of transportation of massive stones in other cultures, the lack of any mention of Stonehenge amongst historians pre-dating Geoffrey of Monmouth, and the discovery of a tablet written in an unknown language near the site, which he took to have been a runic inscription.[23] But, like Jones and Webb, Charleton had other motives beyond mere scholarly curiosity. *Chorea Gigantum* was dedicated to Charles II, a dedication which explicitly referenced the fact that, in 1651, Charles was 'pleased to visit that *Monument*, and, for many hours together, entertain [him]self with the delightful view thereof', even in the midst of the Civil Wars.[24] The liminal verses contributed by Dryden made it clear how this, and Charleton's argument as a whole, was to be understood: 'STONE-HENG, once thought a *Temple*, You have found | A *Throne*, where Kings, our Earthly Gods, were Crown'd.'[25] Charleton, despite disagreeing with their theory, had made explicit what Jones and Webb had only implied: Stonehenge was a lasting monument to the durability and Divine Right of the Stuart monarchy.

Charleton's contribution to the debate was game changing, not for his argument itself, but for his choice of principal source: Ole Worm's *Danicorum monumentorum libri sex* (1643), a study of Danish prehistoric monuments and runestones.[26] Worm, professor of medicine at the University of Copenhagen, had close ties with the English scholarly community, having visited England in his youth and subsequently corresponded with the English antiquary Henry Spelman.[27] In his

---

[22] Charleton, *Chorea Gigantum*, 36ff., esp. 53–4 (for variation between Stonehenge and Danish sites).

[23] Charleton, *Chorea Gigantum*, 28–30 (inscribed tablet), 56 (lack of notice by ancient historians), 59–61 (mechanical skill of the Danes and ease of transportation compared to the building of the pyramids).

[24] Charleton, *Chorea Gigantum*, sig. [a]v.

[25] Charleton, *Chorea Gigantum*, sig. b2v.

[26] Charleton, *Chorea Gigantum*, 28–30 and *passim*; Ole Worm, *Danicorum monumentorum libri sex* (Copenhagen, 1643). For Worm, see H. D. Schepelern, 'Museum Wormianum: dets forudsætninger og tilblivelse' (Copenhagen University Doctoral Thesis, 1971), the Latin and Danish editions of Worm's letters, *Olai Wormii et ad eum doctorum virorum epistolae*, 2 vols. (Copenhagen, 1751) and *Breve fra og til Ole Worm*, 3 vols., ed. H. D. Schepelern (Copenhagen, 1965–8), Klavs Randsborg, 'Ole Worm: An Essay on the Modernization of Antiquity', *Acta Archaeologica* 65 (1994): 135–69, Ole Peter Grell, 'In Search of True Knowledge: Ole Worm (1588–1654) and the New Philosophy', in *Making Knowledge in Early Modern Europe: Practices, Objects, and Texts, 1400–1800*, ed. Pamela H. Smith and Benjamin Schmidt (Chicago and London, 2007), 214–32, and Valdimar Tr. Hafstein, 'Bodies of Knowledge: Ole Worm & Collecting in Late Renaissance Scandinavia', *Ethnologia Europaea* 33 (2003): 5–19.

[27] Ethel Seaton, *Literary Relations of England and Scandinavia in the Seventeenth Century* (Oxford, 1935), 154–5 (for Worm's visit to England).

correspondence with the latter, the same tensions between antiquarian discovery and nationalist aggrandizement seen in Charleton's work had already played out, albeit in a somewhat different context.

On 18 April 1629 Spelman had written to Worm, providing a copy of the inscription found on the Bewcastle Cross in Cumberland and asking Worm whether it was in the Gothic alphabet found in Bonaventura Vulcanius's edition of the surviving fragments of the Codex Argenteus, a sixth-century Gothic manuscript of portions of the New Testament.[28] Worm responded magisterially on 18 July that, 'Runic is nothing other than Gothic' (and therefore to Worm nothing other than Danish) and was the proper name for the alphabet known as Gothic by foreigners, before going on to provide a conjectural emendation and interpretation of the inscription.[29] Spelman, in his following letter, proposed that 'rune' derived from Old English 'ryne', a secret or hidden thing, a conclusion supported by later scholarship.[30] Both sides seem to have valued the scholarly friendship thus formed and the correspondence resulting from it. Later, Spelman was to print his letter to Worm on the etymological origin of 'rune' in his *Glossarium Archaiologicum*.[31] For his part, Worm eagerly awaited the second part of Spelman's *Glossarium* and sent him a copy of his *De aureo cornu* in the spring of 1641.[32] While the two scholars' correspondence might at first appear to be a model of transnational

---

[28] Worm, *Epistolae*, i. 426 (= Worm, *Breve*, i. 170–1). Spelman's transcription is of more than usual interest given the probability that the inscription had been tampered with at some point in the nineteenth century, for which see R. I. Page, 'William Nicolson, F.R.S., and the Runes of the Bewcastle Cross', *Notes and Records of the Royal Society of London* 14 (1960): 184–90. The somewhat squat and blocky runes at Bewcastle reminded Spelman of the specimen of Gothic script, printed with type cut in imitation of the Codex Argenteus, in Bonaventura Vulcanius's *De literis et lingua Getarum, sive Gothorum* (Leiden, 1597).

[29] 'Gothicae enim nil aliud sunt quam Runicae, & illa qua exteris dicta est Gothica, ab iis, qui eam primum in peregrinas advexerunt regiones, nobis Runica est literatura vero & genuino nomine' (Worm, *Epistolae*, i. 431 [= Worm, *Breve*, i. 179]). Worm was only paraphrasing Vulcanius himself, who had also equated runes with the Gothic script in his *De literis*, 43–8. For Vulcanius's runes see Kees Dekker, 'The Runes in Bonaventura Vulcanius *De literis & lingua getarum sive Gothorum* (1597): Provenance and Origins', in *Bonaventura Vulcanius, Works and Networks*, ed. Hélène Cazes (Leiden, 2010), 411–53.

[30] Worm, *Epistolae*, i. 434–5 (= Worm, *Breve*, i. 208–10); cf. *OED, s.v.* This was not the first time an English scholar had turned their attention to runes. Already in the sixteenth century Richard Talbot and Daniel Rogers had studied the Futhark and copied inscriptions off runestones. The latter, in particular, had studied runestones while serving as English ambassador to Denmark and passed a variety of runic material on to Philips van Marnix who, in turn, provided it to Vulcanius for the *De literis*; see Dekker, 'Provenance and Origins', 423–4, and J. A. W. Bennett, 'The Beginnings of Runic Studies in England', *Saga-Book of the Viking Society* 13 (1946–53): 269–83.

[31] Sir Henry Spelman, *Glossarium Archaiologicum* (London, 1664), 493–4; Seaton, *Literary Relations*, 226–7. Spelman's letter is included under the rubric of 'Runicae literae' within the *Glossarium*.

[32] Worm, *Epistolae*, i. 440–3 (= Worm, *Breve*, i. 329–31); ii. 783–4 (= ii. 246–7).

cooperation, Worm's determined equation of 'Gothic' with Danish reveals the nationalist motivations present in his work, as they were in Charleton's. In both cases the study of ancient monuments could bolster the authority of modern nations, whether the Divine Right of English monarchs or the supposed ancient extent of Danish sovereignty.

Their correspondence also highlighted Worm's interest in runic epigraphy, the subject which dominated his *Monumenta Danica*. The majority of the work is a region-by-region survey of surviving runestones throughout Denmark.[33] What set Worm apart was his methodology. The systematic list of runestones was not compiled solely through Worm's own travels, but also through the results of a survey sent by him to parish priests in 1622, prefiguring correspondence networks such as that of the editors of the 1695 edition of Camden's *Britannia*.[34] More importantly, the first book of the *Monumenta Danica* was a short essay on the history and material culture of the ancient Danes, whose theoretical and critical assumptions would become central to the work of later archaeologically minded antiquaries.

Worm categorized the sites known to him according to pre-existing models, but with modifications which allowed for the unique nature of his material. His broad divisions were *delubra* and *arae* (shrines and altars), *sepulcra* (graves), *epitaphia* and *monumenta* (epitaphs and runestones), *fora* (thing-sites), *circi* (circles for duels and other purposes), and *limites* (demarcated places, usually for various religious ceremonies).[35] Of these he was particularly interested in graves and burial traditions, a fascination growing out of his epigraphic researches, and he proposed a theory of development in burial practices which would significantly influence Aubrey's thinking. Danish burial practices, he suggested, could be divided into three eras: a fire era, in which bodies were cremated and their ashes then buried together with grave goods; a mound-burial era, in which bodies were inhumed in barrows with grave goods; and finally the Christian era, in which current burial customs first began to be practised.[36]

As well as constructing a methodological framework, Worm also provided an unusually large corpus of data with which to compare later finds, a corpus for which there was no equivalent in contemporary antiquarian scholarship. Klavs Randsborg has made the important point that 'fresh rich data' had at least as much impact on changing antiquarian theories as

---

[33] Worm, *Monumenta Danica*, 100–526.

[34] Randsborg, 'Ole Worm', 136 and *passim*. See Graham Parry, *The Trophies of Time: English Antiquarians of the Seventeenth Century* (Oxford, 1995), 331–57, for the 1695 *Britannia*.

[35] Worm, *Monumenta Danica*, 1–99 *passim*, esp. 3–4 (for a survey of the divisions).

[36] Randsborg, 'Ole Worm', 145–6; Worm, *Monumenta Danica*, 30–40.

developments in methodology; the paradigm-shifting possibilities of publishing a wide-ranging selection of material such as Worm's should not be underrated.[37] Charleton's *Chorea* is completely indebted, in its basic premises, to Worm's chapter 'of places for considering the election of kings', and the early acquisition by the Bodleian Library of the philologist and antiquary John Selden's copy of the *Monumenta Danica*—along with the rest of his formidably erudite library—meant that it was comparatively easily accessible to English scholars.[38]

Charleton's use of Worm also ensured his favourable reception amongst Danish scholars.[39] Ole Borch (Olaus Borrichius), professor of philology at Copenhagen, wrote to Thomas Bartholin during the course of his travels in England, discussing the Stonehenge controversy.[40] In this letter, dated 10 August 1663, he noted with approval that Charleton had published a work—the *Chorea Gigantum*—in accord with the arguments of Worm and went on to summarize the gist of Charleton's theory. This Danish vision of Stonehenge through the combined lenses of Worm and Charleton was continued by Bartholin's son, also Thomas, in his *Antiquitates Danicarum* of 1689, long after Charleton's work had lapsed into comparative obscurity in English antiquarian circles.[41] Charleton's major contribution to the debate was his association of it with similar investigations in the Scandinavian countries, a trend which Aubrey would subsequently follow, despite having serious reservations about Charleton's work itself.[42]

---

[37] Randsborg, 'Ole Worm', 159. Camden's *Britannia* offers a parallel English example of the ways in which the publication of a large corpus of new data could profoundly affect subsequent antiquarian studies.
[38] Worm, *Monumenta Danica*, 87–91 ('De locis Regum electioni deputatis'). Selden's copy, with its characteristic Greek inscription, *peri pantos ten eleutherian*, on the title-page (for which see Gerald J. Toomer, *John Selden: A Life in Scholarship*, 2 vols. [Oxford, 2009], ii. 796), is now Bodleian T 1.11 Jur.Seld. The 1674 Bodleian Library catalogue records the same volume at its earlier shelfmark of P.1.13 Art.Seld. as well as adjacent copies of Worm's *Antiquitates Danicae* at P.1.12 and his *Fasti Danici* at P.1.14 (Thomas Hyde, *Catalogus impressorum librorum Bibliothecae Bodleianae in Academia Oxoniensi* [Oxford, 1674], 260).
[39] He was also mentioned in several letters between Worm and Erasmus Bartholin, see Worm, *Epistolae*, ii. 985–90 (= Worm, *Breve*, iii. 424–8, 434–6).
[40] Thomas Bartholin, *Epistolarum medicinalium à Doctis vel ad Doctos scriptarum*, 3 vols. (Copenhagen, 1663–7), iii. 516–40. Cf. also Seaton, *Literary Relations*, 238.
[41] Thomas Bartholin, *Antiquitatum Danicarum de causis contemptae a Danis adhuc gentilibus mortis libri tres ex vetustis codicibus & monumentis hactenus ineditis congesti* (Copenhagen, 1689), 139–40.
[42] Bodleian MS Aubrey 11 consists of a series of extracts and notes by him on the *Chorea Gigantum* which suggest that he found it no more convincing than the hypothesis presented in *Stone-Heng Restored*. MS Aubrey 11's date of composition is uncertain, but it must have been written by 11 August 1690 as it is listed among the parts of the *Monumenta* deposited with Robert Hooke at Gresham College on that date (Bodleian MS Top. Gen. c. 24, fol. 13r). In its present form it is bound separately from the *Monumenta*. Aubrey's evident

The penultimate contribution to this controversy was John Webb's *Vindication of Stone-Heng Restored*. It was not published until 1665 but possesses a 6 June 1664 imprimatur and appears to have been composed while *Chorea Gigantum* was still circulating in manuscript form.[43] It added no new information, but only rehearsed Jones's arguments in greater detail. If Aubrey did consult it, he does not mention having done so, and it appears to have had no influence on his own thought.

By the time Aubrey began his own investigations, Stonehenge and its origins had already become a matter for heated antiquarian debate. Jones, Webb, and Charleton had all used comparative approaches to identify the megaliths' builders, relying upon Vitruvius's prescription or Worm's description to provide them with parallels which would clinch an identification. They had gestured towards the possibility of using the megaliths themselves as a potential source, but their material comparatism remained relatively simplistic: almost any stone placed on end could be dragooned into their arguments as a potential parallel to Stonehenge. Likewise, for all of them much more was at stake than simply the identification of the megaliths' builders. Stonehenge had become a site for competing Royalist narratives of kingship, a visible symbol of royal power within the landscape. While Jones and Charleton's divergent interpretations made it clear that this could be manifested in widely differing scholarly theories, any subsequent study of the monument would nonetheless be forced to confront this additional layer of meaning.

TEMPLES OF THE DRUIDS

Aubrey dismissed the works of Jones, Webb, and Charleton as 'several Bookes . . . much differing from one another, some affirming one thing, some another' and claimed, as Charleton had before him, to have made a fresh start with his surveys of Stonehenge and Avebury.[44] Despite this, his methodology was not so very different from the comparatism of his predecessors. He wrote that:

concern to check Charleton against Ole Worm's *Monumentorum Danicorum libri sex* (Copenhagen, 1643) may indicate that the manuscript is contemporaneous with the second recension of the *Monumenta*, reflecting, as it does, an interest in Scandinavian archaeological literature and comparative archaeology in general. It was certainly written after 1685, as Aubrey refers on fol. 9v to a paper in the *Philosophical Transactions* of that year.

[43] John Webb, *A Vindication of Stone-Heng Restored* (London, 1665), 1 ('when *Chorea Gigantum* first came to my sight in manuscript').

[44] Aubrey, *Monumenta* 24–6 (for comments on the debate and its publications and a summary of his own hypothesis).

I doe here endeavour (for want of written Record) to work-out and restore a kind of Algebraical method, by comparing [those monuments] that I have seen one with another; and reducing them to a kind of Æquation: so (being but an ill Orator my selfe) to make the Stones give Evidence for themselves.[45]

By 'Algebraical method', Aubrey meant comparatism; he was using analogies between different kinds of monuments to make them 'give Evidence' which could not be retrieved from the study of a single site in isolation.[46] He also claimed to have placed textual sources in a supporting role, concentrating instead on the physical remains themselves. In so doing, he recognized the necessity of taking as wide a sample as possible and comparing surviving monuments with each other. His intent, he wrote, was to 'proceed gradually à notioribus ad minus nota [from things more known to those less known] that is to say, from the Remaines of Antiquity less imperfect, to those more imperfect'.[47] This necessity apparently provided the first impetus for his attempt to record as complete a survey of British monuments as possible and perhaps for the idea of a *Monumenta Britannica* at all. Aubrey provided an important caveat to his own methodology, however, in the crucial phrase 'for want of written Record'. He turned to artefacts and archaeological sites out of a lack of written sources, not because he believed in the absolute superiority of physical over textual evidence. Aubrey was no prototype Jean Hardouin to use physical evidence to undermine the textual tradition, or even to doubt the relative value of textual versus artefactual sources as bases upon which to reconstruct history.[48] Instead, he came to the study of non-textual sources out of necessity and a conviction that his predecessors had reached faulty conclusions through a failure to give due weight to the sites themselves.

[45] Aubrey, *Monumenta*, 32.

[46] See Schnapp, *Discovery*, 191–2, on Aubrey's methods of 'comparative antiquitie', and Hunter, *Aubrey*, 183, for the suggestion that this mathematical imagery may be related to the emphasis he put on mathematical and logical reasoning in his *Idea of Education of Young Gentlemen*, Bodleian MS Aubrey 10.

[47] Aubrey, *Monumenta*, 32.

[48] Hardouin was to argue on the basis of numismatic studies that the vast majority of classical texts known in the seventeenth century were medieval forgeries. See his *Ad censuram scriptorum veterum prolegomena* (London, 1766) as well as Anthony Grafton, 'Jean Hardouin: The Antiquary as Pariah', *Journal of the Warburg and Courtauld Institutes* 62 (1999): 241–67, Chantal Grell, 'Le vertige du pyrrhonisme: Hardouin face à l'histoire', in *The Return of Scepticism: From Hobbes and Descartes to Bayle*, ed. Gianni Paganini (Dordrecht, 2003), 363–74, and Arnaldo Momigliano's classic placement of Hardouin within the larger narrative of antiquarian studies at the turn of the eighteenth century in 'Ancient History and the Antiquarian', *Journal of the Warburg and Courtauld Institutes* 13 (1950): 302–3.

Working within this methodological framework, Aubrey developed a novel theory. It was clear, he thought, 'that all the Monuments, which I have here recorded, were Temples', an idea derived from Jones, Webb, and (despite Charleton's interpretation of him) Worm.[49] It was also clear that monuments like Stonehenge and Avebury were extant not only in England, but throughout the British Isles, Scandinavia, Germany, and France.[50] This being so, they could hardly have been built by either Jones's Romans or Charleton's Danes, neither of whose spheres of influence had reached all the regions in which those monuments were to be found. Furthermore, there was no doubt that '[t]hese Antiquities are so exceeding old, that no Books doe reach them' and that they savoured not of some classical purity but of an 'antique rudenesse'.[51] Leaving aside the thorny question of the Scandinavian monuments, which Aubrey elsewhere argued were an example of prehistoric architectural imitation, the inescapable conclusion was that the megaliths were works of the ancient Britons and:

> That the Druids being the most eminent Priests (or Order of Priests) among the Britaines: 'tis odds, but that these ancient monuments (sc. Aubury, Stonehenge, Kerrig y Druidd &c.) were Temples of the Priests of the most eminent Order, viz, Druids, and it is strongly to be presumed that Aubury, Stoneheng, &c: are as ancient as those times.[52]

Aubrey was not the first scholar to reach this conclusion. In Scottish historiography there was a tradition associating stone circles with Druids which dated at least as far back as the Aberdonian humanist Hector Boece. Boece, in his 1527 *Scotorum historiae a prima gentis origine*, had described the religious innovations of the mythical Scottish king, Maynus, including 'havand ane huge stane to the grete south' of temples, 'in memorie heirof remains yite to our dayis many huge stanys, drawing to giddir in forme of

---

[49] Aubrey, *Monumenta*, 24.

[50] Aubrey, *Monumenta*, 85. Evidence for Scandinavian circles came from Worm and later from Olof Rudbeck. For German parallels Aubrey subsequently cited Edward Browne (*Monumenta*, 224), 'In this road through *lower Saxony*, I could not but take notice of many *Barrows* or *Mounts* of *Earth*, the burial *Monuments* of great and famous *Men*, to be often observed also in open Countries in *England*, and sometimes rows of great *Stones*, like those in *Wormius* his *Danish Antiquities*: And in one place I took more particular notice of them, where three massy *Stones* in the middle, were encompassed in a large square by other large *Stones* set up on end' (Edward Browne, *An Account of Several Travels through a Great Part of Germany* [London, 1677], 146).

[51] Aubrey, *Monumenta*, 25, 129. Aubrey's 'antique rudenesse' echoes Rudbeck's description of the 'great simplicity' of the Swedish monuments, but contrasts notably with Jones's appreciation of Stonehenge as a monument so 'magnificent' it could only have been built by the Romans.

[52] Aubrey, *Monumenta*, 25.

circulis, namyt be the pepill the ancient tempillis of goddis. It is na litill admiracioun', he added, 'be quhat ingyne and strength sa huge stanys bene brocht to giddir.'[53] While the Druids were not specifically mentioned, Boece elsewhere made it clear that they were the priests of the ancient Scots and there is little doubt that he understood them to be the ones sacrificing amongst the 'mony huge stanys'.[54] By the seventeenth century this had become the orthodox line amongst Scottish historians such as David Calderwood, whose treatment of 'the ethnick religion of the Scots' identified their priests as Druids and noted that 'it is said that Mainus, the third king, caused designe certaine places of the countrie, and compassed them about with hudge stones, circle-wise', closely echoing Boece.[55] It remains to be seen how this percolated into English antiquarian thought, but its shadow reappears more than once in sixteenth- and seventeenth-century texts, including *Stone-Heng Restored* itself, which went so far as to systematically discredit any possible Druidic origin for Stonehenge.[56]

Aubrey's reception of this link between Druids and megaliths came from two earlier English scholars: William Camden and John Selden. In his *Britannia* Camden had given a brief account of the Druids from classical sources but did not elaborate on his texts.[57] He did, however, provide a crucial clue for Aubrey by noting that amongst the hills of Denbighshire, 'there is a place commonly called *Cerig y Drudion*, that is, *The stones of the Druidae*, and certaine little columns or pillers are seen at *Yvoellas*, with inscriptions in them of strange characters, which some

[53] Hector Boece, *Scotorum historiae a prima gentis origine* (Paris, 1527), fol. XVI ('Extant in rei fidem, vel hoc nostro aevo ingentia ea saxa ducta in circos prisca deorum Phana vulgus appellat. Mirabitur profecto quisquis ea spectaverit qua arte, quibus corporis viribus lapides tanta mole in unum locum fuerint congesti'). The translation, by John Bellenden, is in Hector Boece, *The Chronicles of Scotland*, ed. R. W. Chambers and Edith C. Batho, 2 vols. (Edinburgh and London, 1938–41), i. 57–8.

[54] Boece's Druids, 'richt expert in morall and natural philosoquhy' (*Chronicles of Scotland*, i. 73), were an early example of the tradition associating them with some version of the *prisca theologia*, discussed later in this section. Ronald Hutton has seen in the co-option of stone circles into Druidic religion an echo of the recumbent stone circles near Aberdeen and implies that the local landscape of Boece's home in the north-east of Scotland may have first given rise to this association (Ronald Hutton, *Blood and Mistletoe: The History of the Druids in Britain* [New Haven, CT, and London, 2009], 54).

[55] David Calderwood, *The History of the Kirk of Scotland*, 8 vols., ed. Thomas Thomson (Edinburgh, 1842–9), i. 34.

[56] Jones and Webb concluded that '[t]he truth is, those ancient times had no knowledge of publique works, either Sacred or Secular . . . The *Druid's* led a solitary contemplative life, contenting themselves with such habitations, as either meer necessity invented, to shelter them from contrariety of seasons, without *Art*, without *Order*, without any whatever means tending to perpetuity . . .' (Jones, *Stone-Heng Restored*, 4).

[57] William Camden, *Britain*, trans. Philemon Holland (London, 1610), 12–14.

imagine to have beene erected by the *Druides*.[58] Selden followed Camden
in concluding that the monuments at Cerrigydrudion were 'lapides
Druidarum' (stones of the Druids) in his discussion of the Druids in
Janus Anglorum, although he drew no larger conclusion about other
megalithic monuments, lamenting instead that the pillars at Yvoellas
were no longer readable.[59] Aubrey was convinced that 'the Hinge of this
Discourse depends upon Mr Camden's Kerrig y Druidd', a belief that
evidently stemmed from the etymology given by Camden and repeated by
Selden.[60] For Aubrey, the traditional name of a stone circle in Wales was
the last link in the chain needed to conclusively identify stone circles
across Britain with the holy sites of Druids before the Roman invasion;
material and philological evidence worked in tandem to recover the origin
of these contested antiquities.

Having established to his satisfaction that the Druids were the architects
of Stonehenge, Aubrey added to the *Templa Druidum* an appendix 'On
the Religion and Customs of the Druids'.[61] This appendix was in effect a
literature review containing extracts from classical and modern sources
discussing the Druids. The classical texts singled out by Aubrey included
the standard passages on the subject known to the early moderns from
Caesar's *Commentaries*, Lucan's *Pharsalia*, Tacitus's *Histories*, Cicero's *De
Divinatione*, Pliny's *Natural History*, Ammianus Marcellinus, Diodorus
Siculus, Diogenes Laertius, and Ovid's *Amores*.[62] More revealing of
Aubrey's notions of Druidism, however, were his citations of modern
authors. By the time he began to compile the *Templa Druidum* there was
already an established tradition of scholarly interest in the Druids, numer-
ous exemplars of which were known to him.[63] Of these, the works of John
Selden and Thomas Smith reappear most frequently and suggest that
Aubrey's work was imbricated with an antiquarian tradition which saw

---

[58] Camden, *Britain*, 675.

[59] John Selden, *Jani Anglorum facies altera* (London, 1610), 20.

[60] Aubrey, *Monumenta*, 22. That his knowledge of this derived from the *Janus* as well as
the *Britannia* is made likely by his early ownership of a copy (now Bodleian Ashmole 1555)
as well as a reference to Selden's account of the Druids in the appendix of the *Templa*
(Aubrey, *Monumenta*, 133).

[61] Aubrey's unusual choice of name for this appendix ('mantissa') may be partly in
imitation of Ralph Cudworth's *Discourse Concerning the True Notion of the Lords Supper*
(London, 1642) in which Cudworth states that he will 'adde as a *Mantissa* to that discourse
[of Jewish ritual feasting] something of the custome of the Heathens also' (9), cited in the
OED as one of the earliest uses of the word in English.

[62] Aubrey, *Monumenta*, 131–50. See Hutton, *Blood and Mistletoe*, ch. 1, for commentary
on these and other classical texts concerning Druidic practices.

[63] A survey of many of the principal texts on the subject can be found in Hutton, *Blood
and Mistletoe*, 49–85.

the Druids as central to the dispersal of patriarchal wisdom across the ancient world.

Although now better known for his exploration of Hebrew culture, John Selden addressed the Druids and their place in ancient history in a series of works published in the second decade of the seventeenth century. As early as 1605, when he composed his *Analecta Anglo-Britannica* (not published until 1615), Selden had stressed the parallels between the supposed Druidic belief in metempsychosis and the teachings of Pythagoras. By the time he composed his *Janus Anglorum* (1610) this had gained the status of an obvious intellectual kinship, although 'Whether the *Druids*... had their *Metempsychosis* or transmigration of Souls, from *Pythagoras*, or he from them, I cannot tell.'[64] The Druids, in Selden's reconstruction, 'were of the oldest standing among the Philosophers of the Gentiles, and the most ancient among their Guardians of Laws'.[65] Two years later, when he composed the antiquarian notes accompanying Michael Drayton's chorographical poem *Poly-Olbion* (1612), he elaborated yet again on his reconstruction of Druidic practice, this time crediting the Druids with a sort of monotheism: even if 'before our Saviours time, *Britain* acknowledged not one true God, yet it came as neere to what they should have done, or rather neerer, then most of other, eyther *Greeke* or *Roman*'.[66] Selden claimed that the Druids had worshipped a single god under the name of Apollo, quoting ambiguous epigraphical evidence to support his theory.[67] Both here and in the *Janus* he supplemented his philological arguments with a vivid visualization of the Druids, quoting the fifteenth-century German antiquary Conrad Celtis, who claimed that he had seen:

[I]n an Abbey at the foot of *Vichtelberg* hil, neer *Vottland*, six Statues, of stone, set in the Church-wall, some VII. foote every one tall, bare head and foote, cloakt and hooded, with a bagge, a booke, a staffe, a beard hanging to his middle, and spreading a Mustachio, an austere looke and eyes fixt on the earth.

Both Aubrey and Selden had no doubt these were images of Druids.[68] These statues fit perfectly with the picture of patriarchal wise-men, steeped

<hr>

[64] John Selden, *Analecton Anglobritannicon libri duo* (Frankfurt, 1615), 20–36, and see Toomer, *John Selden*, i. 59–60; John Selden, *The Reverse or Back-Face of the English Janus*, trans. Adam Littleton (London, 1682), 15.

[65] Selden, *English Janus*, 16.

[66] Michael Drayton, *Poly-Olbion* (London, 1612), 152.

[67] Drayton, *Poly-Olbion*, 152, citing Joseph Justus Scaliger, *Ausonianarum lectionum libri duo* (Lyon, 1574), 28, and Camden, *Britain*, 770–1, for two Roman inscriptions which he believed were dedications to the Druidic deity.

[68] Selden, *English Janus*, 16; Drayton, *Poly-Olbion*, 154. Celtis himself described the statues as 'septem pedum singulae. nudis pedibus: capita intecti. graecanico pallio &

in the *prisca theologia*, which Selden had elaborated in his works—unsurprisingly to modern eyes, given that they were almost certainly medieval jamb figures of biblical prophets.[69] For Selden the Druids were no savages, but rather the inheritors of an ancient tradition of wisdom and learning, perhaps even the tutors of Pythagoras himself.

A generation later, the young Oxford orientalist Thomas Smith published a virtuosic monograph entitled *Syntagma de Druidum moribus ac institutis* (1664).[70] Smith built upon Selden's work, referencing his etymological arguments as well as the by-then standard inference that the stones at Cerrigydrudion were simply '*lapides Druidarum*'.[71] He went further than Selden in his comparative approach, however, doing for the Druids' sacred groves what Jones, Webb, and Charleton had done for Stonehenge. He saw in them echoes, not only of the grove of Diana Nemorensis, but of the Abrahamic oaks of Mamre, and in an ingenious game of intellectual hopscotch proceeded to link the Druids with patriarchal wisdom, the Persian magi, and the Indian Brahmins in a series of increasingly far-fetched hops and skips. Forget Pythagoras, Smith argued (although he nonetheless had a role to play), the Druids were *the* primeval religious order, dispensing the *prisca theologia* across the entire ancient world.

Aubrey quoted both Selden and Smith extensively in his textual appendix to the *Templa* and citations to their works appear regularly throughout the manuscript of the *Monumenta*. However, their ideas existed in tension with statements he made elsewhere concerning the uncivilized state of the pre-Roman Britons, '2 or 3 degrees I suppose lesse savage then the Americans', and his emphasis that stone circles generally were 'such rude monuments' that even the none-too-sophisticated Anglo-Saxons could have produced something more polished.[72] And yet Aubrey could speculate, along with the Welsh antiquary Thomas Sebastian Price, that Smith's identification of the Druidic groves with the famous cult of Diana at Nemi had some basis, not least in a supposed etymological link with the ancient

---

cucullato. perulaque & barba ad inguina usque permissa & circa naris fistulas bifurcata in manibus liber & baculus dyogenicus saevera fronte & tristi supercilio obstipo capite: figentes lumina terris' (Conrad Celtis, 'De origine, situ, moribus & institutis Norimbergae', in *Quatuor libri amorum secundum quatuor latera Germaniæ feliciter incipiunt* [Nuremberg, 1502] sig. mviiir). For the context of Celtis's (mis)identification of these medieval jamb figures at the monastery of Speinshart see Christopher S. Wood, *Forgery, Replica, Fiction: Temporalities of German Renaissance Art* (Chicago, 2008), 1–12.

[69] Wood, *Forgery, Replica, Fiction*, 3–4.
[70] Thomas Smith, *Syntagma de Druidum Moribus ac Institutis* (London, 1664). Aubrey's own copy, inscribed 'Jo: Aubrey R.S.S.', is now Bodleian Ashmole 1572 and he references it in the appendix (Aubrey, *Monumenta*, 145).
[71] Smith, *Syntagma*, 7–8.
[72] Bodleian MS Aubrey 3, fol. 10v; Bodleian MS Aubrey 11, fol. 10v.

British language.[73] For Aubrey, the ancient culture he studied could go both ways: purveyor of *prisca theologia* or primitive barbarism. This vacillation went hand in hand with his Pyrrhonistic conviction that classical texts could only go so far in making sense of the Druids. 'The Latin Historians', he wrote, 'make great mistakes as to the Lawes & customes of the Jewes who lived at Rome & were much more considerable than the Druids, then why may they not mistake more in the Religion &c: of the Druids who lived farther from their acquaintance & knowledge?'[74] By undercutting any absolute authority on their part, Aubrey could use the classical texts he copied out and quoted so copiously, but was not hampered by their disagreement with his more novel theories.

While Aubrey did not wholeheartedly embrace Selden and Smith's visions of the lost wisdom of the ancient world, his association of their work with his own identification of megalithic sites as Druidic has a striking parallel in another antiquarian dispute which erupted almost simultaneously in Sweden. This latter debate arose independently of the English controversies over Stonehenge and the Druids, but it involved analogous issues of control over a national past, tendentious interpretation of evidence, and rejection of textual in favour of artefactual or site-based sources. Later, Aubrey himself would make use of the texts produced during this controversy, drawing upon both the English and the Swedish traditions in his writings of the 1680s and 1690s. Even before that point of contact, however, a closer examination of the Swedish debate provides an illuminating parallel to the English one, helps clarify the ways in which early modern nationalisms profoundly shaped the arguments that Aubrey and his contemporaries advanced, and provides the tools with which to place those arguments within continent-wide trends in antiquarian research and discourse.

THE SWEDISH ATLANTIS AND
ANTIQUARIAN NATIONALISM

Swedish antiquarian scholarship already had a legacy of cultural imperialism, claiming for itself the entire—still only recently rediscovered—saga

---

[73] Aubrey, *Monumenta*, 135, 144. The relevant note at 135 reads: 'from Tho. Price of Llanvillinyn Montgomeryshire. Lucan: lib. 1. et Tarinis Scythica non mitior axa Diana. *Taran* est Britannica Thunderbolt. Item ab eodem *Llundain(i)* Imago Diana.' For the obscure Price see *Dictionary of Welsh Biography Down to 1940* (London, 1949), 793. Aubrey probably knew him through Meredith Lloyd or Edward Lhuyd.

[74] Aubrey, *Monumenta*, 147.

corpus, all runic texts, and a variety of other materials as part of its 'Gothic Renaissance' earlier in the seventeenth century.[75] These claims were made in the teeth of a previous, and still vigorous, Danish scholarly ascendency.[76] The rediscovery of the sagas had been spearheaded by Danes and Icelanders, but in the decades following the Peace of Westphalia and Swedish domination of the north their discoveries were contested, appropriated, and reconfigured by Swedish scholars. In the midst of this fight for antiquity, the Swedes turned to non-textual artefacts and sites as potential sources with which to buttress their competing understandings of ancient Scandinavian history.[77]

In 1666 Johann Scheffer, a Strasbourg-born scholar and something of an outsider at the University of Uppsala, had published his *Upsalia*, an urban antiquarian study in the tradition of Flavio Biondo and the architectural and topographical antiquaries of the fifteenth and sixteenth centuries.[78] In it he argued that pagan Uppsala was built on the site of the present town, not at the village of Gamla (Old) Uppsala, a few miles away, and that the pagan temple described by the eleventh-century chronicler Adam of Bremen was not to be confused with the church at Gamla Uppsala, which was, Scheffer argued, only a few hundred years old.[79] This argument went against historical orthodoxy as set forth in Erik Olofsson's fifteenth-century *Historia Suecorum Gothorumque* and elsewhere.[80] In 1672 Scheffer's colleague Olof Verelius published his *editio princeps* of *Hervarar saga ok Heiðreks* and went out of his way, in a note discussing the burial of the legendary lovers Ingibjörg and Hjalmar in a

[75] For surveys of this trend in Swedish historiography see Seaton, *Literary Relations*; Ernst Ekman, 'Gothic Patriotism and Olof Rudbeck', *Journal of Modern History* 34 (1962): 52–63; Stina Hansson, 'The Lament of the Swedish Language: Sweden's Gothic Renaissance', *Renaissance Studies* 23 (2009): 151–60; William Poole and Kelsey Jackson Williams, 'A Swede in Restoration Oxford: Gothic Patriots, Swedish Books, English Scholars', *Lias* 39 (2012): 1–67.
[76] The Danish scholarly tradition bore late fruit in an English context when it was rediscovered by the poet and antiquary Thomas Gray in the mid-eighteenth century, for which see Kelsey Jackson Williams, 'Thomas Gray and the Goths: Philology, Poetry, and the Uses of the Norse Past in Eighteenth-Century England', *Review of English Studies* 65 (2014): 694–710.
[77] See generally Allan Ellenius, 'Johannes Schefferus and Swedish Antiquity', *Journal of the Warburg and Courtauld Institutes* 20 (1957): 59–74.
[78] Johann Scheffer, *Upsalia cujus occasione plurima in religione, sacris, festis... illustrantur* (Uppsala, 1666). See Flavio Biondo, *Italia illustrata*, ed. and trans. Jeffrey A. White (Cambridge, MA, 2005).
[79] For the famous temple and its golden chain see Adam of Bremen, *History of the Archbishops of Hamburg-Bremen*, trans. Francis J. Tschan (New York, 1959), 207–8.
[80] Erik Olofsson, *Historia Suecorum Gothorumque*, ed. Johan Loccenius (Stockholm, 1654).

barrow there, to contest the age of the church at Gamla Uppsala.[81] Verelius, in a move reminiscent of both Jones and Aubrey, measured and illustrated the remains of the church and found its structure reminiscent, not only of the building described by Adam of Bremen, but also of the arch of Janus Quadrifrons in Rome.[82] Like Jones and Webb he attempted to naturalize an unidentified monument into the classical framework of early modern scholarship. In the following years both sides published additional squibs until forbidden to continue by Uppsala's chancellor, Count Magnus Gabriel De la Gardie, but their main lines of argument changed little.[83] Scheffer was a more conservative textual critic and a more reticent interpreter of archaeological evidence while Verelius, acting on the assumptions of Gothic antiquity common amongst the Swedish nationalist historians, was quick to find similarities between medieval Scandinavian and classical culture, both in texts and in archaeology. Arguments by architectural comparatism were common to both sides, but given the lack of any real evidence to analyse (the church at Gamla Uppsala was, as Scheffer had supposed, only built in the eleventh century but survived in a very damaged form), no broader conclusions could be drawn.[84]

Both methodologically and ideologically, the Uppsala temple debate not only bore a resemblance to the Stonehenge controversies of previous decades, but also set the stage for the greatest and most problematic product of the Swedish antiquarian tradition: Olof Rudbeck's *Atlantica sive Manheim* (Rudbeck had already weighed in on Verelius's side during the earlier debate).[85] Published between 1679 and 1702 in four volumes and an accompanying elephant folio of plates, the *Atlantica* brought every resource of philology and antiquarianism to bear on Sweden's ancient past, resulting in the inescapable conclusion that Uppsala was none

---

[81] Olof Verelius, ed., *Hervarar Saga på Gammal Gotska med Olai Vereli uttolkning och notis* (Uppsala, 1672), 62–6.

[82] Verelius, *Hervarar Saga*, 64 and figures I–V facing 64–5.

[83] Ellenius, 'Johannes Schefferus', 63–6.

[84] The archaeology of the Christian and pre-Christian ritual complexes at Uppsala, together with the other, in some cases still unidentified, remains surrounding them continues to be explored; cf. John Ljungqkvist, Per Frölund, Hans Göthberg, and Daniel Löwenborg, 'Gamla Uppsala: Structural Development of a Centre in Middle Sweden', *Archäoligisches Korrespondenzblatt* 41 (2011): 571–85.

[85] Olof Rudbeck, *Atland Eller Manhem... Atlantica sive Manheim*, 4 vols. (Uppsala, 1679–1702). For Rudbeck's life and work the basic sources remain the *Atlantica* and his letters as edited by Claes Annerstedt, *Bref af Olof Rudbeck d.ä. rörande Uppsalas universitet*, 4 vols. (Uppsala, 1893–1905). The best modern studies are those of Gunnar Eriksson, *The Atlantic Vision: Olaus Rudbeck and Baroque Science* (Canton, MA, 1994) and *Rudbeck 1630–1702: Liv, lärdom och dröm i barockens Sverige* (Stockholm, 2002).

other than Plato's Atlantis.[86] Rudbeck opened his first volume with a methodological chapter on the 'necessary preparations for a valid knowledge of antiquarian matters'.[87] In it he distinguished six possible sources: *traditio* (oral history), *historia* (or 'saga', in the Swedish parallel text), *geographia* (geography), *suffragia naturae* (the authority of nature), *aedificia* (monuments), and *cippi* (standing stones), and outlined the ways in which they could profitably be used together. His summary of the importance of the study of ancient monuments paralleled the lines of argument Aubrey would take in the *Monumenta*, arguing that the 'great simplicity' of the prehistoric sites he had examined, was 'the most certain index of great antiquity', certainly much greater than that of Rome.[88] Nonetheless, had Rudbeck stopped there his archaeological methodology would have been little different from that of Scheffer or Verelius. His innovation was the development of a theory of stratigraphy, outlined in chapter 6 of the *Atlantica* ('in which the old Swedish race is deduced out of ancient tumuli and burial mounds') and experimentally tested.[89]

Rudbeck had observed that the undisturbed surface of the earth was covered with a layer of humus, made up of vegetation and airborne debris. To prove the nature of its accretion he left an empty pot exposed to the elements over the course of the winter and noted the presence of a fine layer of this humus at its bottom the following spring. Continuing these tests on sites known to have been untouched since significant disturbance ten and fifty years before, respectively, Rudbeck observed what seemed to be a constant rate of sediment accretion. He then extrapolated from this data to reach a general equation of deposition rates which could be used to date the age of an object found at any given level within a layer of undisturbed topsoil. Using this technique he dated numerous sites around Sweden, including the barrows outside Gamla Uppsala, which he concluded—in line with modern archaeological scholarship—were built *c.*600–1000 CE.[90]

---

[86] For the wider context of Atlantis and Atlantean theories in the early modern period see Pierre Vidal-Naquet, 'Hérodote et l'Atlantide: Entre les Grecs et les Juifs: Réflexions sur l'historiographie du siècle des lumières', *Quaderni di Storia* 16 (1982): 3–76, and Pierre Vidal-Naquet and Janet Lloyd, 'Atlantis and the Nations', *Critical Inquiry* 18 (1992): 300–26.

[87] Rudbeck, *Atlantica*, i. 1–15.

[88] Rudbeck, *Atlantica*, i. 14–15 ('Rudera & parietinae praesertim arcium antiquarum, in his locis multò quam apud gentes alias frequentius occurrunt. Et haec monimenta e rudi tantum materia congesta praecipuè commendat operis maxima simplicitas, quae ultimae vetustatis certissimus index est. Romanos quidem arcus triumphales & alia magnifica aedificia post se reliquisse, e ruderibus, quae passim adhuc conspiciuntur manifestum evadit: atqui temporibus antiquissimis ea operis elegantia minimè respondet').

[89] Rudbeck, *Atlantica*, i. 125–44 ('in quo gentis Sveonicae vetustas ex antiquorum tumulis seu collibus sepulcralibus colligitur').

[90] Rudbeck, *Atlantica*, i. 125–44 and plates, tab. 31, fig. 104 (a cross-section of several layers of topsoil measured by relative age). See also Eriksson, *Atlantic Vision*, 15–16.

Rudbeck's work was remarkable not only for its novel methodology, but also for its reliance on that methodology, and on physical remains in general, as the ultimate basis for his arguments. He described the *Atlantica* as a house with foundations, walls, roof, ornaments, and decorations. The last of these were philological and etymological arguments, the walls and roof were 'the writings of the ancients' and:

> The foundation is what I call the country of Sweden, its lakes, mountains and streams and other such things, all of which features remain undisturbed until the stone, mentioned by Daniel, who himself planted it, falls from heaven crushing everything.[91]

Rudbeck stands in relation to Scheffer and Verelius much as Aubrey stood to Jones, Webb, and Charleton. He built upon the arguments of his predecessors, adopting their comparative methodologies but taking a dramatically material, non-textual turn in his own scholarship and using artefacts and sites as sources through which to reconstruct a previously unknown ancient past. As with the other scholars discussed in this chapter, methodological innovation moved in an uneasy alliance with a series of nationalist presuppositions; while his use of stratigraphy helped Rudbeck prove the antiquity of his burial mounds, their Suevo-Atlantean nature had never been in any doubt to him. As Edward Gibbon would later comment of Rudbeck, 'whatever is celebrated either in history or in fable this zealous patriot ascribes to his country'.[92]

Aubrey came into contact with Rudbeck and Verelius's ideas in 1681 when their student Johan Heysig arrived in London, acting as a travelling tutor to the young nobleman Baron Erik Axelsson Sparre.[93] Aubrey was, however, already familiar with the basic concept underlying Rudbeck's stratigraphy, having encountered it a decade before in the 1671 English translation by Henry Oldenburg of the Dane Nicolaus Steno's 1669 *De solido intra solidum naturaliter contento dissertationis prodromus*.[94] In their

---

[91] Rudbeck, *Atlantica*, i. 560; English translation from Eriksson, *Atlantic Vision*, 45. Rudbeck refers to the vision of the stone at Daniel 2.34–5 ('the stone that smote the image became a great mountain, and filled the whole earth').

[92] Edward Gibbon, *The History of the Decline and Fall of the Roman Empire*, 3 vols., ed. David Womersley (London, 1994), i. 234. See also Anthony Grafton, *The Footnote: A Curious History* (Cambridge, MA, and London, 1999), 182–3.

[93] Poole and Jackson Williams, 'A Swede in Restoration Oxford', 1–67.

[94] Nicolaus Steno, *De solido intra solidum naturaliter contento dissertationis prodromus* (Florence, 1669). Translated as Nicolaus Steno, *The Prodromus to a Dissertation Concerning Solids Naturally Contained Within Solids*, trans. H[enry] O[ldenburg] (London, 1671) and republished in Robert Boyle, *Essays... of Effluviums... To Which is Added The Prodromus to a Dissertation... By Nicholas Steno* (London, 1673), although only a minority of copies of the Boyle also contain the *Prodromus* (see John F. Fulton, *A Bibliography of the Honourable Robert Boyle, Fellow of the Royal Society*, 2nd edn. [Oxford, 1961], 75–6).

most basic form, Steno's theories established several propositions concerning the behaviour of solids, deriving from these a theory of stratification and sedimentation which allowed for an explanation of fossils and for a reading of layers of earth as successive stages of geological history—Rudbeck's sediment deposition experiments writ large.[95] Aubrey's marginalia in his copy of Steno make it clear that he read and agreed with the Dane's theories. Among his notes are a series on the flyleaf including 'Origin of the Strata', 'Some strata remaining since the Creation', and 'The Beds wherin Bones of Animals are most certainly since the Creation'.[96] We also know that Aubrey read and approved of Rudbeck's parallel experiments and, together with Christopher Wren and Robert Hooke, made observations on the changing ground level of London since the Roman period.[97] Like Rudbeck, he had become increasingly fascinated with the possibility that physical remains traditionally at or beyond the edge of the antiquary's purview could be used to explain otherwise unknown tracts of the ancient past.

But Aubrey's seemingly 'modern' antiquarianism—his emphasis on material objects, his comparatism, his knowledge of stratigraphy, his questioning of traditional, text-based arguments—should not beguile us into believing he existed outside of contemporary national, religious, or ethnic controversies. Like the other scholars who participated in the debates over Stonehenge or the temple at Uppsala, he combined intellectual ingenuity and methodological innovation with certain nationalist goals and assumptions, never explicitly expressed but ever-present in his work. In Rudbeck's case such goals were obvious: a desire to aggrandize contemporary Sweden and justify its new role as a major power by finding for it a suitably illustrious ancient past. Aubrey was no different, only subtler. Rather than building an Atlantean monument to national

---

[95] Steno, *De solido, passim*. See also the summary in William Poole, *The World Makers: Scientists of the Restoration and the Search for the Origins of the Earth* (Oxford, 2010), 102–3.

[96] Aubrey's copy of the *Prodromus* is Bodleian Ashmole C. 10. For these notes see the back flyleaf. Aubrey's reception of Steno's theories was somewhat complicated by his belief that they had been stolen by Oldenburg from Robert Hooke. On the front pastedown of his copy of the *Prodromus* he wrote, 'Memorandum, Mr H. Oldenburgh by stealth sent a copie of Mr Hookes Lectures of Solids in Solids read about 1664, to Mr Steno; to be printed Mr Hookes excellent Notions in Italie & Mr H. Oldenburg translated them [i.e., Steno's *Prodromus*, which Aubrey took to be Hooke's lectures] into English' (Bodleian Ashmole C. 10).

[97] He noted, 'In Rudbeckii Monumenta Suecica are excellent Remarques concerning the growing of Earth, which is worth the reading; and there is also a Scale of it's growth, for every 1000, or 500 yeares. "—annis 100—quam nunc humus atra et herbis obsita segit crassitie partis quinta digita unius. Annis 500 digitum circiter unum. stratam super stratum haec autem omnia ab oriente versus occidentem jactata fuisse apparet." cap. VI.' (MS Aubrey 1, fol. 66r). For the ground level of London see Aubrey, *Monumenta*, 505.

aspirations, he took pride in his Welsh ancestry, identified himself as Welsh despite his birth and education in Wiltshire, and firmly believed that his adopted people were descended from a sophisticated Romano-British culture which had been largely destroyed by the brutish Anglo-Saxons.[98]

Aubrey was immensely proud of his Welsh forebears.[99] At one stage he had attempted to insert his pedigree into Edmund Gibson's 1695 edition of Camden's *Britannia* and throughout his life he made frequent visits into Wales, at first to his own estates there and later, after the reversal in fortune which led to the sale of his properties, to the seat of his cousin Sir John Aubrey of Llantrithyd.[100] This self-identification was strengthened by an early acquaintance with the Welsh lawyer and antiquary Meredith Lloyd, who served as a conduit through which Aubrey came into contact with seventeenth-century Welsh antiquarian scholarship, whether in the form of linguistic data on the Celtic languages or reports concerning Welsh monuments such as the Eliseg Pillar and the Bedd Rhita Gawr cairn.[101] Likewise, towards the end of his life Aubrey's friendship with

---

[98] For concise summaries and discussions of the question of nationalism in the seventeenth-century Celtic world see Colin Kidd, *British Identities before Nationalism: Ethnicity and Nationhood in the Atlantic World, 1600–1800* (Cambridge, 1999), *passim*, and John Kerrigan, *Archipelagic English: Literature, History, and Politics, 1603–1707* (Oxford, 2008), esp. 115–40. A more general theoretical reinterpretation of pre-modern nationalism is given by Caspar Hirschi, *The Origins of Nationalism: An Alternative History from Ancient Rome to Early Modern Germany* (Cambridge, 2012).

[99] The senior branch of the Aubreys had been settled at Abercynrig in Brecknockshire for many generations and deduced their descent from a legendary 'Stiant Awbrey' of Norman extraction who allegedly came to Britain in the train of William the Conqueror (Lewys Dwnn, *Heraldic Visitations of Wales and Part of the Marches*, 2 vols., ed. Sir Samuel Rush Meyrick [Llandovery, 1846], ii. 57). Aubrey's own connection to the Abercynrig family was highly attenuated, however; his great-grandfather William Aubrey (*c.*1529–1595), 'second son, of Thomas Aubrey the 4th son of Hopkin Aubrey, of Abercuvrig', had been born in Brecknockshire but made his career in Elizabethan London (*ODNB*, *s.n.*, and Aubrey, *Lives*, i. 60–74).

[100] Aubrey proposed this to Lhuyd in his capacity as subeditor for Wales. In a letter of 1 April 1694 Lhuyd gently rebuffed him: 'you'l be so kind as to excuse me, for takeing no notice of Aubreys. For to celebrate those Norman families whom some persons of good account in Wales, call by a name signifying *Grassatores* [i.e., robbers or footpads], and to take no notice of our own Gentry; as it would be in me no sign of an honest patriot, so it would give several just occasion of offence.' He then foisted the whole matter off onto Thomas Tanner, as being more properly pertinent to Wiltshire (Edward Lhuyd, *Life and Letters of Edward Lhuyd*, ed. R. T. Gunther [Oxford, 1945], 234–5). Needless to say, Aubrey's pedigree was absent from the published edition.

[101] Aubrey, *Monumenta*, 118, 794–5, 914–15 (for etymology), 550–1 (Eliseg Pillar), 808–9 (Bedd Rita Gawr). For Lloyd see *Dictionary of Welsh Biography*, 585–6; Richard Williams, *Montgomeryshire Worthies*, 2nd edn. (Newtown, 1894), 176. Lloyd was living near Aubrey at a girdler's shop under the King's Head Tavern in Fleet Street, 5 February 1655, when he addressed a letter from there to his cousin, the antiquary Robert Vaughan of Hengwrt ('A Catalogue of Curious and Valuable MSS. in Hengwrt Library, A.D. 1658',

Edward Lhuyd also brought him into contact with a group of young
Welsh scholars at Oxford, chiefly based in Jesus College, who regularly
begged to be remembered to him at the end of Lhuyd's letters.[102]
These associations either reinforced or helped to define Aubrey's own
perception of his cultural identity and his relationship to the British
past.[103] He identified the Welsh as direct descendants of Romano-British
culture and had little time for the savage Anglo-Saxons and Danes, whose
contribution to British civilization is regularly denied throughout his
works. By a bold act of historical revision the English also became
descendants of the same Romano-British culture in Aubrey's writings
and he developed a *longue durée* narrative of Britain's history which
effectively both Celticized and Romanized British culture at the expense
of German and Scandinavian influences.[104] While not so flagrant as the
antiquarian imperialism of Rudbeck or Verelius, Aubrey's interpretation
of British history was essentially conditioned by his own cultural and
national loyalties.[105] This does not detract from his scholarship, but to
ignore it is to ignore one of the essential presuppositions which informed
so much of early modern antiquarianism: a commitment to the centrality
and significance of the antiquary's own perceived ancestral nation or
culture.

Cambrian Register 3 [1818]: 302–3). He and Aubrey likely first met in the London legal
community of the mid-century. As well as antiquarianism, Lloyd was also interested in
natural philosophy, was cited by Aubrey as a source for several alchemical statements (cf.
Hunter, *Aubrey*, 22), and gave him a copy of Henricus Regius's Cartesian *Philosophia
naturalis*, 2nd edn. (Amsterdam, 1654). Aubrey's copy is now Bodleian Ashmole F 22 and
is inscribed on the flyleaf 'Sum Johannis Aubrii R.S.S. | The Gift of my worthy Friend |
Mr Meredith Lloyd'.

[102] Notable amongst these were Ellis Anwyll, MA, of Jesus College, Oxford, and later
rector of Llaniestyn, Carmarthenshire (Joseph Foster, *Alumni Oxonienses: The Members of
the University of Oxford, 1500–1714*, 4 vols. (Oxford, 1891–2), i. 28), John Davies, MA
and later DD, of Jesus (Foster, *Alumni Oxonienses*, i. 381), Christopher White, a chemist
associated with the university (Foster, *Alumni Oxonienses*, iv. 1613), and William Wynne,
MA, Fellow of Jesus, and editor of David Powel's *History of Wales* (London, 1697) (Foster,
Alumni Oxonienses, iv. 1696). For their greetings to and associations with Aubrey see
Lhuyd, *Life and Letters*, 177, 184, 207, 238. Jonathan Edwards, principal of Jesus, also
took an active interest in Aubrey and his work (Lhuyd, *Life and Letters*, 216–17, 235).

[103] At least some of his Welsh friends accepted Aubrey's self-identification. Lhuyd wrote
on 2 March 1693 that the bearer of the letter was 'Mr. Thomas, *a countryman of ours*'
(Bodleian MS Aubrey 12, fol. 241r, emphasis added).

[104] See, for example, Aubrey on ancient embanking and draining: 'we must conclude
that these great Dreyns were donne by [the Romans]: who were skilfull in all Arts: and the
Saxons were barbarous & ignorant' (*Monumenta*, 1023).

[105] For the growth of modern Romantic, nationalist interest in the Welsh past which
had its roots in the beliefs of Aubrey and his contemporaries, see the survey by Prys Morgan,
'From Death to a View: The Hunt for the Welsh Past in the Romantic Period', in *The
Invention of Tradition*, ed. Eric Hobsbawm and Terence Ranger (Cambridge, 1983):
43–100.

Aubrey has been praised by both historians and archaeologists for his perceptive conclusion that megalithic monuments such as Stonehenge and Avebury pre-dated recorded British history and were built by an indigenous people rather than Romans, Danes, or other interlopers.[106] However, the genesis of the arguments in the *Templa Druidum* was far more complex and equivocal than such praise would suggest. As well as developing or adapting new methodologies and bringing to the study of prehistoric monuments a new emphasis on comparatism and contextualization, Aubrey also deployed older mythical histories and conjectural philologies to support his Druidical theories, and ultimately founded his interpretation upon his own emotive identification with what he saw as a Romano-British Welsh culture. As comparisons between the Stonehenge debate in England, Worm's hunt for ancient monuments in Denmark, and the Uppsala controversy in Sweden show, understanding the ancient past in seventeenth-century Europe was a project situated within a shifting web of national, cultural, and local loyalties which could both motivate and at least partially determine the conclusions of antiquarian scholarship.

---

[106] Michael Hunter, 'The Royal Society and the Origins of British Archaeology', *Antiquity* 65 (1971): 113–21, 187–92; Hunter, *Aubrey*, 182–3 and *passim*; Stuart Piggott, *Ancient Britons and the Antiquarian Imagination: Ideas from the Renaissance to the Regency* (London, 1989), 113–15; Schnapp, *Discovery*, 188–96, among others.

2

Monumenta Britannica

Ancient Traces in the British Landscape

In 1663, when the debate over Stonehenge was still at its height, the future James VII and II had asked Aubrey to 'give an account of the old Camps and Barrows on the Plaines' near Bath.[1] It was not until five years later, after the first draft of the *Templa Druidum* had been composed, that Aubrey began to fulfil the Duke of York's request. As he began to compose the new manuscript, he emphasized his unique qualifications. Francis Bacon, he wrote, wished in *The Advancement of Learning* that active men 'would or could become writers' and Aubrey's frequent journeys to and from his estates in Wiltshire and South Wales eminently qualified him as an active man, while his 'ingenious', scholarly turn of mind meant that he 'could not but make somewhat a deeper inspection into [ancient monuments] than one of the Vulgar'.[2] In short, he was the perfect gentleman for the job.

This essay would eventually form the nucleus of the second part of the *Monumenta Britannica*, of which the *Templa Druidum* was the first. The extent and focus of the work changed dramatically over the course of Aubrey's life. In 1673 John Locke encouraged him to publish the *Templa*, going so far as to promise the Earl of Shaftesbury's financial assistance, but Aubrey held fire.[3] At the time he was involved with John Ogilby's abortive endeavour to produce a major new antiquarian history of Britain and thought that the *Templa* might make up a

---

[1] Aubrey, *Monumenta*, 21.

[2] Aubrey, *Monumenta*, i. 237, paraphrasing Francis Bacon, *The Advancement of Learning*, ed. Michael Kiernan (Oxford, 2000), 143.

[3] Letter from Aubrey to Locke, dated Shrove Tuesday (i.e., 11 February) 1674 and published in Maurice Cranston, 'John Locke and John Aubrey', *Notes and Queries* 197 (1952): 383–4. See also Maurice Cranston, 'John Locke and John Aubrey', *Notes and Queries* 195 (1950): 552–4. Cranston, however, is incorrect in thinking that the 'Scriblings' are Aubrey's Wiltshire manuscripts. The date and context makes it far more likely they refer to the *Templa*.

portion of it.[4] When that project failed, he continued adding to the manuscript and by 22 May 1680 was writing to Anthony Wood that he had decided to rename the entire work 'Monumenta Britannica for reasons I will tell you hereafter. So Olaus Wormius called his Monumenta Danica. The next thing I goe about shall be to transcribe it faire, & print it.'[5] Once again publication was delayed, however, and he did not make a complete transcript of the manuscript until 1689, by which time '[t]he first draught was worn-out with time & handling: and now, me thinks, after many years lying dormant, I come abroad like the Ghost of one of those Druids'.[6] It is this version of the *Monumenta* which survives as the two impressive folio volumes of Bodleian MS Top. Gen. c. 24–5.

In its final form Aubrey divided the *Monumenta* into three parts. The *Templa Druidum* was the first. The second consisted of six chapters on camps, castles, military architecture, Roman towns, pits, and horns. The third was a similarly miscellaneous collection of eight chapters on barrows, urns, sepulchres, ditches, highways, Roman pavements, coins, and embanking and draining.[7] Behind this chaotic, Borgesian encyclopaedia of antiquarian materials lay an inexhaustible curiosity and a series of novel methodologies for thinking about the physical remains of the ancient past. By choosing to study camps and barrows rather than cameos and bas-reliefs, Aubrey moved away from the main stream of antiquarian thought and its tendency to focus on artefacts in isolation or, at most, as one facet of a site. Instead he firmly located his subjects in their wider contexts, justifying his claims to the Baconian role of active scholar, and using the

[4] Ogilby had been in the process of producing a vast geographical work, designed to rival Blaeu's *Atlas*, since 1669, and had already published *Africa* (1670), *China* (1671), and *Asia* (1671); see Katherine S. van Eerde, *John Ogilby and the Taste of His Times* (Folkestone, 1976), esp. ch. 7. Aubrey was hired in August 1672 to write 'the History of all England' for Ogilby's next volume (Bodleian MS Wood F 39, fol. 181r), an undertaking which had been scaled down by May 1673 to an antiquarian survey of Surrey (Bodleian MS Aubrey 12, fol. 206r). Aubrey undertook the survey in the summer of 1673, enjoying himself immensely and writing to Anthony Wood that it was 'the pleasantest Pilgrimage that ever any man has had I thinke since the reformation' (Bodleian MS Wood F 39, fol. 221r), but in October Ogilby scrapped the entire project, leaving Aubrey fuming and out of pocket. 'God deliver me from such men', he wrote to Wood (Bodleian MS Wood F 39, fol. 231r). His *Perambulation of Surrey* survives as Bodleian MS Aubrey 4 and was later published in greatly expanded form as John Aubrey, *The Natural History and Antiquities of the County of Surrey*, 5 vols. (London, 1718–19). See Hunter, *Aubrey*, 37, and Powell, *Aubrey*, 149–52.

[5] Bodleian MS Wood F 39, fol. 340r.

[6] Aubrey, *Monumenta*, i. 26. For his completion of a transcript of the *Monumenta* by October 1689 see Bodleian MS Wood F 39, fol. 402r.

[7] As he prepared it for publication in the 1690s, Aubrey also added a series of other smaller tracts to the third section which had not previously formed a part of the *Monumenta* (see Chapter 3).

landscape as a way of thinking his way into the creation and use of the sites he studied. His method was analogical, reaching an understanding of novel or strange sites—whether Offa's Dyke or Silbury Hill—by relating them back to more familiar monuments and using those perceived relationships as a way of reconstructing the cultures which had produced them. This necessarily entailed recourse to texts, but over the decades during which the *Monumenta* was composed, Aubrey became increasingly willing to move outside textual histories, drawing upon current literature for accounts of the Great Wall of China or Homeric burial practices, but going beyond his initial determination to locate discoveries within the familiar frameworks of classical works such as Caesar's *Commentaries*.

The remainder of the *Monumenta* was less spectacular in its conclusions than the *Templa Druidum* and has attracted correspondingly less attention as a result. In many ways, however, it provides a clearer, more sophisticated view of Aubrey's methods than the *Templa* and demonstrates how his understanding of the ancient past gained in nuance over the course of his life. While maintaining his focus on Romano-British culture, Aubrey was becoming increasingly open to comparisons which linked it with other ancient civilizations, a tendency which saw its fullest expression in his genealogies of architecture and folklore in the 1670s and 1680s.[8] The portions of the *Monumenta* discussed in this chapter represent a midpoint between the focused nationalist arguments of the *Templa*, and the claims for a pan-European, if not global, ancient culture made in his later writings. They also demonstrate with particular clarity Aubrey's comparative methods; analogy, for Aubrey, was a tool which could naturalize and explain otherwise baffling evidence and, in the process, make legible worlds far outside of the humanist textual tradition.

READING THE LANDSCAPE

Meric Casaubon's characterization of antiquaries as those for whom 'visible superviving evidences of antiquitie represent unto their minds former times, with as strong an impression, as if they were actually present, and in sight' struck a chord with Aubrey.[9] The quotation and its surrounding context appear twice in the *Monumenta* and a similar act of antiquarian visualization lay behind the lyrical passage with which Aubrey opened his study of camps and fortifications:

---

[8] See Chapters 3 and 5 respectively.
[9] Aubrey, *Monumenta*, i. 259; quoting Meric Casaubon, *A Treatise of Use and Custome* (London, 1638), 97–8. See Introduction.

The prodigious graffes and rampires [i.e., trenches and ramparts] of the old Encampings seemed justly to claim Admiration in the beholder. The greatnesse, and numerousness of the Barrowes (the Beds of Honour where now so many Heroes lie buried in Oblivion) doe speake plainly to us, that Death & Slaughter once rag'd there, and that here were the Scenes, where terrible Battles were fought: wherein fell so many thousands, mentioned by the Historians. By the burying places it might be presumed where about the Engagement began and which way the Victor made his persuit: and by the Imperial Camps (where now Sheep feed, and the Plough goes) one may trace out which way the victorious Roman Eagle tooke her Course.[10]

Aubrey was describing an act of imaginative reconstruction which balanced simultaneous visions of the present landscape and its ancient past conjured up by those 'visible superviving evidences' of the camps and barrows. Here he was moving beyond an antiquarian approach which surveyed a site—as at Stonehenge or Avebury—to one which took in a panoramic view of an entire landscape and all the human activity that had taken place within it. He also drew out the tensions between the recovery of the past, the 'presumptions' which followed from a close examination of the landscape, and the impossibility of complete knowledge, the oblivion in which the British heroes lay buried. This tension, and the discomfort of partial knowledge, were all the more acute in a historical context largely devoid of the comfort of textual sources. This delicate balancing act between observation and imagination, present only in the background in the *Templa Druidum*, became a guiding principle in the remainder of the *Monumenta*.[11]

Under the rubric of 'camps' Aubrey included not only Roman encampments but other sites of varying ages, including many now known to be prehistoric hill forts. In identifying and describing Roman camps, Aubrey already had an extensive literature to rely upon. At the beginning of the chapter he directed his readers to pseudo-Hyginus's *De castris Romanis* and to the discussion of military encampment in the surviving fragment of book six of Polybius's *Histories*, both conveniently collected in a new edition edited by R. H. Schellius and published in Amsterdam in 1660.[12] To this he appended Edward Grimeston's English translation of the fragment of Polybius in its entirety and subsequently added a draft of a model Roman camp taken from Sir Henry Savile's dissertation on Roman

[10] Aubrey, *Monumenta*, i. 237–9.
[11] Aubrey's privileging of imagination in the scholarly process has also been discussed by Alain Schnapp, *The Discovery of the Past*, trans. Ian Kinnes and Gillian Varndell (London, 1996), 191.
[12] Aubrey, *Monumenta*, i. 241; [Rabodus Hermannus Schellius, ed.], *Hygini gromatici, et Polybii Megalopolitani, de castris Romanis, quae exstant* (Amsterdam, 1660).

warfare in the notes to his 1591 edition of Tacitus.[13] Drawing upon previous antiquaries' fascination with the practicalities of Roman warfare as well as from two standard classical sources on the subject, Aubrey was able to develop a rule for identifying Roman remains: a Roman encampment should be square or rectangular, thus, the remains of a square or rectangular encampment in the British landscape could reasonably be supposed to be Roman.

Aubrey's difficulty lay in relating the sites he had identified as Roman back to the history of ancient Britain in so far as it could be recovered from classical authors. The first pages of the chapter, which probably date from its initial composition in 1668, are replete with extracts from Caesar's *Commentaries* describing the invasion of Britain by the Romans.[14] Aubrey originally imagined that the camps he had discovered in Kent, Surrey, and Middlesex could be equated with those constructed by Caesar during his invasion and, at least to begin with, seems to have been unfazed by the long duration of Roman occupation and the possibility that sites could be Roman but could also date from hundreds of years apart. He was, however, prepared to consider that camps in different parts of the country might represent later waves of Roman invasion or settlement and wondered whether subsequent invading generals would have learnt from Caesar's mistakes and landed farther west, 'perhaps in Sussex as did William the Conqueror'.[15]

If square camps were Roman, the problem of round camps remained. In the recension of 1668, Aubrey drew a map of south-western Britain as it would have appeared in Roman times but with modern towns superimposed on the Roman landscape (see Figure 2.1).[16] On this he reiterated that 'the Roman Campes are allwayes Square, or at least squarish' (he had observed elsewhere that natural features sometimes meant that camps had

---

[13] Aubrey, *Monumenta*, i. 260–1; Sir Henry Savile, 'A view of certaine militar matters, for the better vnderstanding of the ancient Roman stories', in *The End of Nero and Beginning of Galba: Fower Bookes of the Histories of Cornelius Tacitus...* (Oxford, 1591), sep. pag. 49–75. This was subsequently translated into Latin by Marquard Freher and published separately as *Commentarius de militia Romana* (Heidelberg, 1601). At Aubrey, *Monumenta*, i. 243–57, he has pasted in pages 291–304 of *The History of Polybius the Megalopolitan... Also the Manner of the Romane Encamping...*, trans. Edward Grimeston (London, 1634). It was, at the time, the best English translation of Polybius available.

[14] Aubrey, *Monumenta*, i. 265–9, 278. Locating the actions described in the *Commentaries* within a contemporary British landscape was an approach also taken by Aubrey's friend Edmond Halley in the latter's 'Discourse Tending to Prove at What Time and Place, Julius Cesar [*sic*] Made his First Descent upon Britain', *Philosophical Transactions* 16 (1686–92): 495–501. Halley, however, focused on the coastline rather than on inland fortifications.

[15] Aubrey, *Monumenta*, i. 281.   [16] Aubrey, *Monumenta*, i. 594–5.

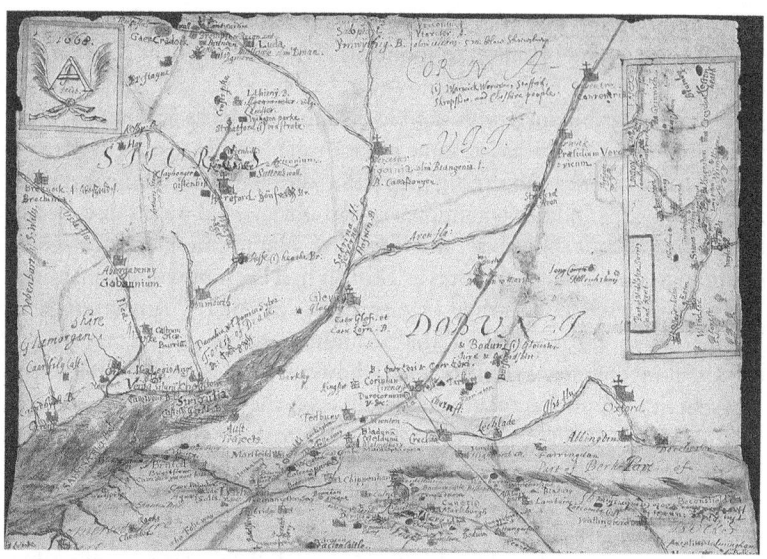

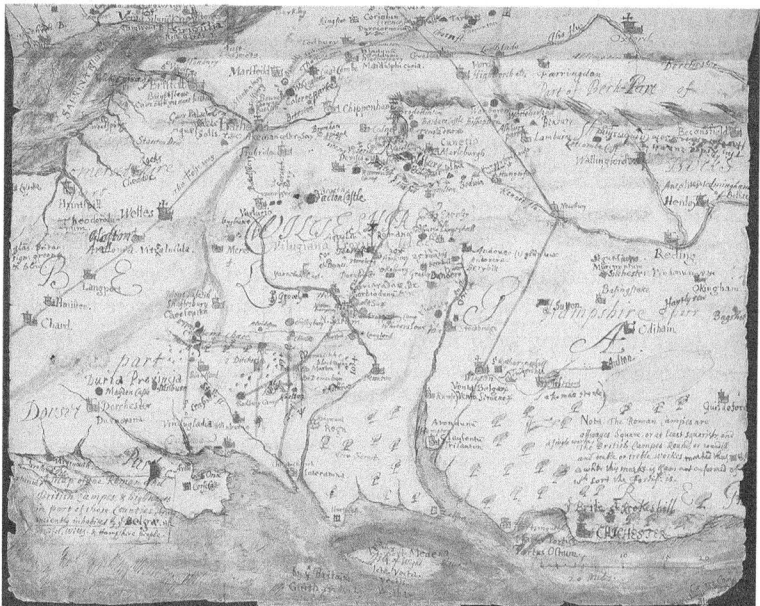

Figure 2.1 Aubrey's 1668 'Map of the Roman and British Campes, & highwayes' in south-western England (Bodleian MS Top. Gen. c. 24, fols. 250v–251r).

to be built around obstacles, distorting their shape), but added that 'the
British Campes [are] Round, or roundish'.[17] At a subsequent point in the
composition of the *Monumenta*, however, he altered his ideas and began to
identify circular hill forts with double or treble ramparts as 'Danish', that
is, built by Viking invaders at some point in the Middle Ages. That this—
like his later theories concerning megalithic sites—may be connected with
a reception of Scandinavian antiquarianism is suggested by his discussions
of Yarnbury Castle, Wiltshire, and Fripsbury, Hampshire.[18] In these cases,
etymologies identifying the sites as Danish had been provided to Aubrey
by Petrus Zitzscher, 'a learned Danish Gent', in 1681.[19] Any attempt to
locate this in the context of the Scandinavian scholarly connections
explored in chapter 1 is frustrated, however, by a lack of evidence.
Zitzscher's own intellectual contacts and even the reason for his presence
in England are unclear; he does not seem to have had Royal Society
connections.[20] Nonetheless, it is notable that it was around this time
that Aubrey began to take greater account of Scandinavian antiquities
than before.

Aubrey was proud of his classification of hill fort forms, expressing
disbelief that William Camden had been unable to tell the difference
between Roman and Danish camps (in spite of having access to Savile's
Tacitus, one of Aubrey's major sources for Roman fortification) and
noting smugly that Robert Plot 'knew not how to distinguish' between
the two 'till I told him'.[21] Plot, in his 1677 *Natural History of Oxford-Shire*
had commented on 'the large square *Entrenchments*' and the 'small *Fortification[s]*' in the county, that 'in general 'tis like they were *works* of the
Saxons, these being all *square*, though the *last* [Beaumont Castle, near
Mixbury in Oxfordshire] by its name should indeed be *Norman*'. Of two
other fortifications he opined that ''tis most probable they were made by
the *Danes* (they being both *round*)'.[22] Aubrey, in his own copy of the
Natural History, made short work of Plot, noting of '*works* of the *Saxons*',

[17] Aubrey, *Monumenta*, i. 595.   [18] Aubrey, *Monumenta*, i. 287, 289.

[19] Petrus Zitschler, or Zitzscher (1652–1697) was a Danish pastor who had studied at
Helmstädt, Wittenberg, Leipzig, and Jena, later embarking on a grand tour of the Neth-
erlands, England, and France (P. G. Witsen Geysbeek, *Algemeen Noodwendig Woordenboek
der Zamenleving*, 7 vols. [Amsterdam, 1836–61], vii. 5407). He provided two more Danish
etymological arguments for the *Monumenta* (*Monumenta*, i. 355, 519), but does not appear
elsewhere in Aubrey's manuscripts.

[20] His name does not appear in Gail Ewald Scala, 'An Index of Proper Names in
Thomas Birch's *The History of the Royal Society*', *Notes and Records of the Royal Society of
London* 28 (1974): 263–329.

[21] Aubrey, *Monumenta*, i. 289, 293.

[22] Robert Plot, *Natural History of Oxford-Shire* (Oxford, 1677), 336.

''tis false', and against 'made by the *Danes* (they being both *round*)', 'This note the Dr [i.e., Plot] had from J. Aubrey.'[23]

Aubrey's determination to create a fixed typology of fortifications is of a piece with his concern to use analogy as a method of pattern-building. As with megalithic sites, he could proceed from known to unknown quantities by comparing their visual appearance. However, his determination that square camps were Roman and round camps were British or Danish leaves a gaping hole in his history of Britain's military occupation. Here, as elsewhere, the Anglo-Saxons have no place in his narrative, leaving the dichotomy of Roman–Briton at centre stage, with a little later support from the Scandinavians.

The two subsequent chapters, discussing castles and the remnants of ancient military architecture, were complementary to that on camps. Camps were only identifiable by their earthworks, but Aubrey distinguished castles as those sites which had remnants of stonework remaining, if not entire structures, and were thus, in theory, more easily identifiable as the product of a specific era. Despite this, Aubrey was more enthusiastic than precise in his identification of Roman structures, failing to transfer his post-Conquest methodologies into a pre-Conquest context. He identified the Norman ruins of Old Sarum as Roman—having eliminated the Saxons as possible candidates by quoting William of Malmesbury that they did not build with stone.[24] In this he was probably influenced by William Camden, who mentioned the 'ruins yet remaining' at 'Old Sorbiodunum' in a Roman or immediately post-Roman context in his *Britannia*.[25] A similar Camdenian influence, augmented by Aubrey's own observations, can be seen in his conviction that the thirteenth-century Caerphilly Castle was Roman on the basis that there were 'severall Busts, scilicet Roman heads and bodies to the wast, in the Roman habit' in the hall there; Camden had written that it 'hath beene of so huge a bignesse, and such a wonderfull peece of worke beside, that all men wel nere say, it was a garison-fort of the *Romans*'.[26] His identification of these sites as Roman may seem all the more surprising since, in the following chapter, he gave detailed sketches and descriptions of genuine Roman fortified architecture at Colchester, Silchester, London, and elsewhere, but it is worth remembering that his own comparative architectural methods were the first of their kind and reliant upon the presence of specific architectural forms, particularly windows.[27] The absence of those forms, combined

---

[23] This copy is now Bodleian Ashmole 1722.   [24] Aubrey, *Monumenta*, i. 400–7.
[25] William Camden, *Britain*, trans. Philemon Holland (London, 1610), 246–7.
[26] Aubrey, *Monumenta*, i. 400–7; Camden, *Britain*, 642.
[27] Aubrey, *Monumenta*, i. 422, 425, 429. See Chapter 3.

with existing antiquarian interpretations, made a watertight case not just
for Aubrey but also for his younger contemporary Edward Lhuyd. Lhuyd,
writing his additions to the 1695 *Britannia*, still argued that it was 'highly
probable' Caerphilly had been built by the Romans, despite finding no
evidence of Roman textual remains there except for two puzzling coins
with Latin inscriptions, communicated to him by Aubrey's cousin Sir
John Aubrey of Llantrithyd.[28] Without surviving Roman architecture of
the sort that could still be found in Italy or elsewhere on the continent,
British antiquaries lacked a comparative framework which would have cast
doubt on the traditional origins of these structures.

Aubrey began his chapter on Roman towns and cities with a short
survey of the Roman occupation of Britain. He found an origin for
fortified Roman settlements in the need to have walled defences against
the native Britons, comparing their incursions upon the Roman province
to 'the Descent which the Indians A.D. 16..., lately made on the New-
England-men for want of walled Townes'.[29] This comparison between the
Roman occupiers of Britain and the English settlers in North America
gains additional depth when measured against Aubrey's attempts at asserting cultural continuity between the two in his *Remaines of Gentilisme*. The
majority of the chapter, however, is more concerned with the specifics of
uncovering Roman settlements than in the appropriation of Roman
culture for the English so in evidence in the *Remaines*. Following on
from this comparison, Aubrey paraphrased from John Milton's 1670
History of Great Britain to establish a *terminus post quem* for Roman
building in Britain: 'In Constantine's time here were great store of
Workmen and excellent Builders...Theodosius (tempore Valentiniani)
raysed on the confines many strong Holds, nunc infestabatur Britannia
Scotis, Saxonicis, Pictis.'[30] In other words, Roman architecture was being
erected in England well into the fifth century CE.

This passage shows a noticeable growth in Aubrey's understanding of
Roman Britain from his earlier determination to see in every Roman camp
one of Caesar's way stations. Now he was at pains to emphasize the
continuity of active Roman rule and building into the late antique period
instead of reducing all Roman traces in Britain to a blueprint from which
Caesar's invasion could be recovered. In doing so he anticipated John

[28] William Camden, *Camden's Britannia*, ed. Edmund Gibson et al. (London, 1695),
615.
[29] Aubrey, *Monumenta*, i. 437. Aubrey was here presumably referring to King Philip's
War and the raids made by the Native American coalition on New England towns in
1675–6.
[30] Aubrey, *Monumenta*, i. 437. His source is John Milton, *The History of Britain*...
(London, 1670), 88–93.

Horsley's history of Roman Britain, which, following Ammianus Marcellinus, emphasized the Emperor Theodosius's (379–95) role in 'recover
[ing] the provincial cities and forts, which had been very much damaged
by the enemy'.[31] In 1668 Aubrey's beliefs about Romano-British culture
had not yet been expressed, or perhaps even developed, but by the time
this passage was composed he had begun to formulate the ideas which
appeared in the *Remaines of Gentilisme*. If later English culture was the
product of a long-term fusion between Roman and native British civilizations, it only stood to reason that Roman architecture would have gradually settled across the British landscape during a period of several
hundred years.

Taking a wide view of the ancient landscape also led Aubrey to entertain
new methodological possibilities, even if he did not systematically put
them to use. In a 'Philosophicall Corollary' to his description of Roman
Silchester he noted that Seth Ward and John Wilkins had told him that,
when viewing the ruins there in 1658, 'one might discerne in the Corne-
ground ('twas about April) the signe of the Streets, passages, and also of
the Hearths. quod NB. That expression of Ovid is applicable here, "Iam
seges est ubi Troia fuit".'[32] Ward and Wilkins's anecdote must have made
an impression on Aubrey, for he quoted the same line from Ovid as the
epigraph to part two of the *Monumenta*, but he does not seem to have
followed up his own *nota bene*.[33] What the two future bishops had
described were negative cropmarks caused by the subterranean remains
of Roman buildings, a phenomenon which was later noticed by Stephen
Hales in 1733 and Gilbert White in 1789, but which only entered the
archaeological toolbox in the twentieth century.[34] However, it tells us less
about Aubrey's friends' bright idea than about the way in which he
conceptualized and naturalized ideas. By linking the observation with
the line from Ovid—'now corn grows where Troy stood'—Aubrey was
bringing it into his own mental world, built upon a corpus of classical texts
whose tags and images could serve as hooks on which to hang new and
unfamiliar material. Here, Ovid's Troy was not only anchoring a new idea,
but naturalizing the still foreign, because unknown, landscape of Roman

[31] John Horsley, *Britannia Romana: Or the Roman Antiquities of Britain in Three Books*
(London, 1732), 73.
[32] Aubrey, *Monumenta*, i. 441. The quotation ('now corn grows where Troy stood') is
from Ovid, *Heroides*, 1.53.
[33] Aubrey, *Monumenta*, i. 231.
[34] The phenomenon of cropmarks—in this instance based on observation of snow
thawing more slowly above concealed drains—was observed by Stephen Hales in his
Haemastatics (1733) and its potential application to Roman archaeology was noted by the
naturalist Gilbert White in his *Natural History and Antiquities of Selborne*... (London,
1789), 15–16. See Hunter, *Aubrey*, 193.

Britain into the textual world of humanism. For all that Aubrey read the landscape with a precision and perspicacity uncommon for his era, this more stable, better-known textual landscape was his native home.

BURIAL MOUNDS IN HOMERIC BRITAIN

From the moment of the Duke of York's request, Aubrey had tended to see fortifications and burial sites as linked; the latter being, one might say, the inevitable product of the former in so far as battles inevitably generate burials. Interpreting barrows and other tombs posed different questions from his work on camps, however. At the inception of his project, Aubrey had no doubt that barrows were 'the Beds of Honour where now so many Heroes lie buried in Oblivion', but in the course of the *Monumenta* he proposed two separate theories explaining their origin.[35]

At first, he had believed that the ancient Britons were buried where they fell in battle and that '[b]y the burying places it might be presumed where about the Engagement began and which way the Victor made his pursuit'.[36] That this might have been somewhat impractical seems not to have fazed Aubrey, who not only referred to it in his introduction to the chapter on camps, but returned to the theory as a hermeneutic tool when discussing a series of prehistoric barrow cemeteries in Dorset:

> At Woodyates ... hath been a terrible fight. there are, but a little within the line, nineteen barrowes and some of them very great: here are also 2 or 3 circular trenches with a little tump or two viz: [bird's-eye views of two tumuli] which in probabilty were the places for combustione cadaverum [burning of bodies] ... one may plainly see here that the Chace of the Victory runs westwards ... This great fight by Woodyates I take to be \perhaps was/ that between the Romans and Boadicea: it agrees so well with the Description of Cornelius Tacitus. where the entrance (as a throate) was narrow but grew broader ...[37]

Aubrey was suggesting that the warriors slain in this supposed battle were subsequently cremated and buried in the places where they had fallen.

Aubrey's emphasis on the crematory tumuli probably derived from readings of Ole Worm and Sir Thomas Browne—the latter's *Hydriotaphia, Urne Buriall, or a Discourse of the Sepulchrall Urnes Lately Found in Norfolk* (1658) is quoted extensively in the subsequent chapter—though it

---

[35] Aubrey, *Monumenta*, i. 239.   [36] Aubrey, *Monumenta*, i. 239.
[37] Aubrey, *Monumenta*, i. 533, recalling Tacitus, *Annales*, XIV. xxxiv.

may also owe something to the theories of his friend James Long.[38] Indeed, discussing the barrows on the Downs in another context he proposed a radically different interpretation of their presence which seems to have been based on a hypothesis by Long:

> On the Downes are Barrowes almost everywhere <u>on high ground</u>: for they affected to have their Ashes lie drie. It is to be noted that where Barrows are, there is alwaies for the most part one circular Trench, or more without any Barrow: which Colonel James Long, ingeniously ghesses to be the place for the Combustion of the dead bodies, and for performing the Ceremonies, within which circle, every body was not permitted to enter
> —— procul ô, procul ite profani.[39]

Here theories of burial upon the site of death were dropped in favour of a carefully sited cemetery. Aubrey bolstered this latter theory with modern analogies:

> My conceit is that the Seaven Barrowes &c: (where are severall together) were not tumuli, or barrowes erected upon the account of any great person slain there in Battle: but in those times they chose to lye drye upon such hilly ground: and those of the same familie would desire to be neer one another; as the Kings at Westminster abbey, and at St Dionyse in France.[40]

These passages were probably written later than that concerning the 'battle' at Woodyates and suggest the same evolution in thought which occurred in his understanding of camps, beginning at a chronologically compressed point where almost any feature could be related back to the initial Roman invasion of Britain, but gradually opening out to a recognition of a much longer timeline. A comparison of the two passages also suggests that Aubrey's conception of ancient British society had become more complex. His earlier writings paid scant attention to any Britons who were not either heroic warriors or Druids and any discussion of ancient kingship was entirely absent, but the passage just quoted opened up the possibility for some sort of social structure in which kings or heroes could be buried along lines made recognizable by modern analogies.

Investigation of barrows led naturally to an investigation of their contents. Aubrey's chapter on urns related them back to their physical contexts and used them and their analogies to enrich his reconstruction of

---

[38] Cf. Aubrey, *Monumenta*, ii. 728–61, for the quotations from Thomas Browne, *Hydriotaphia* (London, 1658).

[39] Aubrey, *Monumenta*, ii. 705. The quotation is a slight variation on Virgil, *Aeneid*, 6.258 ('procul o procul este, profani', 'away, o away, you profane ones!'), and is the exclamation of the Sybil warning away the uninitiated from the grove through which Aeneas will reach the Underworld.

[40] Aubrey, *Monumenta*, ii. 705.

ancient British society. It opened with a long series of excerpts from Sir Thomas Browne's *Hydriotaphia* that served to contextualize Aubrey's own more focused case studies.[41] Browne famously began *Hydriotaphia* with a history of the practice of cremation across all cultures, and the first lines Aubrey chose to quote in the *Monumenta* are of particular importance:

> [T]he practice of Burning was also of great Antiquity, and of no slender extent. For (not to derive the same from *Hercules*) noble descriptions there are hereof in the Grecian Funerals of *Homer*, in the formall Obsequies of *Patroclus*, and *Achilles*; and somewhat elder in the *Theban* warre, and solemn combustion of *Meneceus*, and *Archemorus*, contemporary unto *Jair* the Eighth Judge of *Israel*. Confirmable also among the *Trojans*, from the Funerall Pyre of *Hector*, burnt before the gates of *Troy*.[42]

Aubrey, if he did not take this passage immediately to heart, certainly came to the same conclusion. As we have seen earlier in this section, he theorized that barrows were part of larger ritual complexes which also included crematorial areas, and in finding analogies for these supposed practices, he turned immediately to the passage from Homer cited by Browne. Following the excerpts from *Hydriotaphia* are quotations from the funeral of Patroclus, the funeral of Elpenor, and the burial of Achilles, amongst other Homeric fragments.[43] Much as hill forts and megaliths could be domesticated and understood through reference to classical and biblical antiquities, so the British warriors and their obsequies could be understood through comparison with Homeric heroes. In thinking about the rituals that would have surrounded burial in barrows, Aubrey turned first to Homer, noting that, 'I shall first set downe Homer's descriptions of burying and raysing Tumuli: and then subjoine those of Virgil.'[44]

For Aubrey, then, pre-Roman British culture was essentially comparable to that of archaic Greece as seen in classical texts, and a close reading of the *Iliad* and the *Odyssey* could serve as a means of explicating the otherwise unrecoverable culture of the prehistoric Britons. This was not quite the same thing as the exclusively textual antiquarianism which existed alongside Aubrey's more visual approach. He was certainly using texts to understand what he had found, but not in lieu of artefacts. Instead he was using them as something supplementary, a way of siting those artefacts within a known universe, of domesticating them and making them intelligible. In this respect, he was engaging in an antiquarian

---

[41] Aubrey, *Monumenta*, ii. 729–61.

[42] Browne, *Hydriotaphia*, 4, quoted in Aubrey, *Monumenta*, ii. 729.

[43] Aubrey, *Monumenta*, ii. 758–9 (funeral of Patroclus); 761 (funeral of Elpenor); 763 (Nestor's directions on the burial of the dead); 765 (burial of Achilles).

[44] Aubrey, *Monumenta*, ii. 699.

technique that can be seen in the writings of early travellers to the eastern Mediterranean. David Constantine has discussed Edmund Chishull's attempts to find continuity in the Turkish landscape through quotations of Homer or other ancient poets apposite to what he himself observed, in other words domesticating and interpreting a profoundly foreign space.[45] Chishull, in a journal entry for 29 April 1698, contrasted the emptiness of the Caystrian plain in Lydia, on which could only be observed, 'a stone bridge of three considerable arches, built directly along the bank of the river; and therefore now serving to no other purpose, but only to witness that the stream had changed its chanel', with 'the sweetness of that immortal verse', 'The Asian mead by the streams of Caystrius'.[46] He and Aubrey both took texts familiar to them and used them as lenses through which to understand otherwise foreign and perplexing environments, whether they were temporally distant (ancient Britain) or spatially and culturally so (the modern Ottoman Empire).[47]

Urn burials were the sites of most early attempts at excavation and, as such, Aubrey's chapter on urns reads somewhat differently from the remainder of the *Monumenta*. Rather than measuring and describing sites, Aubrey recorded excavations, detailing their dates, their finds, and their instigators. The original impetus for excavating urns seems to have been the assumption that they would contain buried treasure, but Aubrey also recorded a number of instances where a less pecuniarily informed antiquarian curiosity led to impressively thorough excavation. Amongst this latter category was the dig conducted by Sir Edward Harley (and unnamed local labourers) at a barrow near Leintwardine, Herefordshire, in 1662:

Sr Edward Harley Knight of the Bath Governour of Dunkirk and my ever honoured friend . . . caused one of these Barrowes to be digged A° 1662, and found therein a great deale of coales, and some pieces of burnt bones: but in the middle he found an Urne about two foot and a half high, full of coales and ashes and some pieces of burnt bones: I had a little piece of the Urne it is of a kind of darke muske colour (umbre) a quarter of an Inch thick and the middle of it is as black as a coale.[48]

---

[45] David Constantine, *In the Footsteps of the Gods: Travellers to Greece and the Quest for the Hellenic Ideal* (1984; repr. London, 2011), 40.

[46] Edmund Chishull, *Travels in Turkey and Back to England* (London, 1747), 19 (= Homer, *Iliad*, ii. 461). 'Ἀσίω ἐν λειμῶνι Καϋστρίου ἀμφὶ ῥέεθρα.'

[47] Anthony Grafton, *What Was History? The Art of History in Early Modern Europe* (Cambridge, 2007), 121, has observed the 'convertibility of time and space' in early modern antiquarianism, of which Aubrey's and Chishull's reactions are examples.

[48] Aubrey, *Monumenta*, ii. 765.

Unlike Browne, Aubrey refrained from attempting to identify the burial as Roman, or, indeed, as anything specific, contenting himself with a careful description of what was discovered (he included a drawing of the urn itself in the margin).

The excavation of burial mounds was also of interest from a scientific point of view as they were believed to sometimes contain the so-called 'ever-burning lamps' referred to in numerous classical texts. That lamps were sometimes found in Roman burials was well established, but legends of such lamps being discovered still lit were more difficult to verify.[49] One of the standard sources amongst early modern scholars for evidence of the legend was a report that such a lamp had been discovered in the supposed tomb of Cicero's daughter, Tullia, but whatever element of truth the story contained was quickly submerged in a sea of imprecise citation and conjecture.[50] By the mid-seventeenth century, it was generally assumed that if such lamps had existed, they would have been fuelled with naphtha and it was with this assumption in mind that Robert Plot gave a paper to the Philosophical Society of Oxford concerning their possible construction in 1684.[51]

Aubrey came up against this legend twice in his research for the *Monumenta*. The first instance was in a letter from William Sydenham to his uncle, Thomas Sydenham, dated 1675, detailing a barrow excavation much like Harley's.[52] Having previously noted that the centre of the

[49] The most systematic contemporary discussion in English is John Wilkins, *Mathematicall Magick*... (London, 1648), 232–56.

[50] Aubrey would have known the story from Sir Thomas Browne, *Pseudodoxia epidemica*... (London, 1646), 161, and perhaps elsewhere. An early and oft-quoted reference to the opening of Tullia's tomb was that by Guido Panciroli (1523–1599), who wrote that it had been opened and the lamp seen 'in the time of Paul III' (i.e., 1534–49), cf. Guido Panciroli, *The History of Many Memorable Things Lost, Which Were in Use Among the Ancients*, 2 vols. (London, 1715), i. 115–16. A collection of translated contemporary documents relating to the opening in 1485 of the tomb which first gave rise to this legend is in Rodolfo Lanciani, *Pagan and Christian Rome* (Boston, MA, and New York, 1896), 295–301, which suggests that the identification with Tullia was not universally accepted during the initial excavation.

[51] Robert Plot, 'A Discourse Concerning the Sepulchral Lamps of the Ancients, Shewing the Possibility of Their Being Made Divers Waies', *Philosophical Transactions* 14 (1684): 806–11. The potential use of naphtha had already been proposed by Browne, *Pseudodoxia*, 161, and Fortunio Liceti, *De lucernis antiquorum reconditis libb. sex* (Udine, 1652), 222–4.

[52] Aubrey, *Monumenta*, ii. 769–71 (the letter is also published in Kenneth Dewhurst, *Dr. Thomas Sydenham (1624–1689): His Life and Original Writings* [London, 1966], 166–7). William Sydenham was the son of the parliamentary officer of the same name, lost his estate in suspicious circumstances, and died in jail in 1718 (G. G. Meynell, *Materials for a Biography of Dr. Thomas Sydenham (1624–1689): A New Survey of Public and Private Archives* [Folkestone, 1988], 76, 97–8), while his uncle Thomas (1624–1689) was the well-known physician, author of *Methodus curandi febres* (1666), and friend of John

barrow was 'perfectly like an Oven curiously clayed round', Sydenham
wrote that:

> I must not omitt the chiefest thing that at the first opening this Oven one of
> my Servants thrust in his hand and pulling it quickly back againe
> I demanding the reason of him, hee told me it was very hott: I did also
> putt in my hand and it was warme enough to have baked bread: severall
> other persons did the like, who can all testifie the trueth of it ... I thinke it
> would puzzle the Royall Societie to give a reason of the heate of the Oven
> being fifteen hundred yeares old.[53]

Sydenham offered no explanation for the natural phenomenon he had
encountered. Aubrey, however, saw it as corollary evidence for the existence of eternal lamps and commented in the margin that it could be
related to a passage in 2 Maccabees describing burning petroleum (its first
identification as 'naptha') and also, allegedly, to Pliny's description 'of
Tullia's Urne'.[54] He was, however, mistaken in his second citation: Pliny
made no mention of any such object.

Aubrey's interest in ever-burning lamps throws some light on an
unusual printed item bound into the *Monumenta*'s chapter on Roman
pavements. It is a single sheet, dated 1685 and headed 'A Strange and
Wonderful Discovery Newly made of Houses Under Ground, At *Colton's-
Field* in *Gloucester-Shire*'.[55] The short narrative that followed purported to
relate the story of two labourers, engaged in digging a gravel pit, who came
by chance upon the entrance to a series of subterranean rooms, at the end
of which stood an automaton dressed as a Roman soldier. When they
approached it, the figure struck out three times, at the third blow breaking
the glass in which an ever-burning lamp was suspended and plunging
them into darkness. Further investigation was prevented by 'a hollow
Noise like a deep Sigh or Groan', which augured the collapse of the entire
complex, 'our Adventurers' only narrowly escaping.[56]

Stuart Piggott has identified this as a hoax and pointed towards several
common medieval and early modern mythological tropes which appear in
the narrative, but it is worth investigating its more immediate sources in
an attempt to explain Aubrey's interest in this lampoon of antiquarianism

Locke (*ODNB*, *s.n.*; Dewhurst, *Dr. Thomas Sydenham, passim*; Meynell, *Materials for a
Biography of Dr. Thomas Sydenham, passim*). It may have been Sydenham's acquaintance
with Locke which first brought this letter to Aubrey's notice.

[53] Aubrey, *Monumenta*, ii. 769–71.

[54] Aubrey, *Monumenta*, ii. 769, citing 2 Maccabees 1:32–6.

[55] Cf. the discussion of this item in Kate Loveman, *Reading Fictions, 1660–1740:
Deception in English Literary and Political Culture* (Aldershot, 2008), 80–1.

[56] Aubrey, *Monumenta*, ii. 947–9.

and natural science.[57] Leaving aside the vague descriptive passages of the various rooms—'they went into a Parlour, furnish'd according to the fashion of those Times', and so on—the central point in the narrative is the figure and actions of the ancient automaton. This closely followed John Wilkins's discussion of eternal lamps in his *Mathematicall Magick*:

> There is another relation of a certain man, who upon occasion digging somewhat deep in the ground... discovered a fair Vault, and towards the further side of it, the statue of a man in Armour, sitting by a table, leaning upon his left arm, and holding a scepter in his right hand, with a lamp burning before him; the floor of this Vault being so contrived, that upon the first step into it, the statue would erect itself from its leaning posture; upon the second step it did lift up the scepter to strike, and before man could approach near enough to take hold of the lamp, the statue did strike and break it to peeces: such care was there taken that it might not be stoln away, or discovered.[58]

Wilkins's account places more emphasis on the eternal lamp, whilst the broadsheet was concerned with the 'Medals and Coyns' elsewhere in the vault and reduced the lamp to a decorative role. Nonetheless, it is sufficiently close to the language of the broadsheet to clearly indicate that the latter depended upon it for its description of the automaton. It is significant, also, that the source for this story should derive from a work that has multiple points of contact with members of the Royal Society and their writings. The broadsheet claimed to have been printed in 1685, a date that suggests a potential allusion to Plot's experiments on eternal lamps the previous year. A third connection with the Royal Society comes in the form of a reference at the beginning of the broadsheet to 'that Island near *Ireland*, which is described in the Maps, but cannot now be found', a reference to the Irish myth of Hy Brasil, which had exercised Robert Hooke's ingenuity in 1679.[59] The final clue is Aubrey's own annotation on the verso of the sheet, 'This Paper I had from Mr Thomas Pigot M.A. Fellow of Wadham college Oxon. who went to see it. Quaere Mr Edw. Stephens of Cheriton.'[60]

According to Aubrey, Thomas Pigot 'went to see' this mythical excavation and Stuart Piggott has suggested that the broadsheet may have been an elaborate joke by him, either for the 'private amusement' of the Royal

---

[57] Stuart Piggott, *Ruins in a Landscape: Essays in Antiquarianism* (Edinburgh, 1976), 77–99.

[58] Wilkins, *Mathematicall Magick*, 237.

[59] See William Poole and Kelsey Jackson Williams, 'A Swede in Restoration Oxford: Gothic Patriots, Swedish Books, and English Scholars', *Lias* 39 (2012): 21.

[60] Aubrey, *Monumenta*, ii. 949. Edward Stephens of Cherington and Alderley, Gloucestershire, had married the daughter of Judge Matthew Hale and had been noted by Aubrey as a potential source for Hales's life (Aubrey, *Lives*, ii. 784). Aubrey presumably planned to turn to him as a local Gloucestershire informant.

Society or perhaps at their, or Aubrey's, expense.[61] In either case its amusement value, whether for author or reader, rests upon a tension inherent in the antiquarianism of the period: while ancient artefacts were eagerly discussed and sought after, very few scholars actually obtained them through excavation and even fewer actively participated in any excavations which they might have sponsored. Even Aubrey, describing the contents of a barrow tomb, wrote that, 'I never was so sacralegious as to disturb, or rob his urne: let his Ashes rest in peace', and there is no indication that he conducted a single excavation himself.[62] In this atmosphere, the moment of excavation could easily assume a quasi-mythical quality, as in the broadsheet, and the possibility of discovering an eternal lamp was not so distant as it afterwards became.

FORTIFICATIONS AND FLOODS: HUMAN INTERVENTION AND GEOLOGICAL CHANGE

In the final sections of the *Monumenta* Aubrey turned to two other prominent features of the ancient landscape: fortifications and roads. In these chapters he was chiefly concerned with identifying the routes of the Roman roads and ancient ramparts that criss-crossed early modern Britain, but in the process of doing so he reached larger conclusions about how the landscape interacted with society and how both had changed since antiquity.

Writing 'of Ditches', Aubrey began by defining the term. '[T]he word ditch', he observed, 'did anciently signifie a Bank, or Rampire ... the same as dyke', whereas by the time he wrote it had also taken on the opposite meaning, that of a 'fossa [i.e., a dug-out channel], which the Dutchmen call, the graff'.[63] To avoid confusion, Aubrey only referred—counterintuitively to modern ears—to the former dykes as ditches, and it was with these earthworks that the chapter was concerned. It covered Offa's Dyke, Wansdyke, and other examples of man-made defences, included remarks by William Dugdale on Hadrian's Wall in which Dugdale corrected Camden, and saw Aubrey making interpretative arguments from physical evidence similar to those made during his study of hill forts.

Aubrey mapped these large-scale earthworks through a combination of personal observation, mobilization of local contacts, and text-based research. In one of his more complete surveys, that of Offa's Dyke, he

---

began with the conventional theory of its origin, ultimately derived from Asser's *Life of Alfred*, that it 'was made by Offa King of the Mercians (his seat was at <u>Sutton-wall</u> in Herefordshire) It was to separate the Britons from the Saxons, and who (of either partie) was found on the other side of this Dyke armed, was to loose his right hand'.[64] He then gave a description of its course:

> It is to be seen on the top of <u>Bachy-hill</u>, and on Stocky-hill both neer Morhampton-park in Herefordshire: in some places above a mile together. The Graffe is on the Welsh side: viz. Westwards, and the Rampire towards the English side: which evidences that it was made by the Saxons ... (Memorandum the range of Hills lyeing north and south are the first that terminate the fair <u>plain</u> level of Herefordshire toward Wales).[65]

His distinction between the 'Graffe', or excavated ditch, on the western side and the raised earthworks on the eastern was comparatively elementary, but had not been made before and was the more impressive in Aubrey's case, given his resistance elsewhere to crediting the Anglo-Saxons with architectural talent.[66] In this case, the conclusion he had drawn only confirmed something which was already known from written sources— that it had been built by the Mercians against incursions from Wales—but he later applied the same principle to the less well-documented Wansdyke, noting that there 'the Rampire is to the Southward, and the graffe is to the northward'; in doing so he revealed something about the intent behind its construction which was not otherwise known.[67]

This chorographical and physical account of Offa's Dyke was, Aubrey noted in the margin, not based on his observations alone, but also derived from reports by his friend John Hoskins—whose Herefordshire estate, Morehampton Park, lay close to the dyke—and a detailed description of its course which he had received from 'Henry Milbourn Esq Recorder of Monmouth: and a good Antiquarie'. Below this he noted that the Domesday Book might, potentially, contain a reference to the dyke, and left himself a memorandum that 'Mr William Guillim of <u>Langston</u> (Hereff.) can tell me'.[68] Finally, he placed the dyke within a larger landscape, noting

---

[64] Aubrey, *Monumenta*, ii. 885. This story, which originated in the *Policraticus* of John of Salisbury, was well known by the seventeenth century. Aubrey may have derived it from Camden, *Britain*, 623, or Aylett Sammes, *Britannia antiqua illustrata* (London, 1676), 558, which he also read while writing the *Monumenta* (cf. Bodleian MS Top. Gen. c. 24, fol. 102r).

[65] Aubrey, *Monumenta*, ii. 885.

[66] Edward Lhuyd identifies its course in more detail but does not discuss its structure in Camden, *Camden's Britannia*, 587.

[67] Aubrey, *Monumenta*, ii. 889.

[68] Aubrey, *Monumenta*, ii. 885. Before he could contact Guillim, however, Thomas Gale had read through the *Monumenta* and written 'noe mention' next to Aubrey's note.

how it filled the level of western Herefordshire between ranges of hills which made artificial defences less necessary. Throughout, Aubrey deployed a broad range of sources and hermeneutic tools to recover the extent, purpose, and larger significance of the earthworks.

Elsewhere, speaking of earthworks which he believed to be British rather than Saxon, he engaged in the same imaginative reconstruction which he had brought to bear on camps and burial mounds:

> I beleeve that there were several Reguli [petty kings], which often made wars upon one another; & the great Ditches which run on our plaines & elsewhere so many miles, were (not unlikely) their boundaries; & with all served for defense against the incursion of their Enemies, as the Picts wall, & that in China; to compare things small to great.[69]

In this passage from the *Description of the North Division of Wiltshire*, Aubrey reached an understanding of the place and function of an object in the British landscape through analogy with other objects or sites from the ancient world. His 'Picts wall' was Hadrian's Wall, extensively studied by Camden, which provided a natural point of comparison elsewhere in Britain, but his reference to the Great Wall was more geographically adventurous.[70] It reappeared elsewhere in the *Monumenta*, again in the context of Hadrian's Wall:

> The Division of Territories and Kingdomes is of great Antiquity. The Chinese walle every one has heard of: which is their defence against the Incursion of the Tartars. 'According to the Chinese account that famous Wall, built against the irruptions of the Tartars was begun a hundred yeares before the Incarnation.'[71]

The quoted passage was from Sir Thomas Browne's interpretation of a 'prophetic' poem referencing the incursion into China of the Tartars, but it seems likely that Aubrey was only citing Browne for the date of the wall's construction and had other, more sophisticated sources to draw on for its history and cultural contexts.[72] He was well aware of the wall which 'every one has heard of' and it would appear that, despite its vast geographical distance, it was a better-known point of reference for a

---

[69] Bodleian MS Aubrey 3, fol. 10r.   [70] Camden, *Britain*, 789–95.
[71] Aubrey, *Monumenta*, ii. 901.
[72] Sir Thomas Browne, *Certain Miscellany Tracts* (London, 1683), 189. At the very least he was also aware of one of the works of the earlier seventeenth-century Jesuit scholar Martino Martini, whose *Bellum Tartaricum, or the Conquest of China by the Tartars* (London, 1654), Aubrey possessed in English translation. It is now Bodleian 8o A 7 Art and is inscribed on sig. A3r 'John Aubrey. 1655'. See William Poole, 'John Aubrey, the Two George Ents, and the "Paduan" *Laureae Apollinari*', *Bodleian Library Record* 27 (2014), 88–104.

seventeenth-century English scholar than the native earthworks only a few days' ride from London, an instance that serves to confirm just how novel Aubrey's examination of these local, British remains was.[73] Ironically, Aubrey was able to find analogies well known enough to explain these local monuments to his readers by turning to another piece of defensive architecture half a world away.

Aubrey was not content solely with identifying and describing these previously neglected sites; he also made several tentative forays into explaining the changes that had come about in the landscape since the Roman occupation. Discussing the abandonment of the Roman ways, he quoted conversations with Christopher Wren and Elias Ashmole:

> Sr Christopher Wren saies to me, that Roman waies lost in process of time, by the building of Religious Houses; to which places Pilgrims resorted, and so found-out newer and neerer wayes. quod NB. For example Stanstreet causey (in Sussex) is disused; and so are severall others, and Elias Ashmole Esq demonstrates it who by riding often from Wedon to Lichfield by the Watling street way & finding it four miles neerer than by Coventrey, began to guesse that the Watling-street-way began to be neglected for the advantage of Travellers who had better accommodation at Coventrey, after it became a Religious place.[74]

The abandonment of the Roman ways was one of the many dramatic changes in the landscape which Aubrey identified as having taken place since antiquity. On the opening page of the chapter 'Of Embankeing and Dreyning & Currents', he copied out a long passage from Ovid's *Metamorphoses*:

> I have myself seen what once was solid land changed into sea; and again I have seen land made from the sea. Sea-shells have been seen lying far from the ocean, and an ancient anchor has been found on a mountain-top. What once was a level plain, down-flowing waters have made into a valley; and hills by the force of floods have been washed into the sea.[75]

---

[73] Martini's account of recent Chinese history took it as granted that his readers would be familiar with 'that great Wall, which extends from East to West'. His narrative was translated by Thomas Henshaw and paired with a history of China by another Jesuit, Alvaro Semedo, to make one of the standard early modern English Sinological reference works (see Alvaro Semedo, *The History of That Great and Renowned Monarchy of China*, trans. Thomas Henshaw [London, 1655], Martini's quotation is at 257).

[74] Aubrey, *Monumenta*, ii. 921.

[75] 'Vidi ego, quod fuerat quondam, solidissima tellus, | Esse fretum: vidi factas ex aequore terras: | Et procul à pelago conchae jacauere marinae, | Et vetus inventa est in montibus anchora summis; | Quodque fuit campus, vallem decursus aquarum | Fecit, et fluvie mons est deductus in aequor.' Aubrey, *Monumenta*, ii. 1019, citing Ovid, *Metamorphoses*, 15.262–7, with minor spelling variations.

Around this passage, Aubrey noted relevant examples. The solid earth becoming sea was 'as in Cheshire', the land created out of ocean was 'as in the Sea not far from the Barbados about 1666', and the valley caused by sudden flooding was referred back to 'Gassendum de hoc'.[76] This passage and its paratexts echo Robert Hooke's theories of earthquakes and the alteration of the earth with which Aubrey engaged in his *Natural History of Wiltshire*.[77] Aubrey, like Hooke, recognized the possibility that considerable alterations of the earth's surface could occur within a relatively short period of time, and it is within this context that he understood reports such as one by Sir Jonas Moore, surveyor of the fens during the Earl of Bedford's drainage attempts, which he copied into the *Monumenta*: Moore 'told me that in the Fennes in Lincolnshire they found a Roman Causey fourtie foot under the Low-water-mark at Sea. Matthew Paris saieth that in his time it was the Paradise of England.'[78] In this chapter, however, he was intent on distinguishing between natural changes, such as the inundation of the Roman causeway in Lincolnshire, and significant man-made alterations. He began with a categorical statement that, 'the Saxons were barbarous & ignorant'—in keeping with his general low estimation of their culture—so that the Romans must be the builders of all the ancient embankments and drains now known in England, 'though I doe not remember it expressly mentioned in any Historian of any particular place'.[79] He provided a few examples, mostly from the area in and around London, to support his argument and quoted several pages from Dugdale's more comprehensive *History of Imbanking and Drayning*, but the chapter is sparse by Aubrey's standards and does not suggest a significant amount of research on his part.[80]

Instead, the majority of the chapter consists of an essay 'Of St Vincents Rocks, and Bristow', which is dated 1668 and was probably originally

[76] Aubrey, *Monumenta*, ii. 1019. Aubrey was probably referring to Pierre Gassendi, 'Philosophiae Epicuri syntagma', in *Opera omnia*, 6 vols. (Lyons, 1658), iii. 27–36. The other two cataclysms have not been identified.

[77] Robert Hooke, 'Lecture and Discourses of Earthquakes and Subterraneous Eruptions', in *Posthumous Works* (London, 1705), 277–450; Hunter, *Aubrey*, 58–9; Poole, *Aubrey*, ch. 7. Bodleian MS Aubrey 1, fols. 87r–102r (cf. William Poole, *The World Makers: Scientists of the Restoration and the Search for the Origins of the Earth* (Oxford, 2010), 111–12). The immediate sources for most of the conclusions Aubrey drew in this text were Robert Hooke's lectures to the Royal Society on earthquakes, particularly the eleventh lecture, given on 4 January 1688, for which see Ellen Tan Drake, *Restless Genius: Robert Hooke and His Earthly Thoughts* (Oxford, 1996), 285–93 and *passim*.

[78] Aubrey, *Monumenta*, ii. 923. Aubrey's citation of Matthew Paris may be due to the influence of his friend Thomas Gale who had made notes towards a new edition of Paris (see Chapter 6).

[79] Aubrey, *Monumenta*, ii. 1023.

[80] Aubrey, *Monumenta*, ii. 1053–5, quotations from William Dugdale which derive from his *History of Imbanking and Drayning*... (London, 1662), 104, 111.

written as a separate work before later being incorporated into the *Monumenta*.[81] It does, however, address the same issues. Aubrey, noting the absence of any place that could plausibly be identified with Bristol in the *Antonine Itinerary*, proposed that, '[I]n those daies, this now illustrious Place (together with the great Flat of Somersetshire), was under water, that is to say by the over-flowing of the River of Avon, which was pluggd-up, or barred by the bottome of these Vincentian Rocks.'[82] In support of this he quoted a local tradition from Thomas Axe of Orchard, Somerset, that anchors had been 'digged-up in the Meers' nearby.[83] At the foot of St Vincent's Rock lay a series of smaller rocks called the Lidde, which interfered with navigation and which he supposed were the remnants of a larger barrier that had been partially removed by Roman engineers 'at the Declension of their Government'.[84] He then laid out the gradual evolution of the landscape around Bristol, from prehistoric times to the present. It was first underwater, but an earthquake cut the river channel below the rocks—seemingly, unless he was contradicting himself, in Roman times—and it became a marsh.[85] Subsequently, after the Roman engineering works, it had settled into its present state. Aubrey was here combining his historicization of landscape with current theories of geological change. His unstable earth, replete with violent earthquakes and sudden inundations, was derived directly from Hooke's attempts to make sense of the geological evidence while still hanging onto the concept of an earth which was older than the Bible dictated but still comparatively young.[86]

PUBLISHING THE *MONUMENTA*

During his intellectual stocktaking of the early 1690s Aubrey determined to finally publish the *Monumenta Britannica*.[87] His ultimately unsuccessful

---

[81] Aubrey, *Monumenta*, ii. 1029–51, with 'now [1668]' at ii. 1037. Other sections of the chapter were certainly written no earlier than 1675 (cf. ii. 1023).

[82] Aubrey, *Monumenta*, ii. 1031.

[83] Axe was a friend of Robert Hooke, see Felicity Henderson, 'Unpublished Material from the Memorandum Book of Robert Hooke, Guildhall Library MS 1758', *Notes and Records of the Royal Society* 61 (2007): 168.

[84] Aubrey, *Monumenta*, ii. 1033.

[85] His inspiration for this was Edward Browne, *Travels*... (London, 1677), 62, but it bears a resemblance to Hooke's theories of earthquakes as well. As additional evidence for an earthquake he cited the large stones scattered on the downs to either side of the Avon, comparing St Vincent's Rocks, rather implausibly, with Etna and Vesuvius (Aubrey, *Monumenta*, ii. 1037).

[86] Poole, *The World Makers*, 111–12.

[87] This account is indebted to Michael Hunter's archival groundwork on the same subject, see Hunter, *Aubrey*, 89–90.

attempt to do so highlights the easily saturable market for antiquarianism at a time when polite writing was already doing battle with old-fashioned erudition. It also tells us something about the nature of Aubrey's scholarship. Drawing upon a network of friends and acquaintances, both for information and for subscriptions, was one thing, but Aubrey never possessed the backing of a scholarly juggernaut like the university presses of Oxford or Uppsala. While John Fell's editions and polemics could issue regularly from the Clarendon Building and Henrik Curio could laboriously produce the four volumes of Rudbeck's *Atlantica*, Aubrey was an individual scholar limited by his own resources and the vagaries of the book trade, conditions which in the end led to the *Monumenta* remaining in manuscript for another three hundred years.

Aubrey did, however, make the attempt. In the latter part of 1692 he had sounded out several London booksellers concerning the possibility of publication, including Samuel Smith, publisher of the Royal Society's *Philosophical Transactions* and of works by several friends and acquaintances including William Dugdale, John Ray, and Robert Boyle.[88] However, the cost of paper was high and Smith told him that the three- or four-volume work he imagined would be far too expensive to safely publish in the present market. Instead, Smith and some of the other booksellers he approached advised him to obtain subscriptions and publish in Oxford, where a work like the *Monumenta* could apparently be expected to sell more quickly than in London.[89]

Aubrey wrote to Edward Lhuyd on 4 February 1693 that he would have advertisements for subscriptions printed by the following Monday and would send one or two hundred to Oxford, but Anthony Wood's copy of the advertisement is dated 10 April, suggesting it may have taken slightly longer than Aubrey had hoped in its gestation.[90] When it did appear, Aubrey's proposal was to print the entirety of the *Monumenta* together with the *Stromata* (for which see Chapter 3) in 160 folio sheets, 'with abundance of Cuts'.[91] This would have made for a substantial book, 640 pages in length, with the equally substantial subscription price of 18 shillings, 9 up front and 9 upon delivery.[92] The expense of producing such

---

[88] *ODNB, s.n.*   [89] Bodleian MS Ashmole 1814, fol. 102r.
[90] Aubrey's letter to Lhuyd is Bodleian MS Ashmole 1814, fol. 102r. For Wood's dated copy of the subscription advertisement see Bodleian Wood 780.
[91] John Aubrey, *Proposals for Printing Monumenta Britannica* ([London, 1693]).
[92] The price was considerable, but not exorbitant. The *Proposals for Printing by Subscription Cambden's Britannia, English* issued in the same year gave its price as 26s., 12d. to be paid in hand and the rest upon delivery. By the time the *New Proposals* for the same, dated 20 April 1693, were printed the cost of the *Britannia* had risen to a princely 32s. in sheets, 40s. for non-subscribers.

a monumental work was underlined by the slightly nervous caveat that 'there are so few Printed, that care will be taken that none shall be under-sold'.

Nonetheless, it seems likely that, despite the expense, this scheme could have gone ahead. Edmund Gibson encouraged the project, while warning Aubrey against printing in Oxford due to the probability of a delay of four or five years, reminding him that 'the poor Saxon Chronicle could not be finish'd in less time than a year'.[93] Thomas Tanner seconded Gibson's encouragement and promised to solicit Arthur Charlett, master of University College, to seek subscriptions.[94] Charlett must have proved amenable, for by 4 April Aubrey reported to Wood that he was sending him copies of the proposal that week, noting also, with evident satisfaction, that Dryden had attempted to place the *Monumenta* with his own bookseller, 'but he will print only plays and romances'.[95] In the following days, Aubrey drew upon his network of friends and acquaintances in Oxford, sending four quires of the proposal to Tanner for disposal by him and Lhuyd.[96] Some were to go to subsidiary distributors and some directly to known interested parties, as described in Aubrey's letter to Lhuyd of 6 April, where he wrote that,

> I would entreat you to doe me the favour to deliver about 12 [copies of the proposal] to my cosen Levet fellow of Exeter coll: and some to Dr Gregory at Mistress —— and to send 2 or 3 to Mr Lud (or a name like) of Baliol [*sic*] coll: he was Proctor about 2 yeares since. a very civill Gent.[97]

Gibson was also involved in their distribution, promising to 'send them into the North and to Worcester'.[98] By 4 May, Aubrey reported to Tanner that he had been advised by Samuel Smith that Henry Clements in Oxford was the best choice for a printer and thought if subscriptions continued to flow in, he would be able to commence printing by

---

[93] Bodleian MS Aubrey 12, fol. 138cr. This was Gibson's *Chronicon Saxonicum* (Oxford, 1692), a work less than half the size of the *Monumenta*.

[94] Bodleian MS Aubrey 13, fol. 198r.

[95] Bodleian MS Wood F 51, fol. 5r. It is unclear who is meant by this, whether Jacob Tonson, Henry Herringman, or another.

[96] Bodleian MS Tanner 25, fol. 6r.

[97] Bodleian MS Ashmole 1814, fol. 90r. The recipients of Aubrey's proposals were Henry Levett, Fellow of Exeter, 1688–1700, and later physician at St Bartholomew's Hospital and the Charterhouse (Joseph Foster, *Alumni Oxonienses: The Members of the University of Oxford, 1500–1714*, 4 vols. [Oxford: 1891–2], iii. 904), David Gregory, the mathematician and astronomer, who had taken a medical doctorate in 1692 (Foster, *Alumni Oxonienses*, ii. 602; *ODNB, s.n.*), and Adam Lugg of Balliol who had been proctor in 1691 and was later rector of Brattleby and Fillingham, Lincolnshire (Foster, *Alumni Oxonienses*, iii. 949).

[98] Bodleian MS Aubrey 13, fol. 195r.

Michaelmas of that year.[99] Aubrey seems to have asked Tanner to act as an intermediary between himself and Clements, and Tanner reported on 16 May that while he had not seen Clements himself, he knew the printer planned to subscribe for fourteen copies in any case and that Aubrey ought to see him in London.[100]

This optimistic state of affairs did not last. By 19 July Aubrey had obtained only 112 subscriptions, evidently too few to fund the publication without further assistance, and he thought instead of asking the university to subsidize the printing.[101] Initial responses were positive, with Ralph Bathurst, president of Trinity College and his old friend, writing that Charlett was very ready to assist in the *Monumenta*'s publication, but on 24 May 1694 Aubrey wrote sulkily to Lhuyd that, 'Mr Gibson saith, that the University will not print my MSS: but let them lie among the Rubbish.'[102] A few days later, Lhuyd wrote back gently, implying that Gibson was being needlessly pessimistic ('I presume the curators of the Presse have not as yet had any perusal of your works'), but proceeded to reprimand him for apparently spreading a false rumour that he had the support of Jonathan Edwards, principal of Lhuyd's own Jesus College, for the printing of the *Monumenta* in a passage which Aubrey later heavily crossed out.[103] By the summer of 1694, the initially auspicious project seemed to be dead in the water.

Michael Hunter has proposed that the failure of the subscription campaign was due in large part to the simultaneous publication of Gibson's edition of Camden's *Britannia*, proposals for which were dated 20 April 1693, just as Aubrey's own campaign was getting underway.[104] Aubrey certainly felt this was the case and that the *Britannia* was attempting to swallow up his own work without giving him sufficient credit. Tanner was forced to write on 26 December 1693 insisting that his desire to read the *Monumenta* was entirely above board and regretting Aubrey's unwillingness to show him the manuscript after learning that he was amongst the antiquaries drafted by Gibson to prepare the new *Britannia*.[105] Both Tanner and Lhuyd grappled with Aubrey's disinclination to

[99] Bodleian MS Tanner 25, fol. 39r. Henry Clements, senior, was a well-known Oxford bookseller; see Norma Hodgson and Cyprian Blagden, *The Notebook of Thomas Bennet and Henry Clements (1686–1719) With Some Aspects of Book Trade Practice* (Oxford, 1956), 6.

[100] Bodleian MS Aubrey 13, fol. 199r.   [101] Bodleian MS Tanner 25, fol. 66r.

[102] Bodleian MS Aubrey 12, fols. 23–4; Ashmole 1814, fol. 113r.

[103] Bodleian MS Aubrey 12, fol. 257r.

[104] Hunter, *Aubrey*, 89; *New Proposals for Printing by Subscription Camden's Britannia. English* (n.p., 1693).

[105] Bodleian MS Aubrey 13, fol. 204r. Aubrey's fears would seem not to have been entirely fantastical, as Tanner admits in the letter that he concealed his involvement with

allow material from the *Monumenta* to be used in their chapters on
Wiltshire and Wales respectively, eventually prevailing, so that when the
new edition came out in 1695, the pith of Aubrey's Druidic theories was
ensconced within treatments by his two friends of individual megalithic
sites.[106]

The booksellers who handled Gibson's edition of the *Britannia* were
Abel Swale and Awnsham Churchill. Churchill was John Locke's publisher and agent and would go on to publish a number of substantial folios,
including the famous *Collection of Voyages*, Rymer's *Foedera*, and the
English translation of Bayle's *Dictionary*; although these were still in the
future, he was already an obvious candidate for the job.[107] It may be
through his connections with Locke, Tanner, or Lhuyd that Aubrey
proposed the *Monumenta* to Churchill in the summer of 1695.[108]
Churchill had accepted it by 31 August of that year and initially planned
to print it almost immediately.[109] This seems to suggest that Aubrey may
have been overreacting in his response to the new *Britannia*; certainly its
publication had not completely dried up the market for antiquarian texts.
For unknown reasons, however, work at the printers' end stalled and, on
12 November 1696, Aubrey wrote to Lhuyd, complaining of Churchill's
tardiness and planning to ask Locke and Gibson to speak to him.[110]
Before any further progress could be made, Aubrey died in June 1697
and the manuscript of the *Monumenta* remained, unprinted, in Churchill's hands.[111]

the *Britannia* from Aubrey until he was sure that project would go ahead (or, perhaps, that
the *Monumenta* would not).

[106] See Graham Parry, *The Trophies of Time: English Antiquarians of the Seventeenth
Century* (Oxford, 1995), ch. 12, for the composition of the 1695 *Britannia*. Aubrey's work
was acknowledged in its bibliography under the rubric 'Topographical Surveys of *England*
in general' as '*Templa Druidum, Monumenta Britannica*, &c. being large Collections and
curious observations relating to the Antiquities of England, in four Volumes, MS. By Mr.
John Aubrey, Fellow of the Royal Society' (Camden, *Camden's Britannia*, sig. fr).

[107] *ODNB, s.n.*

[108] Churchill also provided Aubrey with bibliographical details of Locke's publications
sold by him in a letter of 15 July 1695 when inviting him to Paternoster Row to discuss the
Monumenta (Bodleian MS Wood F 39, fol. 451r).

[109] Aubrey, *Three Prose Works*, 459–60.

[110] Bodleian MS Ashmole 1829, fol. 78r.

[111] The manuscript remained in the possession of Churchill and his descendants until it
was donated to the Bodleian Library in 1836 (Hunter, *Aubrey*, 91). The extensive scribal
circulation of the *Monumenta* amongst eighteenth-century antiquaries falls outwith the
remit of the present work, but would be a necessary starting point for any investigation into
the subsequent reception of Aubrey's ideas. Known copies include: (1) a lost transcript by
Thomas Gale made shortly before Aubrey's death (see Stuart Piggott, *William Stukeley: An
Eighteenth-Century Antiquary* [Oxford, 1950], 44; Piggott unsuccessfully searched for it in
Gale's manuscript collection, now in the library of Trinity College, Cambridge), (2) a series
of extracts from Gale's transcript, chiefly from the *Templa Druidum*, made by William

It is tempting to speculate what influence the *Monumenta* might have had if it had been published. Alain Schnapp has described Aubrey as flying the phrase 'comparative antiquitie...like a banner' and it is undoubtedly true that the comparative methodologies Aubrey brought to bear throughout his work were exceptional in the antiquarian scholarship of the time.[112] Whether naturalizing megaliths into world history, reasoning out the cultures behind burial mounds and hill forts, tracing ancient fortifications and roads across the landscape, or looking to Ovid and Robert Hooke to explain cataclysmic geological change, Aubrey's analogical reasoning broke new ground in the study of the ancient physical past. Placed in a wider context, however, it was not as unusual as it seemed but rather derived from a rich seventeenth-century tradition of comparative thought: a tradition better known for its approaches to the study of religion.[113] Aubrey's innovation was to apply this existing method to artefacts which had more often been looked at in isolation. Through the emotive reconstruction of the past which Meric Casaubon had described, he took items as distinct as 'a (coarse) gold coyne of Arviragus' with a rude horse stamped on its reverse and 'the white Horse cutt in the hill called White-horse hill in Berkshire', recognized their similarity, and concluded something new about the ancient landscape of Britain.[114]

Stukeley and dated 10 December 1718 (Wiltshire Archaeological & Natural Historical Society Library MS 889), (3) a transcript of the original by Stukeley's correspondent John Hutchins (British Library MS Add. 78660), (4) a transcript of Hutchins's transcript by Richard Gough made in 1769 (Bodleian MS Gough Gen. Top. 14), and (5) a transcript of Gough's transcript made by Edward Meredith of Christ Church College, Oxford, for John Britton in 1814 (Wiltshire Archaeological & Natural Historical Society Library MS 890). See also Hunter, *Aubrey*, 206.

[112] Schnapp, *Discovery*, 191.

[113] See Guy G. Stroumsa, *A New Science: The Discovery of Religion in the Age of Reason* (Cambridge, MA, and London, 2010).

[114] Namely that the Uffington White Horse dated from roughly the reign of Domitian (81–96 CE) or before if it was commemorated on a coin of Arviragus (for whom see *Biographia Britannica*, 6 vols. in 8 (London, 1747–66), i. 205–6). Cf. David Miles, Simon Palmer, Gary Lock, Chris Gosden, and Anne Marie Cromarty *Uffington White Horse and Its Landscape: Investigations at White Horse Hill, Uffington, 1989–95, and Tower Hill, Ashbury, 1993–4* (Oxford, 2003), 18–19, 63, 77–8.

3

The Old Roman Fashion

Architecture and Its Histories

The study of architecture fell within the purview of the antiquary from a very early date. Flavio Biondo's *Roma Instaurata* (1444–8) had inaugurated a tradition of antiquarian investigations into classical architecture which was developed in the works of sixteenth-century polymaths such as Pirro Ligorio and Andrea Palladio until, by the early seventeenth century, when Cassiano dal Pozzo began to assemble his vast 'paper museum'—of which drawings of Roman buildings formed a major part—architecture had become as central to antiquarian scholarship as numismatics or epigraphy.[1]

This thread of antiquarianism was both scholarly and practical. It was scholarly in so far as it rested on a widely held belief that architecture was a valuable source for the recovery of ancient culture: the ongoing excavations in Rome, including, most spectacularly, the rediscovery of the catacombs, were ample proof of that.[2] This was balanced, however, by an awareness of the practical applications of such research. Many of the leading scholars of Roman and Greek architecture were architects themselves and their researches fed directly into new building projects. Andrea Palladio is perhaps the most famous example, but scholarship and practice were rarely far apart and their intersection led to innovation in both, whether this took the form of a new style of neo-classical architecture or a new precision in the study of ancient monuments. Aubrey's contemporary, the French architect Antoine Desgodetz, is a particularly good example of this cross-fertilization.[3] Desgodetz's *Les edifices antiques de*

---

[1] For a survey of this literature, see Johann Albert Fabricius, *Bibliographia antiquaria*, 2nd edn. (Hamburg and Leipzig, 1716), 147–64.

[2] See Antonio Bosio, *Roma sotteranea* (Rome, 1632) and Irina Oryshkevich, 'Through a Netherlandish Looking-Glass: Philips van Winghe and Jean l'Heureux in the Catacombs', *Fragmenta* 5 (2011): 101–20.

[3] Wolfgang Herrmann, 'Antoine Desgodets and the Académie Royale d'Architecture', *The Art Bulletin* 40 (1958): 23–53.

Rome (1682) was prepared under French government sponsorship as an aide to contemporary architects, but provoked both scholarly and practical responses: the theoretical revisionism of Claude Perrault, the architectural emulation of Robert Adam, and the game-changing archaeological investigations of Robert Wood.[4]

This also meant that antiquarian scholarship on architecture, just like architectural scholarship on antiquities, was anything but unpolemical. Classicizing architects and antiquaries developed narratives of architectural development which privileged a recovery of ancient at the expense of medieval practices, and that developed a rhetoric of politeness and civilization, seen in neo-classical buildings, which contrasted with the rudeness and barbarism of the Gothic. In this milieu a neo-classical country house could be both an exercise in antiquarianism and a statement of humanist good taste. Aubrey's own forays into architecture exemplify this. Although he never built or oversaw any building himself, he was at the centre of a network of men who did: Christopher Wren, Robert Hooke, John Evelyn, and other Restoration virtuosi. Beginning with designs for a neo-classical 'villa' and gardens at his family home of Easton Pierse, Wiltshire, in 1669, Aubrey continued to engage with the architectural tradition and its implications throughout the following decade. This resulted in his *Chronologia Architectonica*, a methodology for dating post-Conquest English architecture, as well as an essay, 'Of Mausolea', this time using funeral monuments as a generic example which could help anchor the otherwise mystifying forts and barrows of the English landscape in a narrative of post-Babelic cultural diffusion.

In all three works Aubrey responded to the visual allure of the architectural past, but this response became progressively more nuanced over time. From a beginning in which his imagined architectures, themselves a *bricolage* of ancient and modern traditions, were both consolation and aesthetic delight, a deeply emotional response to the loss of his childhood home, he progressed to a theory of architecture as a tool with which to establish chronology, a set of physical objects which could provide a literal foundation for the abstract division of time. He also learnt to *see* with an eye to minute variation, paralleling architects like Desgodetz in his exchange of impressionistic descriptions for carefully delineated, precise sketches. Finally, he began to understand ancient architecture in much the

---

[4] Antoine Babuty Desgodetz, *Les edifices antiques de Rome* (Paris, 1682). For Wood's use of Desgodetz in an explicitly antiquarian and archaeological context see Robert Wood, *The Ruins of Palmyra, otherwise Tedmor, in the Desart* (London, 1753) and Robert Wood, *The Ruins of Balbec, otherwise Heliopolis in Coelosyria* (London, 1757), as well as C. A. Hutton, 'The Travels of "Palmyra" Wood in 1750–51', *Journal of Hellenistic Studies* 47 (1927): 102–28.

same way he would later view ancient rituals and custom in the *Remaines of Gentilisme*: as the half-visible traces of past links and inheritances between cultures and, ultimately, as a thread which could tie the particularities of England and the English landscape into the grand narrative of humanity's distant past.

TUSCULUM IN WILTSHIRE: IMAGINING THE VILLA OF EASTON PIERSE

'My talent has been crushed by my long endurance of woes: no part of my former vigour remains.'[5] This was Aubrey's melancholy assessment of his life, mediated through lines from Ovid's *Tristia*, in 1669. At his father's death in 1652, he had inherited a small estate already encumbered with lawsuits and haemorrhaging money at a worrying rate. First to go were his Welsh lands, but breaking the entail upon them required a 'chargeable and taedious lawe-suite' which Aubrey later believed had cost him £1,200.[6] Despite, or because of, this storm clouds continued to gather: 'then debts and lawe-suites, *opus et usus* [toil and wear], borrowing of money and perpetuall riding'. His family's Herefordshire manors of Bushelton and Stratford were disposed of to scholarly acquaintances: Dr Thomas Willis and Herbert Croft, Bishop of Hereford, respectively.[7] Aubrey had already been once disappointed in his attempts to marry an heiress when Katherine Ryves, to whom he was engaged, had died some years before, but in an attempt to revive his flagging fortunes he began to court Joan Sumner, a member of a Wiltshire gentry family, in the mid-1660s. What happened next is not entirely clear—it seems that Sumner discovered the extent of Aubrey's debts after lending him a large sum of money during their engagement and began to have second thoughts—not only did the marriage fail to proceed, but Aubrey found himself in a lawsuit with his prospective bride.[8] When he copied out the passage from Ovid he knew there was no going back: his childhood home at Easton Pierse and his farm at Broad Chalke, the only properties left of his patrimony, would be sold.

It was at this point that Aubrey composed a farewell love-letter to his home. The *Designatio de Easton-Piers in Com: Wilts.*—'per me (heu!) infortunatum Johannem Aubrey R.S. Socium'—was part epitaph, part

---

[5] Ovid, *Tristia*, V.xii.31–2 ('contudit ingenium patientia longa malorum, et pars antiqui nulla vigoris adest'), quoted in Bodleian MS Aubrey 17, fol. 20v.

[6] Aubrey, *Lives*, i. 433–4.   [7] Aubrey, *Lives*, i. 434.

[8] Aubrey, *Lives*, i. 434, 441. See Powell, *Aubrey*, 115–27.

fantasy.[9] Intermixed with shadowy watercolours of the manor house at Easton Pierse and the surrounding countryside are luminous images of an imagined rebuilding in the latest neo-classical style (see Figure 3.1). This 'villa' was both a fantastical consolation prize, dreamt of at the moment when the more prosaic, real Easton Pierse was about to be lost, and Aubrey's first major engagement with the study of architecture, past and present.

Aubrey's 'villa' was, first and foremost, a Restoration-era country house in the style of Inigo Jones or Roger Pratt. Its double pile shape with visible quoins, a hipped roof, and cupola closely echo Pratt's Coleshill House, begun in 1651.[10] This is not surprising. While there is no evidence that Aubrey and Pratt were directly acquainted, they shared several close friends and colleagues. John Evelyn, who would later contribute annotations to the *Chronologia Architectonica*, had been Pratt's 'old acquaintance at Rome', while Christopher Wren served with Pratt on the committee which supervised the rebuilding of London after the Great Fire and would later debate the evolution of primitive architecture with Aubrey and Robert Hooke.[11] If there was a specific link between Aubrey and Pratt it was probably Evelyn, whose 1659 drawings of a proposed residential college, outlined in a letter to Robert Boyle, contain a building and a rough sketch of a garden which almost exactly match Aubrey's dreams for Easton Pierse and which show the influence of Coleshill and Pratt's other designs.[12] The three men, in turn, shared an admiration of the earlier work of Inigo Jones, particularly his banqueting house at Whitehall which Evelyn thought a 'glorious object' compared to the 'fantastical and licentious manner of building' brought in by the 'Goths, Vandals and other barbarous nations'.[13]

[9] Now Bodleian MS Aubrey 17.
[10] For Pratt's Coleshill and its context see Roger Pratt, *The Architecture of Sir Roger Pratt*, ed. R. T. Gunther (Oxford, 1928), 92–7; Nigel Silcox-Crowe, 'Sir Roger Pratt, 1620–1685: The Ingenious Gentleman Architect', in *The Architectural Outsiders*, ed. Roderick Brown (London, 1985), 1–20; Colin Platt, *The Great Rebuildings of Tudor and Stuart England: Revolutions in Architectural Taste* (London and Bristol, PA, 1994), 37–40.
[11] John Evelyn, *The Diary of John Evelyn*, 6 vols., ed. E. S. de Beer (Oxford, 1955), iii. 153; Lisa Jardine, *On a Grander Scale: The Outstanding Career of Sir Christopher Wren* (London, 2003), 254, 257–9. See also Gillian Darley, *John Evelyn: Living for Ingenuity* (New Haven, CT, and London, 2006), 47–8, 188–9 (for Pratt), 219–23 (for Wren).
[12] Michael Hunter, *Establishing the New Science* (Woodbridge, 1989), 181–4; Alice Friedman, 'John Evelyn and English Architecture', in *John Evelyn's 'Elysium Britannicum' and European Gardening*, ed. Joachim Wolschke-Bulmahn and Therese O'Malley (Cambridge, MA, 1998), 161–3.
[13] Friedman, 'John Evelyn and English Architecture', 165. For the classical sources upon which Jones drew for the banqueting house see Vaughan Hart and Richard Tucker, '"Immaginacy set free": Aristotelian Ethics and Inigo Jones's Banqueting House at Whitehall', *RES: Anthropology and Aesthetics* 39 (2001): 151–67.

Figure 3.1 Aubrey's 1669 imagined rebuilding of his home at Easton Pierse, Wiltshire (Bodleian MS Aubrey 17, fol. 8r).

As Evelyn's impassioned words make clear, this choice of architectural style was something more than just selecting a pleasing design from a pattern book; it was a statement of cultural values. Rejecting one past—the 'licentious' Gothic—in favour of another, more polite, more classical antiquity had wide-ranging ramifications. It was no accident that Aubrey described his fantasy Easton Pierse as a villa (and was, perhaps, the first Englishman to do so).[14] He and his contemporaries were attempting to realize their vision of the classical world, reviving 'the old Roman Architecture' but only as part of a larger dream in which Cicero's Tusculan villa could be transported wholesale into the home counties of seventeenth-century England.[15]

This longing for a baroque reimagining of a pastoral Roman country house is writ large in Aubrey's *Designatio*. Liberally spiced with classical quotations, its paratexts revolve around the theme of Aubrey's loss, imagined through quotations from Ovid describing the beauty of the countryside at one moment and Daedalus's hatred of Crete and his exile from his native land the next.[16] On its title page Aubrey gave as an epigraph the *locus classicus* from Horace: 'this is what I prayed for!—a piece of land not so very large, where there would be a garden, and near the house a spring of ever-flowing water, and up above these a bit of woodland'.[17] Elsewhere in the text he turned once again to Ovid: 'then she looked round on the ancient woods, the grottoes, and the grass, spangled with countless flowers. She declared the daughters of Mnemosyne to be happy alike in their favourite pursuits and in their home.'[18] On the facing page he quoted Horace again, distilling his emotions into a single line: 'I praise the lovely country's brooks, its groves and moss-grown rocks.'[19] These classical effusions were apparently matched by another thirteen or fourteen sheets 'in verse & prose' by Aubrey himself, entitled

[14] Villa in the Latin sense of an *ancient* country house was already in English usage by this period and the *OED* is aware of two earlier references in a continental context, but Aubrey and Evelyn appear to have been the first *virtuosi* to use the term to mean a *modern* English building (*OED*, *s.v.*). It had, however, already appeared in a Scottish context as early as 1613; see Michael Bath, 'Philostratus Comes to Scotland: A New Source for the Pictures at Pinkie', *Journal of the Northern Renaissance* 5 (2013), online at <http://www.north ernrenaissance.org/philostratus-comes-to-scotland-a-new-source-for-the-pictures-at-pinkie/> (accessed 13 January 2016).

[15] Bodleian MS Top. Gen. c. 25, fol. 168r.

[16] Bodleian MS Aubrey 17, fol. 2r, quoting Ovid, *Metamorphoses*, VIII.184.

[17] Bodleian MS Aubrey 17, fol. 1r, quoting Horace, *Satires*, II.vi.1–3.

[18] Bodleian MS Aubrey 17, fol. 1v, quoting Ovid, *Metamorphoses*, V.265–8. Aubrey has written 'Maeonidas' for 'Mnemonidas', supplanting the Muses' mother, probably quite unconsciously, with Homer Maeonides, the Maeonian bard.

[19] Bodleian MS Aubrey 17, fol. 2r, quoting Horace, *Epistles*, I.x.6–7.

Villa, or a Description of the Prospects from Easton-Piers.[20] Although this manuscript is lost, Michael Hunter has identified likely drafts of a small portion of it in one of Aubrey's mathematical notebooks. There Aubrey wrote that 'in such fine solitude as these shades the Muses [were] wont in vision to appear to their worshippers... to build in the mans phancy, magnificent \stately/ castles, palaces, gardins'.[21]

The praises of bucolic existence which open the *Designatio* are followed by drawings of both the existing and the imagined houses at Easton Pierse, the magnificent palaces and gardens of the Worcester fragment. While Aubrey's sketches of the surrounding countryside occur later in the volume, it would be a mistake to suppose that the classical texts with which he frames the work as a whole are solely lyric responses to this soon-to-be-lost landscape (though they are that as well). They are the textual colonization of a real landscape, the Wiltshire Downs in the 1660s, by an imagined one, the hills and groves of northern Italy in the first century CE. The extent to which this colonization was complete, at least in Aubrey's visions, is seen in the imagined vistas looking away from the new house: a long walk lined on either side with Lombardy poplars or, more dramatically, a cartouche which may also be a window and which reveals a vista of rolling hills, a forested river course, two ancient towers, and two pyramids.[22] The cartouche reproduces a detail from an engraving which had previously appeared in his friend Evelyn's translation of Roland Fréart's *Parallel of Ancient and Modern Architecture* (1664). Through a classical archway we see a hilly Italian landscape above which clouds are gathering; in the distance two pyramids dominate a wooded plain.[23] This is a real place, whatever fantastical touches have been added by the engraver. Fréart specified it as a 'very antient Sepulchre to be seen near Terracina' on the southern border of the Papal States, in 'a wild and uncultivated place' and identified the source of the engraving as a plan taken by the sixteenth-century antiquary Pirro Ligorio who 'discovered and (as one may say) disinterr'd it (for 'twas almost buried amongst the brambles)'.[24] This vista was transported by Aubrey in its entirety from Latina to Wiltshire: the never-built villa would have looked out on the Appian Way.

---

[20] It was evidently a companion piece to the *Designatio*, but written two years later in 1671 while Aubrey was staying with Sir Robert Henley in Hampshire (see Bodleian MS Wood F 39, fol. 369v). See Hunter, *Aubrey*, 239–41, and Kate Bennett, 'John Aubrey and the Rhapsodic Book', *Renaissance Studies* 28 (2014): 322–3.

[21] Worcester College, Oxford MS 5.4, unpaginated (cf. Hunter, *Aubrey*, 240).

[22] Bodleian MS Aubrey 17, fols. 15r (poplars), 17r (pyramids).

[23] Roland Fréart, *A Parallel of the Antient Architecture with the Modern*, trans. John Evelyn (London, 1664), 35.

[24] Fréart, *Parallel*, 34.

Aubrey's engagement with architecture began both practically and theoretically as plans for a house which was never, and could never have been, built. His villa was overtly classicizing, almost to the point of being displaced from England into Italy, and reflected the latest designs of Aubrey's architecturally minded colleagues in the Royal Society. Paradoxically, however, as he was composing this paean to neo-classicism, he was also preparing a text devoted to the study of the belittled and unfashionable Gothic architecture which surrounded his Horatian retreat.

DATING THE MEDIEVAL, PRAISING THE CLASSICAL

In the same year in which he compiled the *Designatio*, Aubrey asked his new friend Anthony Wood, 'as you looke upon your papers, pray lay aside some remarks for me chronologicall as concerning guessing by Windowes. I have something improved it here since: and about the Priory by Easton.'[25] Aubrey's 'guessing by Windowes' meant establishing the date of medieval buildings by their window styles, now a common practice, but not one which was in the mainstream of seventeenth-century antiquarian methodology. His notes on this method of guessing eventually became a document entitled *Chronologia Architectonica*, part of a 'stromata' (Greek for a patchwork or miscellany) which now forms an appendix to the second volume of the *Monumenta Britannica* (Bodleian MS Top. Gen. c. 25).[26] Of the tracts contained in the *Stromata*, the *Chronologia Architectonica* was the first to be composed—its title page is dated 1671—and eventually became the largest in size (fifty pages in Aubrey's numeration).[27] It was

[25] Bodleian MS Wood F 39, fol. 123r (Aubrey–Wood, 7 August 1669).
[26] The *Stromata* contains chronologies of architecture, scripts, heraldry, and clothing, an essay on inventions and innovations ('*Nouvelles*'), and a series of tracts on histories of weights and measures, values of money, and the price of corn. The title page of the *Stromata* indicates that it had previously been appended to his *Description of Wiltshire* and suggests the possibility that some of the tracts eventually included in Aubrey's *Miscellanies* (London, 1696)—those on day fatality, omens, and dreams—had once been considered for inclusion within it (Bodleian MS Top. Gen. c. 25, fol. 150r). This manuscript genealogy implies that these tracts were not originally conceived as an integral part of either the *Monumenta* or the *Description* or, indeed, necessarily intended to be taken as an interrelated whole. Instead, they are largely free-standing—though the four *Chronologiae* were inspired by and to some extent inform each other—and were probably appended to the larger works out of a desire to ensure their publication. The *Architectonica*, in particular, includes directions for its organization when sent to the printers, see Bodleian MS Top. Gen. c. 25, fol. 153r. The note at the top of this page ('begin to print this Treatise at page. 31') was probably added when Aubrey was contemplating the publication of the *Monumenta Britannica*.
[27] Bodleian MS Top. Gen. c. 25, fols. 152r–179r.

planned as a visual history of architecture in England, from Roman times
to the present, and H. M. Colvin has seen in it the first sympathetic and
reasonably accurate treatment of Gothic architecture.[28] Aubrey, Colvin
argued, stood apart from the common early modern consensus that, as Sir
John Clerk of Penicuik wrote, the Goths had 'introduced a bad manner not
only in Architectory but in all other arts & sciences . . . we have been for
upwards of 200 years endeavouring to recover ourselves from this Gothi-
cism'.[29] Colvin thought that to Aubrey 'must go the credit for being the
first to think historically about medieval English architecture', and saw him
essentially as a precursor to the nineteenth-century architectural historian
Thomas Rickman, a scholar willing both to sympathize with the style and
to see in it a clear process of historical change extending from the late
antique to the early modern.[30]

However tempting it is to place Aubrey in a narrative of growing
aesthetic appreciation for the Gothic, these views are untenable. Aubrey
does appear to have been the first antiquary to attempt a chronology of
medieval architectural styles, but his ideological conception of architectural progress was entirely at odds with those of the nineteenth-century
Romantic antiquaries of Rickman's generation. In the 'diatribe' prefacing
the *Chronologia* Aubrey set out his views on the development of architectural style, seeing a decline from the 'primitive beautie' of Roman architecture into the 'barbarous' and 'fantastick' styles of the Middle Ages, and
a subsequent gradual recovery, shepherded by Palladio and Inigo Jones,
until once again 'the old Roman fashion is become the common Mode'.[31]
By contrast with Rickman, who defined the architecture of the early
Middle Ages as the 'Roman mode debased' but who believed that the
architecture of the thirteenth and fourteenth centuries represented 'the
perfection of the English mode', Aubrey's architectural chronology is a
straightforward one of decline and recovery; Roman architecture degen-
erated into Gothic, but was gradually restored to its antique purity.[32] This
parabola of change maps on to the understanding of the Middle Ages
elsewhere in his work. Aubrey had no sympathy for the barbarian successors of the Romans, seeing them as both superstitious and ignorant of

[28] H. M. Colvin, 'Aubrey's *Chronologia Architectonica*', in *Concerning Architecture: Essays
on Architectural Writers and Writing Presented to Nikolaus Pevsner*, ed. John Summerson
(London, 1968), 1–12.
[29] Colvin, 'Aubrey's *Chronologia Architectonica*', 2, citing Sir John Clerk of Penicuik,
'The Country Seat' (1727).
[30] See especially Colvin, 'Aubrey's *Chronologia Architectonica*', 3, 11. For Rickman see
his *An Attempt to Discriminate the Styles of Architecture in England, From the Conquest to the
Reformation . . .* , 3rd edn. (London, 1825). The first edition was published in 1817.
[31] Bodleian MS Top. Gen. c. 25, fols. 168r–169r.
[32] See Rickman, *Attempt to Discriminate*, 4–5.

technical skills.[33] Moreover, the generic 'Goths' of this larger narrative could be identified by Aubrey as the brutish Saxons, whose culture he had summed up elsewhere in the preface to his *Description* of Wiltshire:

> here was a mist of ignorance for 600 yeares. They were so far from knowing Arts, that they could not build wall with stone. They lived sluttishly in poor howses, where they ate a great deale of beefe & mutton, and dranke good Ale in a browne mazard [i.e., a cup or bowl]: and their very Kings were but a sort of Farmers.[34]

Though Aubrey was aware of the evolution from Romanesque to Gothic, for him all post-Roman architecture fell under the epithet of 'Barbarous fashion' until 'the old Roman Architecture began to be revived', first in Italy in the time of Henry VII and then in England in the reign of Edward VI.[35] In identifying the moment when the new style came to England, he focused on the two great architectural projects sponsored by Edward Seymour, Duke of Somerset: Somerset House on the Strand in London and Longleat House, not far from Aubrey's home in Wiltshire. For both projects, Aubrey maintained, Somerset had 'sent for Architects & Workmen out of Italie'.[36] He gave no further description of Somerset House, but sketched a quick pen-portrait of Longleat, presumably from first-hand experience. It was, he wrote, 'three stories high (above the stately vaulture under ground) adorned with Dorique, Ionique, and Corinthian pillars. Leaded on the top.'[37] He contrasted this with Elizabethan architecture, which 'made no growth: but rather went backwards' with its 'greate wide Windowes, which were not only cold, but weakned the Fabrique' of the building. Burghley House and Audley End he identified as examples of this inferior style.[38]

While Aubrey cited Andrea Palladio and, implicitly, his *I quattro libri dell'architettura* (1570) as an origin point for the 'Roman Architecture', his real hero in its revival was Inigo Jones, whose banqueting house at Whitehall (1619–22) he singled out as 'so exquisite a piece, that if all the Books of Architecture were lost, the true art of Building might be

---

[33] See, for comparison, Bodleian MS Top. Gen. c. 24, fol. 29r, in which he describes the Goths and quotes the essayist Balzac that they 'seemed to come to hasten time and precipitate the end of the world, [and] declared so particular a warre to written things, that it was not wanting in them, but that even the Alphabet had been abolished' (Jean-Louise Guez, Seigneur de Balzac, *The Roman: The Conversation of the Romans and Maecenas, in Three Excellent Discourses* [London, 1652], 92).
[34] Bodleian MS Aubrey 3, fol. 10v.   [35] Bodleian MS Top. Gen. c. 25, fol. 168r.
[36] Bodleian MS Top. Gen. c. 25, fol. 168r.
[37] Bodleian MS Top. Gen. c. 25, fol. 168r.
[38] Bodleian MS Top. Gen. c. 25, fol. 168r.

retrieved thence'.[39] In the wake of Jones, Aubrey concluded, 'the old Roman fashion is become the common Mode'.[40] Certainly it was the mode which he chose for the imagined villa at Easton Pierse. Crucially, though, it is the 'old Roman fashion'; not a new style based upon Roman architecture, but Roman architecture itself. Aubrey's vision of architectural history was essentially circular. Paradoxically, this meant that there was no place for any exaltation of the Romanesque and Gothic architecture with which the majority of the *Chronologia* was concerned; at best it could only be tolerated.

This does not, however, vitiate Colvin's placement of Aubrey as the first historian of Gothic architecture.[41] The *Architectonica* was undeniably original in its emphasis on the specific shapes of architectural forms and the ways in which these could be arranged into a recognizable, chronological pattern of change. Olivia Horsfall Turner has argued that this was due to the influence of Aubrey's contemporaries in the Royal Society, notably Christopher Wren, as well as Meric Casaubon via his *Treatise of Use and Custome* which Aubrey cited in the *Monumenta*.[42] She links Casaubon's emphasis on 'bare forms or matter' to a growing interest in palaeography and the established dating techniques for epigraphic evidence in the same period, seeing in these the methodological origins of Aubrey's architectural schema.[43] While the chronology of epigraphic styles had been developed earlier, it is suggestive that the *Architectonica* should date from the same period as both Aubrey's own *Chronologia Graphica* and the more famous palaeographical treatise, Jean Mabillon's *De re diplomatica* (1681).[44] When composing the *Architectonica* Aubrey had noted to himself that '[t]were an easy matter to make a Scriptura Chronologica of the severall hands from the Conquest till now, which

[39] Bodleian MS Top. Gen. c. 25, fol. 169r. For Palladio's new 'Roman Architecture' see Bruce Boucher, *Andrea Palladio: The Architect in his Time*, rev. edn. (New York, 1998) and Pierre Gros, *Palladio e l'antico* (Venice, 2006). For Inigo Jones's participation in this tradition see Giles Worsley, *Inigo Jones and the European Classicist Tradition* (New Haven, CT, 2006), Christy Anderson, *Inigo Jones and the Classical Tradition* (Cambridge, 2007), esp. 166–83, and Vaughan Hart, *Inigo Jones: The Architect of Kings* (New Haven, CT, and London, 2011), esp. ch. 7.

[40] Bodleian MS Top. Gen. c. 25, fol. 169r.

[41] The point has previously been made by Olivia Horsfall Turner, ' "The Windows of this Church are of several Fashions": Architectural Form and Historical Method in John Aubrey's "Chronologia Architectonica" ', *Architectural History* 54 (2011): 171–93.

[42] Horsfall Turner, ' "The Windows of this Church are of several Fashions" ', 180, and cf. the present work's introduction.

[43] Horsfall Turner, ' "The Windows of this Church are of several Fashions" ', 180–1. Aubrey's paraphrase of Casaubon's argument is at Bodleian MS Top. Gen. c. 25, fol. 5v.

[44] The *Chronologia Graphica* is now at Bodleian MS Top. Gen. c. 25, fols. 185r–196r; Jean Mabillon, *De re diplomatica* (Paris, 1681).

would be of good use'.[45] In 1672 he followed through with his idea, taking advantage of an extended visit to Hothfield, the estate of his friend Nicholas Tufton, 3rd Earl of Thanet, to use the earl's ancient deeds as the basis for such a 'Chronologia Scriptoria' which attempted to identify, date, and systematize scripts on the same plan as the *Architectonica* did for building styles.[46] However, regardless of the systemizing tendencies which may have underlain the *Architectonica*'s compilation, why did Aubrey choose to focus on the dating of a series of architectural examples from the Conquest to the mid-sixteenth century? If he viewed this as a period of 'Barbarous' and 'fantastick' fashions, why did he record its morphologies with such care?

The answer to this can be found in his methods. Early in the work he noted that 'I found by Mr Anthony Woods Antiquities of Oxford, in what Kings reigne & yeare of the Lord such or such a part of a college was built.'[47] This is borne out by the text, in which the majority of the precisely dated examples are from Oxford colleges. Aubrey had recognized early on that the shape of windows was the surest indicator of the age of a building and the text consists chiefly of watercolours of windows, in greater or lesser detail depending on which feature he wished to emphasize (see Figure 3.2). Below these Aubrey added notes such as that appended to a drawing of a Perpendicular Gothic window:

> At All-Souls Colledge in Oxford built tempore Henry 6. 1437. Memorandum there are two windows of double Lights, as here. A windowe at the Parsonage house at Streete in Somerset, just of this fashion. v. the glasse in the inside. The old window of the old Hall at Easton-Piers is of this very fashion. In these western parts are many windowes of this fashion.[48]

Aubrey derived the initial date from materials gathered by Wood, then used his knowledge that the style of windows changed rapidly and predictably to identify similar buildings which could thus be determined to be of a similar age. The bulk of the *Architectonica* was not a history of architecture, as such, though Aubrey attempted to briefly sketch such a

[45] Bodleian MS Aubrey 3, fol. 3v.

[46] Bodleian MS Top. Gen. c. 25, fols. 189r–190v. Aubrey returned to this project in 1689, preparing the final version of the *Chronologia Graphica* and taking into account the publication of Mabillon's *magnum opus* as well as Edward Bernard's *Orbis eruditi literatura à Charactere Samaritico deducta* ([Oxford], 1689) in the meantime (Bodleian MS Top. Gen. c. 25, fol. 185r).

[47] Bodleian MS Top. Gen. c. 25, fol. 153r; Anthony Wood, *Historia et antiquitates Universitatis Oxoniensis*, 2 vols. (Oxford, 1674). Aubrey could, however, have had access to Wood's manuscripts by virtue of their friendship and correspondence before the *Historia et antiquitates* were published.

[48] Bodleian MS Top. Gen. c. 25, fol. 163r.

Figure 3.2 A characteristic sketch from Aubrey's *Chronologia Architectonica*: the rose window in the south transept of Westminster Abbey (Bodleian MS Top. Gen. c. 25, fol. 172v).

history in his introduction, but rather a handbook for the dating of buildings whose age would otherwise be unknown. Aesthetic considerations could be left aside in favour of the obvious benefits of establishing an architectural chronology.

Aubrey's schematization of Gothic architecture went beyond window style. The *Architectonica* did not address the fabric of buildings, but it did include reflections on the technological and physical changes associated with visual changes in architecture, one notable example of which Aubrey had from Sir William Dugdale:

> Sir W. Dugdale tells me, that he finds by W. Malmesbury &c: that glasse was not used but in churches, & great persons chiefe Roomes: and I remember that before the Civil-warres, poor peoples windowes were not glassed: nor yet in Herefordshire, Shropshire, &c: even at free-holders houses.[49]

---

[49] Bodleian MS Top. Gen. c. 25, fol. 167ar.

The *Chronologia* participated not only in an antiquarian tradition which prioritized the construction of a chronological framework, but also owed a debt to the Royal Society's fascination with technology and technological change, which Aubrey engaged with at more length elsewhere in works such as his *Nouvelles*, a record of inventions and innovations in English culture.

Like many of Aubrey's works, the *Architectonica* was looked over and annotated by several of his acquaintances at various stages in its composition. The most important annotations are those by John Evelyn, who had also influenced Aubrey's designs for the villa at Easton Pierse, as discussed in the section 'Tusculum in Wiltshire', and who shared his vision of a neo-Roman Britain. Evelyn contributed additions to Aubrey's historical preface, chiefly notices of significant buildings, offered sociological explanations for the changes in window fashions, and provided comparisons between English and Italian architecture.[50] An example of Evelyn's interventions can be found in his response to Aubrey's complaint that, in sixteenth-century houses 'the fashion of those times was to have the side of a roome all one window: which was cold, & weake'.[51] What was for Aubrey merely an uncomfortable imperfection on the road to the Palladian ideal, was for Evelyn a space which shaped the social discourse of the age. These 'great bay-windows', Evelyn wrote, 'were in stead of Withdrawing-rooms & there lay large Cushions to leane upon. Where after dinner they us'd to retire & discourse in private of businesse. They had also commonly a Curtaine to draw before them, for privacy.'[52] Somewhat unexpectedly, Evelyn emerges as the more thoughtful observer of past customs in this exchange.

The *Chronologia* was a handbook, a guide to 'guessing by Windowes'.[53] Aubrey had recognized the value of architecture as a tool for establishing chronologies, but this recognition existed in tension with his own fervently held beliefs in the superiority of the 'old Roman fashion'. His ideal was the stoic retreat he had created in the *Designatio*, not any Gothic pile with its 'licentious' and 'fantastical' ornament and, as a result, his approach to medieval architecture was essentially pragmatic. Perceived irregularities which might be unacceptable in medieval architecture could, however, be not only acceptable but paradigmatic in the architecture of remote antiquity. Aubrey, together with his friends Wren and Hooke, would return to the issue of architectural evolution in the 1670s, but in a very

---

[50] For Evelyn's additions see esp. Bodleian MS. Top. Gen. c. 25, fols. 164v, 165v–166r.
[51] Bodleian MS Top. Gen. c. 25, fol. 165r.
[52] Bodleian MS Top. Gen. c. 25, fol. 164v.
[53] For the eighteenth-century afterlife of the *Chronologia* see Hunter, *Aubrey*, 206.

different context: that of the ancient, post-Babelic world. There, rude or baffling architectural forms could hold the keys not only to the later development of classical styles, but to the origins of man-made features in the ancient British landscape.

THE TOWER OF BABEL AND PORSENNA'S TOMB

When composing a portion of the *Monumenta Britannica* in the 1670s, Aubrey stepped back for a moment from the sketches and descriptions of individual ancient sites which composed the vast majority of his materials, and prefaced a series of chapters on barrows, urns, and sepulchres with a short architectural treatise 'Of Mausolea'.[54] This essay aimed to map out a genealogy of ancient burial architecture. It began with the Tower of Babel, proceeded through the Egyptian pyramids and the Mausoleum at Halicarnassus to the monument of Almansor, the earthen burial mounds of the Chinese, and Lars Porsenna's tomb.[55] Aubrey traversed widely across ancient history for examples and made use of the modern scholarship available on each of the monuments he discussed. He evidently imagined the finished text would be richly illustrated and made numerous notes towards the insertion of images within the text, of which the following— intended to be inserted immediately after his discussion of the Tower of Babel—is a characteristic example:

> De la Val, in his Travells, speakes of the Tower of Babel: and also of Ezechiel's Tombe: and also of Absolom's Pillar. which was cutt out of a Rock: which Sir Christ Wren sayes 'twas a pretty thing: insert his draught of it here: and also desire him to shew me his excellent draught of Porsenna's Monument.[56]

Wren appears as a source at other points in this essay and his presence helps establish its context within contemporary understandings of ancient architecture.[57] Amongst Wren's incomplete architectural manuscripts is a 'Discourse on Architecture', whose aim was to 'reform the Generality to a

---

[54] Aubrey, *Monumenta*, ii. 670–83.

[55] For the tower of Babel in early modern thought see Arno Borst, *Der Turmbau von Babel: Geschichte der Meinungen über Ursprung und Vielfalt der Sprachen und Völker*, 4 vols. in 6 (Stuttgart, 1957–63).

[56] Aubrey, *Monumenta*, ii. 671. See Pietro Della Valle, *Viaggi*, 4 vols. (Rome, 1650–63), i. 516 (Absalom's pillar), 712–21 (Babel and Ezekiel's tomb). I am grateful to Noel Malcolm for directing me to the Italian original of the *Viaggi*, rather than its contemporary English translation.

[57] He was also Aubrey's source for more information on Porsenna's tomb and on Chinese burial customs (Aubrey, *Monumenta*, ii. 675, 679).

truer tast in Architecture by giving a larger Idea of the whole Art, beginning with the reasons and progress of it from the most remote Antiquity'.[58] His discussion of postdiluvian building began with Babel—'the first Peece of Civil Architecture'—continued with the pyramids, the pillar of Absalom, Solomon's temple, and the walls of Babylon, and concluded abruptly with Porsenna's tomb.[59] On one hand, the structures discussed by Aubrey and Wren belonged to a common fund of marvellous ancient buildings, frequently studied and reconstructed in the early modern period, but as Lydia Soo has argued, the references to Wren in the *Monumenta* together with the striking parallels between the two works suggest that they were more closely related.[60]

The most likely point of contact between Aubrey and Wren was their mutual friend Robert Hooke, also named as a source in 'Of Mausolea'. On 4 October 1677, Hooke had met Wren at a tavern and 'Discoursed of Porsennas Tomb'.[61] They disagreed and the following day Hooke drew 'a rationall porcena', continuing the conversation with Wren at regular intervals throughout the month.[62] Aubrey was living with Hooke in the latter's lodgings in Gresham College during the autumn of 1677 and, as such, was in an ideal position to discuss with Hooke, and probably also with Wren, the funereal buildings of the ancient world, material which he subsequently incorporated into the *Monumenta*.[63] Aubrey, however, was not concerned with recovering the larger history of ancient architecture, as were Wren and Hooke, but rather with developing a specific genealogy within which British monuments could be located.

Aubrey's discussion of the Tower of Babel began with the *locus classicus* of Genesis 11:3, but then moved on to its present appearance:

> This tower of <u>Belus</u> is now a great hill, the arch't brickwork being covered over with dust and earth. The Basis of it is as big as the middle Moore-fields:

[58] Christopher Wren, *Wren's 'Tracts' on Architecture and Other Writings*, ed. Lydia M. Soo (Cambridge, 1998), 188.

[59] Wren, *'Tracts'*, 188–95.

[60] Lydia M. Soo, 'Reconstructing Antiquity: Wren and His Circle and the Study of Natural History, Antiquarianism, and Architecture at the Royal Society' (Princeton University PhD Thesis, 1989), *passim*, and Wren, *'Tracts'*, 8.

[61] Robert Hooke, *Diary of Robert Hooke, M.A., M.D., F.R.S., 1672–1680*, ed. Henry W. Robinson and Walter Adams (London, 1935), 317.

[62] Hooke, *Diary*, 320–2 (and see Hooke's drawing of Wren's proposed reconstruction at 321). Pierre de la Ruffinière du Prey has suggested that Wren's interest in Porsenna's tomb coincided with plans for the mausoleum of Charles I (du Prey, *Hawksmoor's London Churches: Architecture and Theology* [Chicago, 2000], 14–16).

[63] This can be proven through his correspondence with Andrew Paschall at that time, including letters from Paschall directed to Aubrey 'at Mr Hookes lodgings in Gresham Coll' on 19 August (Bodleian MS Aubrey 13, fols. 21–22), 25 October (fol. 24), 31 October (fol. 25), and 20 November 1677 (fol. 26).

of which you may read a most accurate account in <u>Samuelis Rayheri</u>
<u>Mathesis Mosaica</u>.[64]

Aubrey was referring to the German mathematician Samuel Reyher's
exegesis of the mathematics of the Pentateuch. Reyher had reconstructed
Babel as something resembling a ziggurat, but pendulously tall.[65] He was
aided by the precise figures for its size given by the twelfth-century
traveller Benjamin of Tudela, who was also the ultimate source for
Aubrey's description of its present state.[66] The final step in this reconstruction was a passing comment in Wren's 'Discourse on Architecture':
'Providence scatter'd the first Builders [of Babel], so the Work was left off,
but the Successors of Belus the son of Nimrod probably finished It and
made it His Sepulchre, upon his Deification.'[67] Wren's discussions with
Hooke appear to have provided Aubrey with the identification of Babel as
a tomb and this, combined with the narrative of Benjamin of Tudela, as
mediated by Reyher's *Mathesis*, allowed him to describe what he understood Babel to be: a squat, four-sided brick tower, now 'a great hill'. It was,
evidently, the architectural forebear of the 'great Mausolea of Earth' which
Wren identified as characteristic of the Chinese, but was also related to
native British sites such as Silbury Hill and Roseberry Topping, descriptions of which immediately follow the essay on ancient mausolea in the
Monumenta.[68]

Aubrey deployed this diverse array of scholarly insights as a frame
within which to site the monuments he subsequently discussed in the
Monumenta. He is sometimes portrayed as a radical freethinker, dismiss-
ing the literal truth of Genesis in his support of Hooke's theories of the
origins of the world, and it is tempting to extend that dismissal to his
understanding of the ancient human past.[69] 'Of Mausolea' quashes such
temptations. Aubrey's view of the ancient past was essentially biblical: a
gradual repopulation of the world after the fall of Babel leading to a

[64] Aubrey, *Monumenta*, i. 673.

[65] Samuel Reyher, *Mathesis Mosaica, sive loca Pentateuchi mathematica mathematicè ex-
plicata* (Kiel, 1679), 177–210. Aubrey also directed his readers towards Athanasius Kircher's
Turris Babel (Amsterdam, 1679), but was evidently less influenced by Kircher's elegant
Baroque phallus than by the ziggurat described by Reyher.

[66] Reyher, *Mathesis Mosaica*, 186–7. Reyher's measurements derive from the edition and
Latin translation by Constantijn L'Empereur of Benjamin of Tudela's *Travels* (*Itinerarium
Benjaminis* [Leiden, 1633], 77). L'Empereur in his copious notes has no comment on the
ruins of Babel.

[67] Wren, '*Tracts*', 189.

[68] Aubrey, *Monumenta*, ii. 683.

[69] See Poole, *Aubrey*, 84–5. Poole notes that this theory came out of conversations with
Hooke and readings in Kircher (in this case his *Mundus Subterraneus*, 2 vols. [Amsterdam,
1665]), but does not discuss the other pairing of Hooke and Kircher in the *Monumenta*.

dissemination of primitive Hebraic culture across Europe. While he was willing to admit that the physical world was much older than commonly supposed, human culture was only a postdiluvian construct with an origin a few thousand years in the past. English sites, including Stonehenge, had been built by the not-so-distant descendants of the architects of Babel.

If Babel had its natural place in Aubrey's narrative, both as 'the first Peece of Civil Architecture' and as the direct precursor of British hill forts and burial mounds, the significance of Lars Porsenna's tomb in his narrative remains to be explained. Aubrey devoted more attention to it than to any other single ancient monument and this cannot be explained solely through the interests of Wren and Hooke (theirs was largely born from an attempt to rationalize the description in Pliny's *Natural History* with a structure that could both feasibly exist within the strictures of physics and accurately represent the historical evidence).[70] In the course of his discussion Aubrey cited five different reconstructions and made notes towards obtaining images of each for the *Monumenta*.[71] In the end, however, Aubrey only copied the reconstruction prepared by Hooke into the *Monumenta* and it would seem that his intense fascination with the monument must have derived either from Hooke or from Pliny himself. The text and paratext surrounding his reproduction of Hooke's vision (see Figure 3.3) suggest a possible reason for this fascination. Beneath the reconstruction Aubrey noted that, 'In the East Indies such another Monument is mentioned in a Book, which Mr R. Hook hath.'[72]

Nearby he noted that a map of Asia he had seen in the Earl of Pembroke's house contained depictions of several pyramids 'and by them is wrote Sepulchra Regum Tartariae'.[73] Aubrey's small drawings of the four 'pyramids' on the map closely resemble the pyramids in Hooke's

---

[70] See Wren's discussion of it in Wren, 'Tracts', 193–5, and Alexander Wragge-Morley, 'Restitution, Description, and Knowledge in English Architecture and Natural Philosophy, 1650–1750', *Architecture Research Quarterly* 14 (2010): 247–54, though the latter focuses on Wren's and Hooke's reconstruction of the Temple of Solomon.

[71] Aubrey, *Monumenta*, ii. 671, 675, 677. The reconstructions were: (1) a draft by Christopher Wren; (2) a 'cutt of Porsenna's Tombe', allegedly in an edition of Girolamo Maggi's *De tintinnabulis* (no such item appears in the discussions of Porsenna's tomb at Girolamo Maggi, *De tintinnabulis liber postumus*, ed. Francis Sweerts [Amsterdam, 1664], 24–5, 122–3); (3) a draft in Benedictus Pererius's 'Roman Antiquities', copies of which Aubrey stated were in the possession of Edmund Wylde and George Ent (no such work is known and in Benedictus Pererius, *Commentariorum disputationum in Genesim Tomi Quatuor* [Mainz, 1612], the chapter on the Tower of Babel (437–59) makes no reference to it nor does Lars Porsenna appear in the index); (4) John Greaves's draft in his *Pyramidographia*, 'but Mr Hooke doeth not approve of it' (Greaves, *Pyramidographia or a Description of the Pyramids in Ægypt* [London, 1646], facing 67); (5) Hooke's own draft, copied by Aubrey into the *Monumenta*.

[72] Aubrey, *Monumenta*, ii. 677.   [73] Aubrey, *Monumenta*, ii. 675.

Figure 3.3 The tomb of Lars Porsenna according to Robert Hooke (Bodleian MS Top. Gen. c. 25, fol. 9br).

reconstruction of the tomb of Lars Porsenna. They are both tall and thin, reminiscent more of obelisks than anything else. In the case of the tombs of the kings of Tartary they are also slightly irregular in shape and resemble nothing so much as Aubrey's drawings and descriptions of British standing stones elsewhere in the *Monumenta*. While the exact map to which Aubrey referred has not been identified, it is likely that his pyramidal tombs were not, in fact, representations of man-made structures, but rather Aubrey's misreading of stylized mountains. The tombs of Genghis Khan and his descendants make regular appearances in the writings of early modern geographers and travellers. They are never described as pyramidal, but are regularly sited in the Altai Mountains; Aubrey's pyramids were almost certainly a misunderstanding of a visual representation of this tradition.[74] Regardless, they provided him with the link he needed. Porsenna's tomb functioned like Babel; it served as an ancient parallel to the monuments Aubrey had discovered and recorded in the British Isles, though in this case it paralleled megaliths rather than burial mounds. Megaliths, in fact, had been subtly displaced from the contexts in which Aubrey located them in the *Templa Druidum* and were introduced into the history of ancient architecture.

These parallels were part of a larger attempt by Aubrey to anchor his discoveries within a recognizable historical framework. In a postdiluvian world, it was only reasonable to suppose that similar forms of architecture could be discovered throughout antiquity, and Aubrey's placing of the prehistoric British landscape within existing narratives of post-Babelic migration was a naturalizing of that strange country into the mapped world of the biblical and classical past, along the same lines as his Homeric interpretations of ancient British culture. As such, it paralleled the work of his Swedish contemporary Olof Rudbeck—although, as yet, Aubrey had not come directly into contact with Rudbeck's writings—more closely than might initially appear. Just as Rudbeck had erected a scaffolding of classical myth around the otherwise alien archaeology of prehistoric Scandinavia, Aubrey had linked the baffling remains scattered across the British landscape to a recognizable tradition of ancient architecture and learning.

Architecture fitted naturally into Aubrey's collection of scholarly interests, both as the flip side of his fascination with megaliths and other man-made aspects of the ancient landscape and as a discipline whose inherited pieties tallied well with his own convictions as to the cultural superiority of Rome. From an initial engagement with it as an amateur designer, he developed a remarkable new antiquarian tool in the *Chronologia Architectonica*, allowing architectural forms to serve as chronological markers, and finally returned to his central focus on ancient culture in the study of funereal architecture in 'Of Mausolea'. Throughout, he participated in the English architectural and antiquarian culture which centred on

[74] See, for example, Samuel Purchas, *Purchas his Pilgrimage* (London, 1613), 337, and Pierre d'Avity, Sieur de Montmartin, *The Estates, Empires, & Principallities of the World* (London, 1615), 707. The story seems to have originated with the fourteenth-century writer Hayton of Corycus's *La Flor des Estoires d'Orient*, which was cited by d'Avity.

scholar-practitioners such as Christopher Wren and Robert Hooke. His fascination with measurement, minutiae, and the careful observation of detail, however, echoed architectural practice across Europe and was part of the larger shift in antiquarian practices which led to an increasing privileging of architectural data, whether derived from ancient or medieval buildings, in the eighteenth century.

4

Writing Lives

Aubrey, Anthony Wood, and Antiquarian Biography

Much later in life Aubrey still remembered the 'mile, fine walke' his eight-year-old self had taken in 1634 to learn Latin grammar from Robert Latimer, Rector of Leigh-de-la-Mere, Wiltshire, 'who had an easie way of teachings: and every time we asked leave to goe forth, we had a latin word from him, which at our return we were to tell him again'.[1] Though this memory remained with him, Aubrey was all too conscious of the transitory nature of more tangible relics of the past when searching in vain for Latin poems presented to their mutual teacher by Latimer's other famous pupil, Thomas Hobbes: 'I searcht all old Mr Latimers papers but could not find them; the good huswives had sacrificed them the oven (Pies) had devoured them.'[2] Throughout his life Aubrey was only too aware of the fragile nature of scholarly achievement and the ease with which a writer's precious papers could be lost and their memory displaced into the wrapper of a fresh pork pie. One of his major roles in the early Royal Society was as a diligent searcher after the manuscripts of deceased scholars, rescuing more than one mathematician or natural philosopher's *collectanea* from oblivion.[3] His concern for these afterlives manifested itself most clearly, however, in the many biographies or 'minutes of lives' which he researched and wrote over the course of his career. Aubrey drew upon established humanist genres including *historia literaria*, table talk, and the intimate scholarly biography pioneered by writers such as Pierre Gassendi, to develop a unique and remarkable antiquarian form of his own in which he went beyond the bare facts of a life to focus on the vital minutiae which

---

[1] Aubrey, *Lives*, i. 430.
[2] Bodleian MS Aubrey 9, fol. 34r (= Aubrey, 'Hobbes', i. 329).
[3] Kate Bennett, 'John Aubrey, Hint-Keeper: Life-Writing and the Encouragement of Natural Philosophy in the pre-Newtonian Seventeenth Century', *The Seventeenth Century* 22 (2007): 358–80.

distinguished an individual personality. This approach existed in an
uneasy tension with the more public biographical antiquarianism of his
friend and collaborator Anthony Wood.

Aubrey's fascination with this form of humanist memorialization
dated back to the very beginning of his career as a virtuoso. As early as
12 December 1655, the intelligencer Samuel Hartlib had written to John
Worthington that one 'Mr. Aubrey an English gentleman is about to write
the Life of that Noble Scholar [i.e., Francis Bacon]. I wish he may do it to
the life.'[4] Aubrey's plan for a life of Bacon may have already been of some
years standing even then, as he had already visited Bacon's former retainer,
Thomas Bushell, at Lambeth in 1650.[5] In the end, however, his notes
towards a life of Bacon did not reach fruition until decades later. Instead it
was a chance meeting in Oxford which decided the course of his biographical scholarship.

On 31 August 1667, Aubrey was buying books from the Oxford
bookseller Edward Forest. Seeing 'lying on the stall' William Fulman's
recently published *Notitia Academiae Oxoniensis* Aubrey enquired after its
author and was told, mistakenly, that it was one Anthony Wood of
Merton College.[6] Being already acquainted with Wood's older brother,
Aubrey sought Anthony out in his lodgings, 'got into his acquaintance,
talk'd to him about his studies, and offer'd him what assistance he could
make' towards Wood's collections for a history of Oxford.[7]

Their collaboration began tentatively, with Wood writing to Aubrey in
November of 1667, reminding him of a promise to 'obtaine some intel-
ligence' concerning John Hoskins of New College (the grandfather of a
friend of Aubrey's of the same name), but Aubrey's fulsome replies soon
led to a vibrant working partnership between the two men; by August
1669 Aubrey could write to Wood, after a visit to Oxford, that 'I never
was more happy in ones company in my life.'[8] The goal towards which
they were working became suddenly more real on 22 October of that same
year when the Delegates of the University Press, led by John Fell, signed a
contract with Wood to publish his history, which would 'be translated

---

[4] John Worthington, *The Diary and Correspondence of Dr. John Worthington, Master of Jesus College, Cambridge*, 2 vols. in 3, ed. James Crossley and Richard Copley Christie (Manchester, 1847–86), i. 68–9.
[5] Aubrey, *Lives*, i. 313–14.
[6] William Fulman, *Academiae Oxoniensis notitia* (Oxford, 1665), which has no authorship attribution on its title page.
[7] For their first meeting see Anthony Wood, *The Life and Times of Anthony Wood, Antiquary, of Oxford, 1632–1695, Described By Himself*, 5 vols., ed. Andrew Clark (Oxford, 1891–1900), ii. 116–17.
[8] Bodleian MSS Aubrey 13, fol. 262r, Wood F 39, fol. 123r. For Hoskins see Powell, *Aubrey*, 251–2.

into Latine for the honour of the University in forreigne countries'.[9] The second volume of this project, eventually published as *Historia et antiquitates Universitatis Oxoniensis* (1674), is organized by college in order of foundation, within which are short biographical notices of benefactors and heads of house, as well as bishops and writers educated there.[10] It was to these biographies that Aubrey chiefly contributed, offering details of birth and death, works written, and other information gleaned from a variety of written and oral sources.[11]

Wood's projects, both the *Historia et antiquitates* of 1674 and its successor, the *Athenae Oxonienses* of two decades later, were part of a pan-European tradition of *historiae literariae*, histories of letters which were vast biobibliographies of ancient, medieval, and early modern writers. These texts could vary in scope from a work like Wood's, which enumerated the scholars produced by a single institution, to that of his contemporary Thomas Pope Blount, which surveyed the entire literary inheritance of Europe and the Near East.[12] They shared in common a structure of short biographies followed by bibliographical details of their subjects' publications and, often but not always, learned judgements (*judicia*) on their value. Although best known in German contexts, where the vast folios of polyhistors like Daniel Georg Morhof and Johann Albert Fabricius brought the genre to its unwieldy zenith, *historia literaria* had a rich history in England dating back to immediate post-Reformation works of salvage and memorialization such as John Leland's *De viris illustribus* (c.1545) and John Bale's *Scriptorum illustrium maioris Brytanniae catalogus* (1559).[13] Wood and Aubrey were both familiar with this tradition, referring repeatedly to Bale, his Catholic counterpart John Pits, and their seventeenth-century successors in their works; Wood, in particular, explicitly allied himself with the *historia literaria* tradition in the

[9] Wood, *Life and Times*, ii. 172.

[10] Anthony Wood, *Historia et antiquitates Universitatis Oxoniensis*, 2 vols. (Oxford, 1674).

[11] Aubrey's determination in seeking out sources shines through in his letters to Wood. On 27 January 1671 he wrote, 'Yesterday I was at Dr Twisses sonnes howse, & left sufficient Instructions for him to wrote to you & answer your method of Queries: which if he does not, he is the turdy son of a Presbyterian' (Bodleian MS Wood F 39, fol. 163r).

[12] Sir Thomas Pope Blount, *Censura celebriorum authorum: sive tractatus in quo varia virorum doctorum de clarissimis cujusque seculi scriptoribus judicia traduntur*... (London, 1690). Cf. Kelsey Jackson Williams, 'Canon before Canon, Literature before Literature: Thomas Pope Blount and the Scope of Early Modern Learning', *Huntington Library Quarterly* 77 (2014): 177–99.

[13] Anthony Grafton, 'The World of the Polyhistors: Humanism and Encyclopedism', *Central European History* 18 (1985): 31–47; Richard Sharpe, 'The English Bibliographical Tradition from Kirkestede to Tanner,' in *Britannia Latina*, ed. C. S. F. Burnett and C. N. J. Mann (London, 2005), 86–128.

preface to the *Athenae*, describing it as 'the Memoires of the University it self, and the History of Learning therein'.[14]

Their engagement with this tradition was borne out by the structure of the biographies in the *Historia* and the *Athenae*. The lives in the *Historia* closely echo the compact sketches of older *historiae literariae*, emphasizing the subject's county of birth, place of education, a handful of biographical particulars, a list of their works in print or manuscript, their date of death, and place of burial. The heavily fact-centred correspondence between Wood and Aubrey, which, on Aubrey's side, regularly took the form of rapid-fire pieces of data or reports of investigations in progress—for example, 'Mr Hugh Holland buried neer the dore [of Westminster Abbey] entering into the Monuments' or 'I very luckily sent to Sir J. Penruddock who now is at Salisbury about his acquaintance H. Holland'—resulted in equally terse and fact-centred biographies in the *Historia*.[15] Individual pieces of information were often lifted almost verbatim from Aubrey's letters and inserted into their proper places in the text. In the case of Holland, Wood paraphrased Aubrey closely, noting that his tomb was 'in Westminster Abbey by the door which leads to the monuments and not far from the poets' tombs'.[16] By comparison with the later work of either scholar the *Historia* is terse and public, focused on deeds and dates rather than habits and minds, but its basic structure—family, education, life, death, works—would remain the preferred method of biographical composition for both Aubrey and Wood.

'MINUTENESSE WILL BE GRATEFULL': BIOGRAPHICAL THEORIES IN THE *LIFE OF HOBBES*

This participation in a well-established tradition of scholarly biography provided Aubrey with an apprenticeship which would bear fruit some

---

[14] Anthony Wood, *Athenae Oxonienses*, 2 vols. (London, 1691–2)., sig. Ar. Wood owned a copy of John Pits, *Relationum historicarum de rebus Anglicis* (Paris, 1619), now Bodleian Wood 658 and cited Bale throughout the *Athenae*. Aubrey was equally well versed in English *historia literaria*, referring at various points in his manuscripts to Bale (Bodleian MS Aubrey 2, fols. 4r, 5r–6r, 20r, 21r–22r) and Pits (Bodleian MS Aubrey 2, fol. 19r), as well as more recent contributions to the tradition such as Francis Godwin's *Catalogue of Bishops* (Bodleian MS Aubrey 2, fol. 5r), Thomas Fuller's 1662 *History of the Worthies of England* (Bodleian MSS Aubrey 1, fol. 106v, Aubrey 2, fols. 2v–3r, 5r, 16r, 61r, 62v, 116r, Aubrey 6, fols. 21r, 119ar, and Aubrey 8, fol. 98r), and David Lloyd's 1670 *State Worthies* (Bodleian MS Aubrey 8, fols. 25r, 28r).

[15] Bodleian MS Wood F39, fols. 172r, 173r.

[16] 'Tumulum accepit in Ecclesia *Westmonasteriensi* juxta ostium quod ducit ad munmenta, & non procul à tumulis Poetarum' (Wood, *Historia*, ii. 80).

years later. In the 1680s and 1690s, he engaged in three separate bio-graphical projects. First, he wrote his *Life of Mr Thomas Hobbes of Malmes-bury*, a biography of the philosopher which was intended for publication from the outset.[17] At about the same time his collaboration with Wood began to evolve into the independent compilation of a substantial quantity of miscellaneous biographical information which he explicitly intended for the use of future generations. This material he variously called 'Minutes', 'Memoires', or 'My booke of lives', but is now better known as the *Brief Lives*.[18] Finally, he prepared a series of *Lives of our English Mathematicians*, which, like the biography of Hobbes, was also ultimately intended for publication.[19]

Of these, his first attempt was least characteristic of the *historia literaria* tradition: a lengthy, stand-alone biography of his friend and fellow Wilt-shireman, Thomas Hobbes. Long before, in 1667, Aubrey had promised Hobbes that he would write his life, and it appears that Aubrey and several others revived the plan shortly after news of Hobbes's death at Hardwick Hall on 4 December 1679. Certainly it was well under way by 16 January 1680, when Hobbes's former amanuensis, James Wheldon, wrote to Aubrey with responses to a series of biographical queries.[20] Wheldon wrote of 'what you designe to get written by way of Commentary on his [Hobbes's] life' and thanked Aubrey for what he, Anthony Wood, and Sir George Ent 'designe for Mr. Hobbes his honour'.[21] The implication was that Aubrey, Wood, and Ent, sometime in December 1679 or the first days of January 1680, had conceived a plan for publishing a biography of their recently deceased friend.[22]

---

[17] The *Life* is now Bodleian MS Aubrey 9 and has been published in Aubrey, 'Hobbes', i. 321–403.

[18] Now Bodleian MSS Aubrey 6–8, and most recently and accurately edited by Kate Bennett in Aubrey, *Lives*. Its modern title ultimately derives from Aubrey's own short title for Bodleian MS Aubrey 6, 'Σχεδιάσματα. Brief Lives', but this obscures a more complex manuscript history (see Aubrey, *Lives*, i. cvii–cxxx). The alternative Greek title is from Σχεδιάσμα, a whim or caprice, but Aubrey's usage probably more closely approximates its naturalized form in English, 'schediasm', an extempore work or jotting (*OED*, *s.v.*).

[19] The *Lives of our English Mathematicians* is now in Bodleian MS Aubrey 8 and has been published in Aubrey, *Lives*, i. 719–56.

[20] Bodleian MS Aubrey 9, fol. 18.

[21] Bodleian MS Aubrey 9, fol. 18r. Sir George Ent, physician and friend of William Harvey, appears on the list of Hobbes's friends which makes up part of the *Life* (Aubrey, 'Hobbes', i. 370). Ent and Wood had been at loggerheads in the past, with Wood complaining that the physician was 'quarrelsome in his liquour' in a letter to Aubrey, 28 February 1675, but were presumably reconciled by this date (Bodleian MS Aubrey 13, fol. 265v).

[22] This would accord well with Wood's note in his diary for 1 January 1680 that he 'sent to Mr. [John] Aubrey a transcript of what I say of Mr. [Thomas] Hobbs with other notes', indicating that Aubrey's biographical project was already in full swing (Andrew Clark, ed.,

Aubrey lacked confidence in his own literary style and soon enlisted an assistant, the young physician Richard Blackburne, one of the 'the best scholars in London of his age, & φιλοHobbist'.[23] The immediate connection seems to have been that Blackburne had been a pupil of Aubrey's friend Thomas Gale when at Trinity College, Cambridge, some years before.[24] Aubrey spoke of him in a letter to Wood dated 10 February 1680 and their collaboration appears to have been decided by 16 February, when Hobbes's former publisher, William Crooke, wrote an anxious letter to Aubrey arranging a meeting with him and Blackburne to pre-empt another, unspecified, plan to publish a life of Hobbes.[25]

An undated letter from Aubrey to Blackburne from about this time suggests that their original collaboration was to consist of Aubrey preparing a draft which Blackburne would then correct and improve stylistically. It had not yet been decided whether the biography was to be in Latin or English and Aubrey was content to give Blackburne carte blanche in revising his initial text, describing him as 'my Aristarchus', in an allusion to the second-century BCE Alexandrian grammarian whose severe editing of the Homeric texts was proverbial.[26] He seems to have envisioned Blackburne editing for style, noting that he should, 'correct and marke what you thinke fitt. First draughts ought to be rude as those of paynters, for he that in his first essay will be curious in refining will certainly be unhappy in inventing.'[27]

By the following month this working relationship had soured. It had been decided that Blackburne would translate Aubrey's *Life* into Latin and, writing to Wood on 7 March, Aubrey complained that he was 'a great

The Life and Times of Anthony Wood, Antiquary, of Oxford, 1632–1695, 5 vols. [Oxford, 1891–1900], ii. 475–6).

[23] Bodleian MS Ballard 14, fol. 125r. Blackburne was otherwise undistinguished and was elected an Honorary Fellow of the Royal College of Physicians in 1685 (see *ODNB*, *s.n.*).

[24] Blackburne matriculated as a pensioner at Trinity in 1665 and appears to have been taught by Gale throughout his degree (*ODNB*, *s.n.*; John and J. A. Venn, *Alumni Cantabrigienses*, 2 pts. in 10 vols. [Cambridge, 1922–54], part I, i. 160).

[25] Bodleian MS Aubrey 12, fol. 88r. Their concern was perhaps justified, given the sudden market for Hobbesiana. Hobbes's Latin autobiographical poem had been published towards the end of December and Anthony Wood reported that only a 'fortnight after', around 10 January 1680, *The Life of Mr. Thomas Hobbes of Malmesbury, Written By Himself in a Latine Poem, and Now Translated into English* (London, 1680) appeared, so Aubrey and his associates were hardly making the first inroad into the biographical market. Evidence for the publication dates of the poems comes from Wood's copy of the latter, now Bodleian Wood 657 (6).

[26] Aubrey would have known of Aristarchus as a critic or editor through the reference in Horace, *Ars Poetica*, l. 450, among many others, and frequently used the ancient critic's name to refer to the (hoped for, but non-existent) editors of his own works.

[27] Bodleian MS Aubrey 9, fol. 28v.

judge, & consequently magisteriall: he is much against Minutiae'.[28]
Blackburne was being advised by John Dryden and his friend Lord John
Vaughan, sometime governor of Jamaica and correspondent of Henry
Oldenburg, and the latter two had apparently objected to the not always
flattering details contained in Aubrey's draft.[29] By 22 May the disagree-
ment had reached a head and Aubrey fulminated to Wood that:

> This afternoon I shall see the proofe of the first sheet of Mr Hobbes. I hope
> to gett all my originall papers into my hand, & then I will transcribe a faire
> Copie to be preserved in your hands. Pox take your orators & piety, they
> spoile lives & histories. The Dr [i.e., Blackburne] says that I am too minute;
> but a hundred yeere hence that minutenesse will be gratefull . . . He would
> putt it in the <u>High Style</u>.[30]

The proofs were those of Blackburne's Latin adaptation of Aubrey's text,
Thomae Hobbes Angli Malmesburiensis philosophi vita, though it was not
published until the autumn.[31] That Aubrey had decided to transcribe a
fair copy of his original draft and deposit it with Wood suggests that, by
May 1680, he had reached a parting of ways with his former collaborator
and saw his *Life of Hobbes* as something essentially separate from Blackburne's *Vita*.[32]

In the course of his disagreements with Blackburne, Aubrey had begun
to articulate his own theory of biography. 'Now I say the Offices of a
Panegyrist, & Historian, are much different', he wrote. 'A Life, is a short
Historie: and <u>there</u> minutenes of a famous person is gratefull.'[33] This
linking of biography with history also appears in the *Life* itself, which he
described as 'this *Historiola* of our Malmesbury philosopher', but it is
evident that it was not narrative history that Aubrey had in mind.[34] In a
letter to Wood of 27 March, he tellingly remarked, 'I never yet knew a
Witt (unless he were a piece of an Antiquary) write a proper Epitaph, but
leave the reader ignorant, what countryman &c: only tickles his eares with
Elogies.'[35] For Aubrey, biography was a matter of minute detail rather

---

[28] Bodleian MS Tanner 456a, fol. 23r.
[29] Evidence for the involvement of Dryden and Vaughan comes from Aubrey's letter to
Wood of 27 March (Bodleian MS Ballard 14, fol. 131r).
[30] Bodleian MS Wood F 39, fol. 340r.
[31] [Richard Blackburne and John Aubrey], *Thomae Hobbes Angli Malmesburiensis
philosophi vita* (Carolopoli [*sic*], 1681).
[32] It is likely that the fair copy he envisaged was never written. Bodleian MS Aubrey 9,
the surviving version of the *Life*, appears to be that which was sent to Blackburne
(cf. fol. 55v).
[33] Bodleian MS Ballard 14, fol. 131r.
[34] Bodleian MS Aubrey 9, fol. 30r (= Aubrey, 'Hobbes', i. 322).
[35] Bodleian MS Ballard 14, fol. 131r.

than elogium, a position which accorded well with his contributions to Wood's *Historia*. The 'high style' of Blackburne was antithetical to an antiquarian precision of recollection which changed biography from misty hagiography into a recollection of specific facts.

The theory of biography which Aubrey was reacting against derived ultimately not from Blackburne, but from his adviser Dryden, and was subsequently articulated in the poet laureate's *Life of Plutarch* (published in 1683, not long after the *Life of Hobbes*). Dryden's views, in their very proximity to Aubrey's, show up more clearly the crucial points of difference.[36] In his *Plutarch* he gave a taxonomy of history, dividing the subject into annals, narrative history, and biography.[37] Biography, according to Dryden, was 'in dignity inferiour to *History* and *Annalls*, [but] in pleasure and instruction it equals, or even excells both of them'.[38] In his explanation of the role of biography, he seemed, at first, to hold a position similar to that of Aubrey himself, for he observed that:

> There is withal, a descent into minute circumstances, and trivial passages of life, which are natural to this way of writing . . . you are led into the private Lodgings of the Heroe: you see him in his undress, and are made Familiar with his most private actions and conversations.[39]

But Dryden's 'minute circumstances' were not Aubrey's. His distinction of the subject as 'the Heroe' in itself suggests a different viewpoint and this is confirmed by his examples of private actions: 'a *Scipio* and a *Lelius* gathering Cockle-shells on the shore, *Augustus* playing at bounding stones with Boyes; and *Agesilaus* riding on a Hobby-horse among his Children'.[40] In each case the private action illustrated served to illuminate the character of the subject in such a way as to teach a moral or social lesson, harking back to Dryden's initial praise of biography for the 'pleasure and instruction' it gives. Dryden imagined a perfect and polished public hero, a far cry from Aubrey's recollection of General John Lambert once saying, 'that the best of men are but men at the best'.[41] It was this attempt to reduce a life into a lesson against which Aubrey fought.

Aubrey's convictions reappear in his preface to the *Life of Hobbes*. He justified the work by recalling his long-standing promise to the late philosopher to publish his biography and remarking with pride that

---

[36] See also Steven N. Zwicker, 'Considering the Ancients: Dryden and the Uses of Biography', in *Writing Lives: Biography and Textuality, Identity and Representation in Early Modern England*, ed. Kevin Sharpe and Steven N. Zwicker (Oxford, 2008), 105–24.

[37] John Dryden, 'Life of Plutarch', in *Works of John Dryden*, 20 vols., general eds. Edward Niles Hooker and H. T. Swedenberg (Berkeley, CA, 1956–2000), xvii. 270–7.

[38] Dryden, 'Plutarch', 274.   [39] Dryden, 'Plutarch', 275.

[40] Dryden, 'Plutarch', 275.   [41] Aubrey, *Lives*, i. 38.

'nobody knew so many particulars of his life as myselfe'.[42] He then justified his biographical style:

> Amongst innumerable Observables of Him which had deserved to be sett downe these few (that have not scap't \slipt/ my memory) I humbly offer to the present Age and Posterity, tanquam Tabula naufragii; & as plankes & lighter things swimme, and are preserved, where the more weighty sinke & are lost. The Recrementa of so learned a Person \will/ are valueable. And as with the light after sun-sett—at which time, clear; by and by, comes the crepusculum; then, totall darknes: in like manner is it with matters of Antiquitie. Men thinke, because every body remembers a memorable Accident shortly after 'tis donne, 'twill never be forgotten, which for want of writing \registring/ at last is drowned in Oblivion. This reflection haz been a hint, that by my meanes many Antiquities have been reskued, & preserved (I myselfe now growing \inclining/ to be ancient \senescens/)—or els utterly Lost & forgotten.[43]

This is an astonishingly forceful exposition of the biographer's duties. Next to the struck-through *recrementa* Aubrey added a note to 'meliorate this word', but had not, in the end, done so.[44] Meaning dross or refuse, Aubrey was probably aware that *recrementum* had also been used to mean human excrement by the Augustan antiquary Aulus Gellius.[45] Such bluntness was a far cry from Blackburne's polite Latin, but, more than speaking out against the 'orators & piety' which he had fulminated about to Wood, it graphically drove home his belief that the smallest remnants of a personality were worth preserving. This was supplemented by his quotation of Bacon's famous description of antiquities, *tanquam tabula naufragii* ('like planks from a shipwreck'), itself a borrowing from the fifteenth-century Italian antiquary Flavio Biondo, whose *Italy Illuminated* had provided the model for Camden's *Britannia*.[46] Aubrey was doing much more than asserting the need for detail in biography: he was rejecting the hagiographic tradition which had dominated its seventeenth-century

---

[42] Bodleian MS Aubrey 9, fol. 29r (= Aubrey, 'Hobbes', i. 17–18).

[43] Bodleian MS Aubrey 9, fol. 29r (= Aubrey, 'Hobbes', i. 18).

[44] 'The Recrementa of so learned a Person \will/ are valueable' was written in the margin to replace an earlier, cancelled, passage: 'But, for that the recrementa of such a Person are valueable. It is with matters of Antiq.' (Bodleian MS Aubrey 9, fol. 29r).

[45] Aulus Gellius, *Noctes Atticae*, 17.11.2.

[46] Francis Bacon, *The Advancement of Learning*, ed. Michael Kiernan (Oxford, 2000), 66 ('ANTIQVITIES, or Remnants of History, are, as was saide, *tanquam Tabula Naufragij*'). For the transmission of this quotation, see Anthony Grafton, 'The Universal Language: Splendors and Sorrows of Latin in the Modern World', in *Worlds Made by Words: Scholarship and Community in the Modern West* (Cambridge, MA, and London, 2009), 136.

English forms and emphasizing the need for an intimate, antiquarian approach which neglected no facts and took no prisoners.[47]

Tied to Aubrey's association of biography with antiquarianism is a sense of urgency, an apprehension at the fleeting nature of human memory. The biography he advocated was not antiquarianism in the conventional sense—the restoration of what was long past—but rather a sort of preventative or anticipatory antiquarianism in which the planks from the shipwreck were not ancient coins or inscriptions but the specificities of an individual life. He justified his indulgence in these minutiae:

> For that I am so minute, I declare I never intended it; but setting downe in my first rude draught every thing particular, (with purpose, upon review to retrench \cut off/, what was superfluous & triviall), I shewed it to some Friends of mine (who also were of Mr. Hobbes acquaintance) whose judgements I much value: who gave their opinion: & 'twas <u>clearly</u> their opinion to let <u>all</u> stand; for though to soome at present it might appeare too triviall, yet hereafter 'twould not be slighted \scorned/ but goe \passe/ for Antiquity.[48]

Although he appealed to the judgement of his unnamed friends—amongst whom were presumably Anthony Wood and perhaps also George Ent and William Petty—the sentiment is in accord with Aubrey's own, developing theories. The 'soome at present' is surely a backward glance at Blackburne and his advisers. Aubrey the antiquary was vividly aware that the remnants of his own time would one day be 'antiquities', and was concerned to preserve these for future students of his favoured discipline.

The manuscript of the *Life of Hobbes* which now survives (Bodleian MS Aubrey 9) is that of the third draft and has been corrected by both Aubrey and Wood.[49] It originally consisted of twenty-five sheets, marked on the outside 'For Doctor Blackburne with care', indicating that this was the copy used in the composition of Blackburne's Latin life.[50] It began with Aubrey's note to the reader, just discussed, and continued with a sixteen-sheet narrative biography of Hobbes from his birth until his final removal to Derbyshire under the patronage of the Earl of Devonshire in 1675.[51] Although far more detailed and circumstantial, in structure it still echoed the standard biographical forms of *historiae literariae*.

---

[47] For the sea-change in biographical style brought about by what he describes as a 'rhetoric of exemplarity', see Michael McKeon, 'Biography, Fiction, and the Emergence of "Identity" in Eighteenth-Century Britain', in *Writing Lives*, ed. Sharpe and Zwicker, 339–55.

[48] Bodleian MS Aubrey 9, fol. 29r (= Aubrey, 'Hobbes', i. 18–19).

[49] See Bodleian MS Aubrey 9, fol. 28v (= Aubrey, 'Hobbes', i. 19) for it being the third draft (noted in a letter from Aubrey to Wood of 12 February 1680).

[50] Bodleian MS Aubrey 9, fol. 55v.

[51] Bodleian MS Aubrey 9, fol. 30r–46r (= Aubrey, 'Hobbes', i. 321–46).

What followed the *Life* proper was more unusual. In the subsequent sheets Aubrey analysed Hobbes's appearance, mannerisms, and character with antiquarian precision, beginning with his complexion and going on to cover his wit, reading habits, diet, exercises, illnesses, and predominant emotions.[52] The emphasis in these recollections—for they are chiefly Aubrey's personal memories of the philosopher—is on physicality. Aubrey described Hobbes in the same vivid detail as he had scripts or architecture in the *Stromata*, noting that, 'His Skin was soft, and that kind which my Lord Chancellor Bacon in his Hist. of Life and death calles a <u>Goose-skin</u> (i) of a wide texture Crassa cutis, crassum cerebrum, crassum ingenium.'[53] Or, 'Besides his dayly Walkings, he did twice or thrice a yeare play at Tennis (at about 75 he did it) then went to bed there, and was well rubbed. this he did believe would make him live two or three yeares the longer.'[54] These recollections were not inserted for their own sake, but reflected Aubrey's stated intention that even the *recrementa* of a great man were worth preserving. Aubrey was attempting to verbally dissect Hobbes in an effort to reach the wellsprings of the individuality which made him great. The belief underlying this seems to have been that the exceptional could be traced back to identifiable causes, and it was presumably this conviction which caused Aubrey to react with such disgust to Blackburne's smoothing over of the problematic aspects of Hobbes's life.

These anecdotal recollections had developed out of Aubrey's general theory of biography, but they were also indebted to a number of biographical and quasi-biographical texts known across the Republic of Letters. The most obvious antecedent to Aubrey's *Hobbes* was Pierre Gassendi's 1641 biography of the French antiquary Nicolas-Claude Fabri de Peiresc, which had been translated into English in 1657.[55] Gassendi's substantial work (239 octavo pages plus supplementary materials) was divided into six books. The first five presented a chronological narrative of Peiresc's life while the sixth depicted his physical and mental

---

[52] Bodleian MS Aubrey 9, fol. 46r–50r (= Aubrey, 'Hobbes', i. 346–58).

[53] Bodleian MS Aubrey 9, fol. 45v (= Aubrey, 'Hobbes', i. 348). The Latin tag ('coarse skin, coarse brain, coarse nature') does not translate perfectly into English, *crassus* having the additional meaning of dull or stupid. Bacon did not endorse this, but merely observed that 'thick and sponge skin (like, as they say, goose-skinned)' did *not* betoken long life, unlike a firm skin that was 'at once hard and compact' (Francis Bacon, 'Historia vitae & mortis', in *The Instauratio Magna, Part III*, ed. Graham Rees with Maria Wakely [Oxford, 2007], 227).

[54] Bodleian MS Aubrey 9, fol. 47r (= Aubrey, 'Hobbes', i. 351).

[55] Pierre Gassendi, *The Mirrour of True Nobility and Gentility: Being the Life of the Renowned Nicolaus Claudius Fabricius, Lord of Pieresk*, trans. W. Rand (London, 1657). See also Peter N. Miller, *Peiresc's Europe: Learning and Virtue in the Seventeenth Century* (New Haven, CT, and London, 2000), 16–21.

characteristics, daily habits, and peculiarities in the same minute detail which Aubrey would praise ('he went to bed almost as soon as he had supt, and alwayes set his Larum, so as to wake him quickly again').[56] Aubrey may also have taken some theoretical inspiration from Gassendi's dedicatory epistle in which he emphasized 'the simplicity and planness of the Narration' and insisted that 'even the very crums which fall from the Tables of the Gods, seem worthy to be picked up', a sentiment closely aligned to Aubrey's *recrementa*.[57]

The other tradition which Aubrey drew upon was the rapidly expanding genre of '*–ana*' literature and table talk, the collected quips and epigrams of famous scholars.[58] These works, assembled and published by their disciples, played an important role in the cult of personality which surrounded many of the heroic polymaths of the early seventeenth century and were couched in much the same awe-filled but intimate language as Aubrey's biographies. Aubrey may have been familiar with the 1669 *Scaligerana*, the table talk of the philologist and chronologer Joseph Justus Scaliger, which popularized the genre, and he was certainly acquainted with manuscript copies of the first English example of the type, the *Table-Talk* of John Selden.[59] Many of the sayings attributed in these works danced on the edge of heterodoxy and Aubrey was alert to the tensions inherent in writing too plainly about another's life and opinions; copying some of Selden's more free-thinking comments out of a manuscript copy of the *Table-Talk* belonging to the Earl of Abingdon, he noted that it 'will not endure the Test for the Presse'.[60] Taken together, Gassendi and this tradition offered a minute and straight-talking antiquarian counterblast to the hagiographic biographies which dominated the more literary portions of the genre.

Aubrey developed his own variation on the blueprint laid down by Gassendi by following his physical description of Hobbes with a 'Catalogue of his <u>Learned</u> familiar Friends & Acquaintance', setting Hobbes within a larger intellectual context and including several of the

---

[56] Gassendi, *Mirrour*, 163.

[57] Gassendi, *Mirrour*, sig. (a)2r. Aubrey cites Gassendi's *Life* (probably the English translation) elsewhere at Bodleian MS Aubrey 1, fols. 18r, 158r.

[58] For this tradition see Paul J. Korshin, 'The Development of Intellectual Biography in the Eighteenth Century', *Journal of English and Germanic Philology* 73 (1974): 518–22, and A. F. Aude, *Bibliographie critique et raisonné des Ana Français et étrangers* (Paris, 1910).

[59] Joseph Justus Scaliger, *Prima Scaligerana: nusquam antehac edita* (Groningen, 1669). Aubrey certainly knew Scaliger's published correspondence and quoted it at BL MS Lansdowne 231, fol. 178r (= Aubrey, *Remaines*, 123–4). Selden's *Table-Talk* was later published in 1689: John Selden, *Table-Talk*, ed. Richard Milward (London, 1689).

[60] BL MS Lansdowne 231, fol. 133r (= Aubrey, *Remaines*, 55).

mutual friends who would be amongst the first subjects for entries in Aubrey's *Brief Lives* (Sir William Petty and Sir Christopher Wren, among others).[61] This catalogue of emotional debts and credits had the same specificity as the physical description, and placed Hobbes in dialogue with his contemporaries, indicating points of difference as well as points of concurrence (the final sheet included a short addendum listing 'His Chiefe Antagonists').[62] With it Aubrey cut away at the idea of a great man as a being apart from his fellows and set Hobbes amongst the scholars with whom he interacted, showing how his work was a product not only of his own intellect, but of the intellectual currents of his time.

Blackburne's *Vita* was finally published in October or November 1680.[63] Prefaced with laudatory poems by Abraham Cowley, Ralph Bathurst, and allegedly Aubrey (in fact, per Wood, Blackburne) it began with Hobbes's own autobiographical notes, but the vast bulk of the text was taken up with the Aubrey–Blackburne life, the *Vitae Hobbianae auctarium*.[64] The variants between the two are too numerous to list in detail, but they bear out Aubrey's complaints. Blackburne omitted all of Aubrey's information on Hobbes's family and vastly curtailed the account of his early education, noting only that he studied under Robert Latimer and, while still a schoolboy, translated *Medea* into Latin verse.[65] The anecdote of the *Medea* offers a characteristic example of Blackburne's method. Aubrey had written, 'it is not to be forgotten, that before he went to the University, he had turned Euripidis Medea out of Greeke into Latin Iambiques, which he presented to his Master. Mr H. told me, that he would faine have had them, to have seen how he did grow.'[66] Blackburne, however, gave a subtly different story: 'moreover, he made such great progress in Greek and Latin letters while still at grammar school that he had elegantly translated Euripides' *Medea* into Latin verses of a similar meter'.[67] What for Aubrey is a schoolboy folly, albeit an admirable one, is for Blackburne an integral step in Hobbes's literary development.

---

[61] Bodleian MS Aubrey 9, fol. 50r–54r (= Aubrey, 'Hobbes', i. 365–72).

[62] Bodleian MS Aubrey 9, fol. 54r (= Aubrey, 'Hobbes', i. 373–4).

[63] Wood received his copy, given by 'his affectionate friend, and humble Servant Jo: Aubrey', on 6 November 1680 (now Bodleian Wood 434).

[64] Blackburne and Aubrey, *Hobbes vita, passim*. The *auctarium* is at 21–218. In Bodleian Wood 434, Wood has noted against the Latin poem attributed to Aubrey that it was written by Blackburne (sig. A8v).

[65] Blackburne and Aubrey, *Hobbes vita*, 24–5.

[66] Bodleian MS Aubrey 9, fol. 33r–34r (= Aubrey, 'Hobbes', i. 328–9).

[67] Blackburne and Aubrey, *Hobbes vita*, 24–5 ('Tantos autem jam adhuc in ludo literario degens in literaturâ tam Latinâ quam Graecâ progressus fecit, ut *Euripidis Medeam* simili metro Latinis versibus elegantèr expresserit').

The—it may be presumed rather rough—iambics of the original narrative have become polished 'Latin verses' which Hobbes 'tastefully formed'.

Blackburne's *Vita* does retain the structure of Aubrey's *Life*. After the narrative chronology of the life itself, he gives, though in an attenuated and shortened form, Aubrey's account of Hobbes's character, and this is followed, as in the *Life*, by the list of his friends.[68] In Blackburne's account the *amici* have two notable additions. One is Anthony Wood, whose appellation of 'Author celeberrimus' may have been more of a politeness by Blackburne towards one of his sources of information than a true estimation of Wood's fame in London circles.[69] The other is Aubrey, who is described as Hobbes's oldest friend and he 'who first gave me [i.e., Blackburne] the opportunity of writing, and humanely furnished me material'.[70] This faint praise, characterizing Aubrey as little more than a source of information, would seem to support the evidence of a parting of ways that comes from his letters. Nowhere in the printed *Vita* is Aubrey credited as Blackburne's sole source for the biographical material, nor is it stated that the *Vita* is, ultimately, a loose and partial translation of Aubrey's original.

DANGEROUS BIOGRAPHY AND 'MY BOOKE OF LIVES'

Composing the *Life of Hobbes* evidently inspired Aubrey to begin another, more substantial biographical project. In two letters to Anthony Wood, he recalled that on the night of Sunday, 15 February 1680 (three days after finishing the third draft of the *Life*),

> taking a pipe of Tobacco in my chambers it came into my mind to ingrose a sheet of paper close, which I shall enlarge (much) with the Lives of the worthy & ingeniose Knight Sir W. Petty from his cradle; Sir Chr. Wren the like. as also Mr Rob Hooke; which I thinke fitt to be lodged in your hands.[71]

This is the first mention of what Aubrey later came to describe as his *Brief Lives*. His initial inspiration seems to have been to write an independent life of William Petty, but this thought led him to recall a series of 'sheets of

---

[68] Blackburne and Aubrey, *Hobbes vita*, 158–81 (character), 181–7 (*Amicorum elenchus*).

[69] Blackburne and Aubrey, *Hobbes vita*, 186.

[70] Blackburne and Aubrey, *Hobbes vita*, 187 ('qui princeps mihi scribendi ansam praebuit, & materiam humaniter suppeditavit').

[71] Bodleian MS Ballard 14, fols. 126r, 127r.

Minutes' of the lives of John Dee, Francis Bacon, Christopher Wren, Robert Hooke, William Aubrey (his great-grandfather), John Pell, and the 1st Earl of Cork, which he had deposited in the hands of Elias Ashmole about 1675.[72]

From the start, Aubrey conceived of these lives as something quite different from the *Life of Hobbes*. Writing to Wood on 21 February about the projected life of Petty he mused that it 'will be a fine thing, & . . . he shall passe [it] himselfe, & then it shall be left among your papers, for Posterity hereafter, to read (published)'.[73] It is likely that, in the wake of his disagreements with Blackburne (and, through Blackburne, with the more powerful figures of Dryden and Vaughan), Aubrey had decided that, although he believed intensely in the biographical methodology which he had outlined in his *Life of Hobbes*, such biographies should not be immediately published lest they give offence, a conclusion echoing his judgement of Selden's *Table-Talk*. His initial conception seems to have been to write biographies of several of his closest and most respected friends (Petty, Wren, and Hooke), to be preserved in Wood's nascent archive until an imagined posthumous publication.

The following month was one of intense composition. Writing to Wood on 27 March, he reported that,

> I have to my Booke of Lives made a Kalendar of 55 persons, & have donne 10 of them: 3 or 4 leaves in fol a piece . . . it will be a pretty thing . . . I doe it playingly. This morn: being up by 10 I writt two.[74]

To this letter he appended a list of eight of the ten completed lives, though evidently not in the order in which they were written.[75] This list included William Petty, Edward Davenant, Sir John Suckling, Edmund Waller, Thomas Randolph, William Camden, William Oughtred, and Lucius Cary, Viscount Falkland.[76] By 22 May the *Lives* had expanded to fill two quires 'close written' and Aubrey, newly recovered from an illness, wrote again to Wood, worrying about their ultimate fate:

---

[72] Bodleian MS Ballard 14, fol. 127r.   [73] Bodleian MS Ballard 14, fol. 127r.

[74] Bodleian MS Ballard 14, fol. 131r.

[75] This may be presumed as Aubrey speaks of writing the life of Suckling that morning in the same letter, but Suckling is placed third in the list of eight.

[76] Bodleian MS Ballard 14, fol. 132v. These lives are now in Bodleian MS Aubrey 6, fols. 13r–15v (Petty), 39r–42v (Oughtred), 43r–45r (Davenant), 93r–94r (Carey), 109v–110v (Suckling), 111r–113r (Waller), 113v–114r (Randolph), 119ar–v (Camden), and are published in the same order at Aubrey, *Lives*, i. 40–52, 123–32, 132–7, 295–9, 367–72, 373–80, 383–6, 394–7.

They are fine things, but few fitt to be printed in my Life or yours, if you die, your papers will be all in the possession of Dr. J. Wallis (ex officio) as keeper of the Archives: so there 'twill be stiffled, for I am like Almansar in the Play, that spare neither friend nor Foe. but a religious John Telltroth.[77]

Aubrey, always concerned with the fate of his papers, had already decided that the *Lives* should ultimately be lodged with Wood, his former collaborator on the *Historia*.

The structure and content of the first lives followed straightforwardly on from the *Life of Hobbes* and its sources. The biography of Petty closely imitated the structure of the *Hobbes*, beginning with a narrative of his life from birth upwards followed by a written physiognomy and concluding with a list of his writings.[78] All that had been jettisoned was the catalogue of friends. In March, the same month in which he was composing this life, Aubrey had also convinced Petty to sit for a portrait by the engraver David Loggan, probably with a view to matching it with his pen portrait (he seems at this time to have still been planning to prepare Petty's biography for eventual publication).[79]

Subsequently, however, Aubrey changed tack. In his letter to Wood of 17 February, he had considered pairing the life of Petty with those of their mutual acquaintances Wren and Hooke, but instead the lives he wrote after Petty's were of men of the previous generation: the mathematicians Davenant and Oughtred, the antiquary Camden, the poets Randolph, Suckling, and Waller, and the politician Falkland. The overall rationale behind his order of composition seems to have been one of association. Petty and Waller appear amongst his list of Hobbes's friends in the *Life of Hobbes*.[80] In the life of Waller Aubrey noted that he was a familiar acquaintance, not only of Hobbes, but also of Viscount Falkland.[81] In turn, Waller and Hobbes are both listed as intimates in the life of Falkland.[82] Suckling and Davenant seem to be linked in the form of Aubrey's late friend the poet laureate Sir William Davenant (friend to one and relation of the other), who was another friend of Hobbes. The only

[77] Bodleian MS Wood F 39, fol. 340r. Aubrey compared himself to Almanzor, the hero of Dryden's *Conquest of Granada* (cf. *Works of John Dryden*, xi. 1–100).
[78] For Petty and Aubrey see Rhodri Lewis, 'A Babel Off Broad Street: Artificial Language Planning in 1650s Oxford', *History of Universities* 20 (2005): 108–45; Rhodri Lewis, 'William Petty's Anthropology: Religion, Colonialism, and the Problem of Human Diversity', *Huntington Library Quarterly* 74 (2011): 261–88; Harold Love, 'Sir William Petty, the London Coffee Houses, and the Restoration "Leonine"', *The Seventeenth Century* 22 (2007): 381–94; Ted McCormick, *William Petty and the Ambitions of Political Arithmetic* (Oxford, 2009), ch. 2.
[79] Aubrey, *Lives*, i. 48.
[80] Bodleian MS Aubrey 9, fol. 51r (= Aubrey, 'Hobbes', i. 367–8).
[81] Aubrey, *Lives*, i. 374.   [82] Aubrey, *Lives*, i. 297.

odd men out are Oughtred and Camden, who, it may be speculated, Aubrey included due to their pre-eminence in two of his favoured subjects: mathematics and antiquarianism.

Aubrey was not, then, jotting down recollections so much as reconstructing patterns of sociability that had existed in the previous generation and following through the implications of the list of friends he had appended to the *Life of Hobbes*. Though he described writing the *Lives* 'playingly', elsewhere he indicated a sober sense of urgency, recalling to Wood that 'after I had begun it I had such an impulse on my spirit that I could not be at quiet till I had donne it'.[83] As with the *Life of Hobbes*, Aubrey viewed the writing of the *Lives* as an act of conservation, preserving the telling minutiae of individual lives for future generations, as well as highlighting the friendships and debts that linked them together. The number of his early lives which take pains to note the chief friends and acquaintances of the subject underlines this last concern. Aubrey, who was himself at the centre of a circle of scholarly acquaintances and whose autobiography includes a similar catalogue of 'amici', was keen to place each life within its social context.[84]

By 15 June 1680, Aubrey had finished the first set of *Lives* and transmitted them to Wood. Writing on that date he credited Wood with first encouraging him towards the project, an acknowledgement which also appeared in a letter of 27 March in which he had written that 'I am glad you putt me on it.'[85] In other letters of February and March, however, Aubrey had identified the original inspiration as his own. He also asserted his credentials for the job by citing his 'generall acquaintance' and praised 'the moderne advantage of Coffee-houses in this great Citie; before which men knew not how to be acquainted, but with their owne Relations, or Societies'.[86] Such claims would no doubt have rung true for Wood, indebted as he was to Aubrey for a host of oral tradition which subsequently found its way into both the *Historia* and the *Athenae*. When it came to the fate of the *Lives*, however, Aubrey was of two minds. First, he wrote to Wood that 'after your perusall, I must desire you to make a Castration (as Raderus to Martial) and to sewe on some

---

[83] Bodleian MSS Ballard 14, fol. 131r; Wood F 39, fol. 340r.
[84] Bodleian MS Aubrey 7, fol. 4v.   [85] Bodleian MS Ballard 14, fol. 131r.
[86] Bodleian MS Aubrey 6, fol. 12r. Aubrey wrote from experience. In the years leading up to 1680, he was one of the members of a coffee-house club which met at Jonathan's in Change Alley, later to become the London Stock Exchange, and which also included Edmond Halley, Robert Hooke, and Edmund Wylde (cf. Bodleian MS Aubrey 12, fols. 147–8, for a letter from Halley to Aubrey, dated 26 November 1679, giving a partial list of 'our friends that used to meet at Jonathans').

Figgc-lcavcs (i) to be my Index expurgatorius'.[87] This seems to imply at least some thought of immediate use or publication, but it may be that Aubrey was simply thinking of the *Lives*' potential use by Wood in his *Athenae*, for elsewhere in the letter he cautioned, 'now these arcana are not fitt to lett flee abroad, till about 30 yeares hence; for the author & the Persons (the Medlars) ought to be rotten first; But in whose hands must they be deposited in the meane time?'[88] Aubrey's recurring concern that the *Lives* should not 'flee abroad' too soon is in itself evidence that he did envisage their eventual publication, albeit after his death, and the question of their fate, combined with his worry about their potential 'stiffling' should they fall into the hands of John Wallis, may also suggest that he found Wood to be a less than ideal custodian in the meantime. Nonetheless, when in 1681 he drafted an *Auctarium*—a supplement— to the *Lives*, it was subscribed on the title page 'For Mr Anthony Wood at Oxford'.[89]

Both surviving volumes of the *Brief Lives* written by Aubrey in 1680 and 1681 are headed with the same quotation from Bacon with which he began the *Life of Hobbes*: 'tanquam tabula naufragii', 'like planks from a shipwreck'.[90] This explicitly ties the *Lives* back into his larger antiquarian project and, together with their structure and contents, indicates his continued adherence to the principles of biography set out in the preface to the *Life of Hobbes*. The *Lives* were not antiquarianism in a conventional sense, but used antiquarian techniques to develop a lively biographical form which drew on the lionizing culture of early modern scholarship as well as traditional *historiae literariae*. They grew out of a desire to memorialize the great thinkers and men of action with whom he had been acquainted, but Aubrey firmly rejected contemporary hagiographic traditions. Instead he applied the techniques of his own discipline, its systematization, its concern with minutiae, with networks and patterns, to create biographies that focused on individuality, drawing a portrait of their subject for posterity through the enumeration of physiognomy, personality, habits, and characteristic actions.

---

[87] Bodleian MS Aubrey 6, fol. 12r. Aubrey was alluding to the Jesuit scholar Matthaeus Raderus, whose bowdlerized *Martial* had run to twenty-two editions by 1660 (J. P. Sullivan, *Martial, the Unexpected Classic: A Literary and Historical Study* [Cambridge, 1991], 294).

[88] Bodleian MS Aubrey 6, fol. 12r.

[89] Bodleian MS Aubrey 8, fol. 4ar.

[90] Bodleian MSS Aubrey 6, fol. 2r; Aubrey 8, fol. 4ar. Bodleian MS Aubrey 7 contains fragments of the second part of the *Lives*, largely destroyed by Wood, for which, see 'Mathematical Lives' and Aubrey, *Lives*, i. cxxx–cxxxiv.

MATHEMATICAL LIVES AND THE LIMITS
OF AUBREY'S METHOD

Nine years after the *Brief Lives*, Aubrey began a final biographical project: *An Apparatus for the Lives of our English Mathematical Writers*.[91] This small work, only fifteen sheets in length, is dated 25 March 1690 and was composed at the same time as the *Remaines of Gentilisme*, notes towards which are scattered across its title page.[92] Aubrey's intention was to write the framework of the *Apparatus*, then ask Anthony Wood to 'find-out one that is master of a good Latin stile; and to add what is already in his printed Booke'.[93] He appears to have envisaged a collaboration between Wood, himself, and another figure (presumably a more tractable version of Richard Blackburne), resulting in the publication of a Latin history of English mathematicians.[94] He planned to limit his scope to mathematicians living in the reign of Henry VIII or later, but intended to preface the work as a whole with John Selden's poem and accompanying commentary on the English mathematicians of the Middle Ages prefixed to Arthur Hopton's 1612 *Concordancy of Yeares*.[95]

Aubrey's projected work, which would have been one of the first major publications on the history of English mathematics, never materialized, probably due to a cooling of relations with Wood soon after the composition of the *Apparatus*.[96] However, even in its incomplete state, the *Apparatus* is an important antiquarian text and a work different from

[91] Bodleian MS Aubrey 8, fols. 69r–88v. See also Kate Bennett, 'John Aubrey and the "Lives of our English Mathematical Writers"', in *The Oxford Handbook of the History of Mathematics*, ed. Eleanor Robson and Jacqueline Stedall (Oxford, 2009), 329–52, for a study of the *Apparatus* within the larger context of Aubrey's mathematical interests and contemporary portrayals of mathematics and mathematicians.

[92] Bodleian MS Aubrey 8, fol. 69r.

[93] Bodleian MS Aubrey 8, fol. 70r.

[94] Although it seems unlikely that Aubrey would have considering collaborating with him a second time, Blackburne did play a role in the composition of the *Apparatus*, suggesting to Aubrey that he might 'putt-out in print the Lives of our <u>English Mathematitians</u>' at some point before 12 March 1689 (Aubrey, *Lives*, i. 452, ii. 1695).

[95] Arthur Hopton, *A Concordancy of Yeares . . .* (London, 1612); Bodleian MS Aubrey 8, fol. 70r. See Gerald Toomer, *John Selden: A Life in Scholarship*, 2 vols. (Oxford, 2009), i. 17.

[96] Aubrey had been anticipated by Edward Sherburne in an appendix to his monumental 1675 translation of the ancient astronomical poet, Manilius. Sherburne had compiled a 126-page 'Catalogue of the most Eminent Astronomers, Ancient & Modern' which included a large number of British astronomers (Sherburne, *The Sphere of Marcus Manilius Made an English Poem With Annotations and an Astronomical Appendix* [London, 1675], sep. pag. 1–126). Aubrey knew of Sherburne's prosopography and planned to refer to it in the composition of the *Apparatus* (Bodleian MS Aubrey 8, fol. 69r).

either the *Life of Hobbes* or the *Brief Lives*, though they share a similar biographical style and methodology.[97] In the *Apparatus*, Aubrey, for the first time, found himself considering figures with whom he had no oral link to build a biography upon, only their published writings or a biographical entry in one of Wood's collections. As such, the earliest lives in the collection are little more than bibliographies, with an occasional assessment of the works' value by a contemporary mathematician. In many cases, also, there was overlap with the existing biographies in the *Brief Lives*, in which instances Aubrey only referred back to the earlier biography rather than tailoring a new one for the *Apparatus*.

The *Apparatus* is thus noticeable not for what it does, but for what it attempts. It reflects the same preconceptions as Aubrey's *Nouvelles* or tracts on innovations and inventions: an interest in individual achievements, as opposed to a gradual increase in knowledge, and a curiosity to establish a distinctly English lineage of invention and progress.[98] To do this Aubrey turned again to the repertoire of the antiquary, but while the *Brief Lives* had allowed him to make use of his keen observation, the *Apparatus* did not play to his strengths. Though he knew how to use the relevant records, Aubrey's antiquarian interests did not tend towards the methodical searching of parish registers and public archives engaged in by scholars such as Wood and Sir William Dugdale. Instead he was concerned with the visual and the physical: strengths for which biographies of sixteenth-century mathematicians offered little scope. This suggests both the limits and the purpose of Aubrey's unique form of biography. It lacked interpretative power when it ventured beyond the oral history and autopsy upon which his more nuanced lives were based. This was not necessarily a failing, however, for the purpose of Aubreian biography was not to recover, but to preserve. Both the *Life of Hobbes* and the *Brief Lives* were urgent, feverish attempts to preserve knowledge as it was in the process of becoming lost, as 'by and by, comes the crepusculum; then, totall darknes'.[99] The *Apparatus*, in contrast, was an attempt to recover and enumerate the already lost lives of Elizabethan mathematicians and Aubrey's insistence that his work once again be complemented by that of Anthony Wood, who was skilled in understanding the records of the previous century, indicates that he was well aware of his weaknesses and planned to supplement them with the strengths of his friend.

Aubrey had collaborated with Anthony Wood on his *Historia et antiquitates Universitatis Oxonienses* and its sequel the *Athenae Oxonienses* long

[97] See the discussion at Aubrey, *Lives*, ii. 1694–6.
[98] For the *Nouvelles* see Hunter, *Aubrey*, 163–4.
[99] Bodleian MS Aubrey 9, fol. 29r (= Aubrey, 'Hobbes', i. 18).

before the composition of his own *Lives*, and he continued to do so afterwards, depositing the manuscripts of the *Lives* with Wood for long periods and encouraging him to draw upon them, wholesale, for the biographies contained within the *Athenae*. This generosity was repaid by Wood's complete failure to acknowledge Aubrey's assistance in the published *Athenae*, which were printed in 1691–2.[100] Worse, however, was the aftermath. The second volume of the *Athenae*, containing a biography of Edward Hyde, 1st Earl of Clarendon, was published in July 1692. On 11 November of that year, the earl's son dragged Wood into court for libel, having taken exception to Wood's assertion that his father took bribes from office-seekers.[101] It seems likely that the contested statement must have originally derived from the second part of Aubrey's *Brief Lives*, for some time between 11 and 29 November Wood removed pages nine to forty-four of that volume as well as four folios from the first part and perhaps other materials.[102] Aubrey noted with considerable concern that therein were:

> [C]onteined Trueths; but such as I entrusted no body with the sight of but himselfe: whom I thought I might have entrusted with my Life. There are severall papers, that may cutt my throate. I find too late, <u>Memento diffidere</u> was a Saying worthy one of the Sages [*sic*]. He hath also embezill'd the Index of it.[103]

Not long after this, Aubrey established a rapport with Edward Lhuyd, the keeper of the Ashmolean Museum, and proceeded to transfer a large portion of his manuscript writings to him, including the *Lives*.[104] The exact date of deposition is uncertain, but it is likely that they were in the 'Boxfull of Antiquities' which Aubrey sent to Lhuyd on 31 August 1693 and which he did not give outright, but only deposited in the Museum, 'for there are some things reflecting upon Dr Wallis &c not fitt to be seen (yet) by every body'.[105] What he deposited must have been parts one and

---

[100] Wood, *Athenae*, i. sig. ar-v.

[101] The relevant court documents are reproduced in full in Wood, *The Life and Times*, iv. 1–50.

[102] Aubrey, *Lives*, i. cxxx–cxxxi.

[103] Bodleian MS Aubrey 7, fol. 2r. 'Memento diffidere' ('remember to distrust') was a saying 'from one of the sages' quoted in Lucian's *Hermotimus*, 47. Aubrey was quoting the standard Latin version of the Greek original, 'μέμνησο ἀπιστεῖν'.

[104] See Chapter 6. On 10 October 1694 he asked Edward Lhuyd to remove the sheet on which his comments are written from the manuscript, 'which (though true) would make him [i.e., Wood] angry' (Bodleian MS Ashmole 1814, fol. 117r). His rage was evidently not permanent.

[105] Bodleian MS Ashmole 1814, fol. 92r. The 'things reflecting upon Dr Wallis' were no doubt the unflattering life of him at Bodleian MS Aubrey 6, fol. 94v–95r (Aubrey, *Lives*, i. 299–302).

three of the *Lives* (now Bodleian MSS 6 and 8) bound in vellum wrappers, together with the loose sheets remaining from part two, which had been 'gelded' by Wood the year before.[106]

Despite Wood's intervention, Aubrey had substantially succeeded in carrying his plan for the *Lives* through to completion. Having composed them privately he had deposited the manuscripts with his younger contemporary and protégé Lhuyd until such time as they could safely be brought to light. In effect, having performed an act of preventative antiquarianism—the gathering of material which would otherwise have been lost—Aubrey was setting up his own writing to become part of the archive of later generations. More clearly than any of his other antiquarian projects, the *Lives* show Aubrey participating in the sociable memorialization of the Republic of Letters which took the form of *historiae literariae*, lives of great men, editions of correspondence, table talk, donations of archives, lavish funeral monuments, and all the other paraphernalia through which early modern scholars expressed their debt to and continuity with the humanist past. Pertaining to a very different sort of antiquarianism than the *Monumenta* or his architectural works, they nonetheless drew upon similar methodologies and assumptions to preserve the lives of the English *virtuosi* in much the same way as Aubrey had begun to reconstruct pre-Roman Britain a decade before.

---

[106] The modern Bodleian MS Aubrey 7, containing those sheets, was compiled by Edmund Malone during his study of the *Lives* in September 1792 (Bodleian MS Aubrey 7, fol. 1r). For Malone's interventions with Aubrey's manuscripts, undertaken as part of an attempt at editing the *Lives*, see Aubrey, *Lives*, i. cxxxiv–cxxxvii.

5

Ovid in the West Country

The Ancient Origins of Folk Custom

Even before the spectacular combustion of their joint work during the 1692 Clarendon trial, Aubrey and Anthony Wood were acutely aware of the unpleasant results of private papers becoming public. Writing to Wood in a low mood during the autumn of 1688 Aubrey worried

> that you are lookt upon as a Papist and in these tumultuous Turns your papers will be searcht... and you know, that in my Memorandum of Lives, there are some things that may make me obnoxious to Scandalum Magnatum: and I have heretofore writt a letter or 2, which I wish were turnd to ashes. New troubles arise upon me, like Hydra's heads... [w]hen I was comeing one time out of All-soules, the Gape-abouts, at the gate pointed at me, & one sayd Romano-catholicus.[1]

The combination of potentially inflammatory papers with real or suspected Catholicism was a dangerous one for any scholar in the 1680s.[2] The one bright spot in Aubrey's letter was a new project,

---

[1] Bodleian MS Tanner 456a, fol. 34r.

[2] The religious proclivities of both men remain open to question. Wood was widely believed to be a Catholic by his contemporaries, but his own writings suggest a more complicated picture, as seen in diary entries such as one made in February 1678 while visiting his undoubtedly Catholic patron Ralph Sheldon: 'kept a Lent, which I never did before' (*The Life of Anthony Wood in His Own Words*, ed. Nicolas K. Kiessling [Oxford, 2009], 138). Whether he later converted is unknown, but as early as 1672 he appears to have been considered to be a likely potential convert by the English Jesuits; 'all them venerate AW', Aubrey wrote, not entirely in jest, on 18 January 1672 (Bodleian MS Wood F 39, fol. 192r). Aubrey is known for his anticlericalism, distilled into his riposte to Wood when the latter suggested he take orders: 'fough the Cassock stinkes it would be ridiculous' (Bodleian MS Ballard 14, fol. 98r). However, in the dark days following his bankruptcy, when he was living under an assumed name and putting out false stories of his whereabouts to throw bailiffs off the scent, his attitude was quite different. Writing to Wood on 27 October 1671 he rhetorically queried, 'where could a man better withdraw himselfe than into such a learned Society as that of the Jesuits[?]' Nor was this an abstract question. In the same letter he recounted to Wood how the Jesuit Richard Thimbleby had been inviting him 'above this 12 month and stay as long as I will (i) sojourne' at the house for novices in Watten where Thimbleby was rector (Bodleian MS Wood F 39, fol. 141r;

I am perusing Ovids Works, and I have halfe gonne it over, and have pickt up a sheet or more for my Gentilisme, even in his Epistles, and Amoris. Where one would not expect it . . . You see what strange distracted way of study my Fates give me.[3]

Ironically, given Aubrey's concerns at the time, this new work, the *Remaines of Gentilisme*, would become another text which was not fit to fly abroad.[4]

Begun in February 1687, the *Remaines* was a collection of quotations from Catullus, Homer, Horace, Juvenal, Ovid, Persius, Pliny, Propertius, Tibullus, and Virgil concerning the customs and rituals of the ancient world. Aubrey grouped these under relevant headings—everything from the immuring of nuns to the uses of beans—and compared them with modern English folk traditions. He was concerned with customs and practices rather than folklore in the sense of stories or myths, and the material he cited usually consisted of factual accounts of folkways which existed at the time he wrote or which had existed in the recent past. Religious traditions featured largely, with examples including churches, masses for the dead, praying towards the east, and washing hands before prayer, as well as a cluster of entries on important days in the liturgical year.[5] Other broad categories included occupations, objects, foods, and actions. In his other works he had made numerous comparisons between the pastoral world of Greek and Roman poetry and the rural economy of his native Wiltshire, a parallel which also emerged in his entries on occupations such as shepherds, bond servants, rhymers, and goodmen.[6] The objects and foods he mentioned were timeless ones such as garlands,

ODNB, *s.n.*). Although Aubrey never took up Father Thimbleby's offer, he maintained friendly relations with a number of Catholic laymen and priests, including the Provincial of the English Jesuits, George Gray, 'a good grave friendly man' (Bodleian MS Wood F 39, fol. 192r); the gape-abouts on the High Street had good reason for their suppositions.

[3] Bodleian MS Tanner 456a, fol. 35r.

[4] The manuscript of the *Remaines of Gentilisme* is now BL MS Lansdowne 231. It has been edited twice, first by the folklorist James Britten in *Remaines of Gentilisme and Judaisme. By John Aubrey, R.S.S. 1686–87* (London, 1881) and second by John Buchanan-Brown in Aubrey, *Three Prose Works* (Fontwell, Sussex, 1972). Neither edition is ideal, but Britten's is to be preferred in most things as Buchanan-Brown reorders the text beyond recognition. In the present work citations are to the manuscript in the first instance with parallel references to the relevant page of Britten's edition.

[5] BL MS Lansdowne 231, fols. 107v (praying), 108r (masses), 170r (churches), 196r–197r (washing of hands), and, for holy days, fols. 108r (May Day), 138r (Childermas), 154r (Christmas), 159r (Candlemas). The equivalent passages in Aubrey, *Remaines*, are at 17, 18, 48–50, 146, and 18, 63, 88, 93–4.

[6] BL MS Lansdowne 231, fols. 125r (shepherds), 126r (bond servants), 148r (rhymers), 213v (goodmen). The equivalent passages in Aubrey, *Remaines*, are at 45, 47, 81, 170. Cf. Hunter, *Aubrey*, 239–40, for comparisons of Wiltshire to ancient pastoral.

shields, musical instruments, staves, ale, bridal cakes, beans, and the like, while actions varied between traditions associated with the quotidian, such as sneezing or drawing lots, and more ritualized situations, including cockfighting at Shrovetide, the making of offerings at funerals, and trial by fire.[7] Occasionally he mentioned customs associated with a specific form of landscape—examples include high places and springs—or the uses of a mythical figure such as the green man.[8]

It was probably no accident that one part of the *Remaines* was headed by an epigraph taken from the works of the Church Father Lactantius—'primus sapientiae gradus, est falsa intelligere' ('the first step towards wisdom is to perceive falsehood')—which had also famously been used as an epigraph by John Selden for his 1617 *De diis Syris*; Aubrey was writing a work not unlike Selden's massive comparative theology of the ancient Near East.[9] The difference was that, rather than relating Greco-Roman customs and religion to those of the Incas or the Chinese or the Zoroastrians, as had so many of his contemporaries, Aubrey was using them as a tool with which to understand contemporary English folk traditions.[10] The systematic study of other belief systems was one of the core disciplines of early modern scholarship. Aubrey, however, performed the unusual act of othering his own culture and attempted to make sense of the beliefs and rituals which had existed around him since his youth through a model of cultural comparatism which saw those same beliefs and rituals stemming from a common tradition of ancient religious practice.

REMAINS OF GENTILISM: OLD WIVES' TALES AND THE LAUGH OF A FAUN

There was an inherent tension in studying knowledge systems which existed in direct competition with an orthodox Christian worldview.

---

[7] BL MS Lansdowne 231, fols. 115v (cockfighting at Shrovetide), 134r (offerings at funerals), 146r (shields), 155r (lots), 167r (beans), 168r (sneezing), 171r (garlands), 180r (trial by fire), 212v–213r (musical instruments), 215r (staves), 218v (ale), 221r (bridal cakes). The equivalent passages in Aubrey, *Remaines*, are at 35, 64, 69, 90, 102–3, 103–4, 109, 126–7, 167–9, 172–3, 179, 181.

[8] BL MS Lansdowne 231, fols. 162r (high places), 177r (springs), 186r (the green man). The equivalent passages in Aubrey, *Remaines*, are at 98, 121, 134–5.

[9] Lactantius, *Divinae institutiones*, ed. J.-P. Migne (Paris, 1844), I.xxiii; John Selden, *De diis Syris syntagmata II* (London, 1617). *De diis Syris* is discussed in G. J. Toomer, *John Selden: A Life in Scholarship*, 2 vols. (Oxford, 2009), i. 211–56, but the epigraph from Lactantius is not specifically addressed.

[10] For the early modern tradition of cultural comparatism see Guy G. Stroumsa, *A New Science: The Discovery of Religion in the Age of Reason* (Cambridge, MA, and London, 2010).

Unless accommodation could be reached through designating such a system a civil religion—as in the case of the Jesuits and Chinese religion—there was a very real risk that the only theologically coherent choice was to reject the foreign structure in its entirety, labelling it heretical, atheistic, or simply vulgar and wrong.[11] This approach could be extended to local folk cultures and the clergyman Henry Bourne, whose 1725 *Antiquitates Vulgares* was the next major collection of English folklore after Aubrey's, castigated his subject as 'the Produce of Heathenism; or the Inventions of indolent *Monks*', seeing it as his duty to reform, cull, and control what he perceived to be the traditions of the devil.[12]

Aubrey took a different approach. He admitted that 'Old Customes, & old wives-fables are grosse things', but argued that 'there may some trueth and usefulnesse be picked \elicited/ out of them: besides 'tis a pleasure to consider the Errours that enveloped former ages: as also the present', a sentiment evidently related to his quotation of Lactantius discussed earlier in this chapter.[13] For Aubrey, moreover, old wives' tales might be gross (i.e., coarse and rather obvious) in the present of the 1680s, but 'Before Printing' they 'were ingeniose'. In a culture which existed before print, or at least before cheap print was widely accessible, and where 'the ordinary sort of People were not taught to reade', oral culture was a valid system for preserving and transmitting knowledge.[14] Recalling Bacon's list of inventions by which the moderns surpassed the ancients, Aubrey concluded his reflections on this topic by writing wistfully that 'the divine art of Printing and Gunpowder have frighted

[11] Stroumsa, *A New Science*, *passim*, esp. ch. 7; Alexandra Walsham, 'Recording Superstitions in Early Modern Britain: The Origins of Folklore', *Past and Present* 51 (2008): 183–4. Other examples of this tendency include Polydore Vergil, *On Discovery*, ed. Brian P. Copenhaver (Cambridge, MA, 2002); Joshua Stopford, *Pagano-Papismus; or, an Exact Parallel Between Rome-Pagan and Rome-Christian in Their Doctrines and Ceremonies* (London, 1675); Conyers Middleton, *A Letter From Rome, Showing an Exact Conformity Between Popery and Paganism: or, the Religion of the Present Romans Derived from that of their Heathen Ancestors*, 3rd edn. (London, 1733). For Polydore Vergil's treatment of the relationship between pagan and Christian liturgical practice see Catherine Atkinson, *Inventing Inventors in Renaissance Europe: Polydore Vergil's* De inventoribus rerum (Tübingen, 2007), ch. 6.

[12] Henry Bourne, *Antiquitates Vulgares; or the Antiquities of the Common People: Giving an Account of Several of Their Opinions and Ceremonies With Proper Reflections Upon Each of Them; Shewing Which May be Retain'd, and Which Ought to be Laid Aside* (Newcastle, 1725), x–xi.

[13] BL MS Lansdowne 231, fol. 103r (= Aubrey, *Remaines*, 6). For Aubrey's female oral history see Henk Dragstra, '"Before woomen were Readers": How John Aubrey Wrote Female Oral History', in *Oral Traditions and Gender in Early Modern Literary Texts*, ed. Mary Ellen Lamb and Karen Bamford (Aldershot, 2008), 41–53. For an interpretation of Aubrey as an ethnographer or anthropologist see Daniel Woolf, *The Social Circulation of the Past: English Historical Culture, 1500–1730* (Oxford, 2003), 383–6.

[14] BL MS Lansdowne 231, fol. 140v (= Aubrey, *Remaines*, 67–8).

away Robin-good-fellow and the Fayries'.[15] This Baconian allusion, combined with his earlier description of pre-print folk culture as 'ingeniose'—a term which Aubrey elsewhere used specifically to refer to inventions, experiments, or other developments in natural philosophy—suggests that Aubrey had a very specific aspect of folk culture in mind when writing this riposte in its favour. The recipes, magical spells, and traditions associated with custom and ritual were, he believed, ultimately analogous to the philosophical studies of his contemporaries in the Royal Society.[16]

Why did Aubrey believe that credence, or at least respect, should be given to the knowledge system he referred to metonymically as 'Robin-good-fellow and the Fayries'? In part, it was because he was convinced that English folk culture contained visible relics of the religions and cultures of the ancient world—in other words, 'remains of gentilism'.[17] But Aubrey's conviction of the existence of this cultural continuity could, at times, reach a quasi-mystical level which amounted to something more than antiquarian hypothesis. Glossing a couplet from Virgil's *Georgics*, he noted that 'the Fauns are accounted the Countrey Gods, and are thought alwaies to inhabit the woods'.[18] He then described the traditions surrounding 'the first of them', Faunus, grandson of Saturn, from whom '('tis likely) comes our Robin-goodfellow'.[19] A few pages before, under the rubric 'Ho, ho, ho

---

[15] BL MS Lansdowne 231, fol. 140v (= Aubrey, *Remaines*, 68). For Bacon's inventions—printing, gunpowder, and the compass—see Francis Bacon, *Instauratio Magna, Part II: Novum Organum and Associated Texts*, ed. Graham Rees (Oxford, 2004), 167–9.

[16] Aubrey pursued the issue of systemic relativity in a passage on calendars elsewhere in the *Remaines*. How, he queried, can we make sense of claims for the auspicious or inauspicious natures of certain days when 'the Calendars of these computers are very differing; the Greekes differing from the Latins, and the Latins from each other' (BL MS Lansdowne 231, fol. 159r [= Aubrey, *Remaines*, 94])? He made no claims of superior accuracy for any single system.

[17] 'Gentilism' was simply the religion or culture of the gentiles, i.e., pagans (Colin Kidd, *British Identities before Nationalism* [Cambridge, 1999], 13–14). The term had particular currency in Restoration England, perhaps in part through the fame of Theophilus Gale's *Court of the Gentiles*, 2 vols. (Oxford, 1669–70), a work making claims to intellectual and cultural genealogies structurally similar to those made in the *Remaines*.

[18] The lines were 'et vos, agrestum praesentia numina, Fauni, | (ferte simul Faunique pedem Dryadesque puellae!)' (Virgil, *Georgics*, I. 10–11). Although Aubrey quoted the Latin, his gloss is heavily indebted to the annotations in Thomas May's *Virgil's Georgicks Englished* (London, 1628), 29, a copy of which is now Bodleian Ashmole 1561 and is signed at sig. A2 'Jack Aubrey. 1655'. He probably used this in conjunction with the 1632 Cambridge octavo of Paolo Manuzio's edition (Virgil, *Opera... Pauli Manutii annotationes brevissimae in margine adscriptae* [Cambridge, 1632]), now Bodleian Ashmole A. 35, which is signed 'Jo: Aubrey' on the pastedown and contains numerous underlinings and annotations. The translation by May contains no annotations except a note by Aubrey on the front pastedown that it is sometimes bound together with May's *Martial*.

[19] BL MS Lansdowne 231, fol. 150v (= Aubrey, *Remaines*, 84).

of Robin-goodfellow', he had written a recollection which provided the final link in this increasingly idiosyncratic chain of associations. Virgil, he recalled, had written somewhere, perhaps in the *Georgics*, 'of Voyces heard, louder than a Man's'.[20] But Aubrey's friend Lancelot Morehouse 'did averre to me super verbum sacerdotis [on his word as a priest], that he did once heare such a loud Laugh on the other side of a hedge; and was sure that no Human voice could afford such Laugh'.[21] Whether, following the logic of these passages to their conclusion, Aubrey genuinely believed the 'solid and profound mathematician' and Wiltshire curate Morehouse had heard the laugh of a faun is not known.[22] What these passages suggest, however, is Aubrey's belief in the numinous vitality—even in the recent past and amongst the hedgerows of Wiltshire—of what he understood to be an ancient, classical world.

This ancient world was primarily Roman, unsurprisingly given the Roman poets and prose writers upon whom he relied for the majority of his comparisons. The cultural continuity he saw between the Roman world and seventeenth-century England was of a piece with the links he drew between the two in other contexts. Just as a toponym could hint at a Roman settlement or the shape of an ancient fortification could testify to its place in the history of the Roman conquest of Britain, so could a folk tradition form another link in the chain which connected the Romano-British world to Aubrey's present day. The origins Aubrey found for what he had observed in rural England were not exclusively Roman, however. Paralleling his philological writings, Aubrey noted that 'the many Greeke words that remain in the British Language (more than Latin)...doe sufficiently evidence that the Greekes had here Colonies' and both Homer and Theocritus regularly appear as ancient sources in the *Remaines*, as they were in the *Monumenta*.[23] Further afield, he linked the Christmastime tradition of the lord of misrule with the feast of

---

[20] Aubrey was perhaps half-remembering here the description of nature mourning the death of Daphnis in Virgil, *Eclogues*, V. 24–6.

[21] BL MS Lansdowne 231, fol. 147v (= Aubrey, *Remaines*, 81). Morehouse had matriculated sizar from Jesus College, Cambridge, in Easter 1616 (John and J. A. Venn, *Alumni Cantabrigienses*, 10 vols. [Cambridge, 1922–54], Part I, iii. 211) and had subsequently served as curate to Walter Waller, Vicar of Broad Chalke, when Aubrey was a young child (Powell, *Aubrey*, 86).

[22] For Morehouse as a mathematician see Hunter, *Aubrey*, 227, and Aubrey, *Lives*, ii. 1035.

[23] BL MS Lansdowne 231, fol. 113r (= Aubrey, *Remaines*, 27–8). Aubrey repeatedly cites Theocritus's *Idylls* in the *Remaines* (cf. BL MS Lansdowne 231, fols. 112v–113r, 150v, 152v, 167v, etc.) in the English translation by Thomas Creech, *The Idylliums of Theocritus* (Oxford, 1684). Both the *Iliad* and the *Odyssey* also frequently appear (see especially BL MS Lansdowne 231, fols. 190v–198v), but in the original Greek. Aubrey knew the translations by Thomas Hobbes and John Ogilby, but was probably relying on his copy of *Homeri*

the goddess 'Dorcetha' in Babylon, while mazes were derived from the Egyptians via the Greeks and the Danes, and the Welsh tradition of *pbygain* singing came from a similar 'Asiatick Custome'.[24]

At times, this dizzying plurality of ancient origins almost merged into a single universal ancient culture, whose shared symbolic language could be located in texts and objects across the known world. A line from Persius's first satire—'paint up a couple of snakes, my lads, and clear out; the ground is holy'—led Aubrey to recall in succession Swedish inscriptions 'entertoilees with Snakes', serpents' heads in the initial letters of Saint Chad's Gospel at Lichfield Cathedral, serpents in Gothic ecclesiastical architecture, 'Serpents that were fed with the bloud of the Sacrifices' by the Basilidian Gnostics, and the veneration of serpents by Brahmins.[25] Jumping from his own experiences to published works by writers as diverse as the Swedish antiquary Olof Verelius, the German theologian Friedrich Spanheim, and the French traveller Jean-Baptiste Tavernier, Aubrey was following the same associative processes which appear in works such as his history of ancient architecture in 'Of Mausolea'.[26] By implication, the postdiluvian repopulation of the world which allowed for such associations in an architectural context also allowed them in the context of ritual and tradition; if the earth had been entirely repopulated in the relatively recent past, it stood to reason that a variety of cultural continuities could be distinguished even in the present day and in far-flung corners of the world. Aubrey's focus was on one chain of cultural transmission from Rome to England, but he remained aware of a larger ancient world whose culture could be traced back to an origin point on the Ark.

---

poemata duo, Ilias et Odyssea, sive Ulyssea, 2 vols. (Geneva, 1604), which he also cites in Bodleian MS Top. Gen. c. 25, fols. 7v, 15v, 41v, 42v–43ar, 43cr, and 180av–181r.

[24] BL MS Lansdowne 231, fols. 177v (Babylonian), 190r (Egyptian), 206v (Asiatic) (= Aubrey, *Remaines*, 122, 133, 161). Aubrey claimed to follow Samuel Purchas in making the link between the lord of misrule and 'Dorcetha', but Purchas only mentioned her feast 'during which time the Masters were vnder the dominion of their seruants' without drawing the comparison (*Purchas his Pilgrimage* [London, 1613]. 56). Aubrey may or may not have been aware of the woodcut of 'Derceto', depicted as half-fish, half-woman in Athanasius Kircher's *Oedipus Aegyptiacus*, 3 vols. (Rome, 1652), i. 341.

[25] BL MS Lansdowne 231, fol. 119r (= Aubrey, *Remaines*, 38–9); Persius, *Satires*, I. 113–14.

[26] Aubrey drew on Olof Verelius, *Manuductio compendiosa ad runographiam Scandicam antiquam, recte intelligendam* (Uppsala, 1675), *passim*, for snakes in runic inscriptions, Friedrich Spanheim, *Introductio ad historiam et antiquitates sacras* (Leiden, 1675), 325, for the Basilidian heresy, and Jean-Baptiste Tavernier, *The Six Voyages of John Baptista Tavernier* (London, 1677), II.i.34, for a snake in an Indian storehouse (Aubrey had misremembered this last as veneration of snakes by Brahmins).

Within the broad remit of 'gentilism' Aubrey included material which can be divided into three recognizably distinct categories: folkways, magic, and religious custom. He treated each category differently. Folkways, the most numerous, were also the least problematic. In recording, for example, a tradition that the sun shining on Candlemas portended a cold winter, Aubrey would simply note it down, albeit with the occasional whiff of scepticism, in this particular case provided by a citation to Thomas Browne's debunking of such traditions in the *Pseudodoxia Epidemica*.[27] By and large, however, traditions required no special explanation beyond the link made between them and whichever classical text they served to gloss.

Magic and religion were altogether different matters. In some instances Aubrey would note down a magical receipt, such as one for invisibility which required the powdered skin of a serpent killed at midnight, without commenting on it beyond noting its source, in this case 'a booke in octavo in high Dutch. Dr Ridgeley the Physitian hath it, who told me of this.'[28] In other cases, however, his interrogation of what might seem to be 'an old filthy Rhyme used by base people' or 'meer Wantonesse of Youth' revealed something more. Noting the rhyme 'When I was a young Maid, and wash't my mothers Dishes | I putt my finger in my Cunt and pluck't out little Fishes', Aubrey related it back to a passage in the eleventh-century confessor's guidebook contained within the *Decretals* of Burchard of Worms, 'where there is an interrogation, if she did ever putt a little fish into her Pudenda, and let it die there, and then fry it, and give it to her Lover to eate'.[29] Reflecting on this, he congratulated himself that 'out of these simple Rhythmes I have pricked out the profoundest natural Magick that ever I met with in all my life'.[30] The presence of the interrogation in Bishop Burchard's text situated what would otherwise simply have been an 'old filthy Rhyme' within a theological framework that guaranteed its role as 'natural Magick'; further proof that the neglected oral culture of Aubrey's day had once been ingenious.

Magic, for Aubrey, was very close to natural philosophy and the testing of a magical spell could easily be conceived of as an experiment. While he seems not to have found anyone willing to test the fish spell, Aubrey did carefully record a bathetically unsuccessful attempt at verifying another

---

[27] BL MS Lansdowne 231, fol. 159r (= Aubrey, *Remaines*, 93).

[28] BL MS Lansdowne 231, fol. 130v (= Aubrey, *Remaines*, 181).

[29] Burchard of Worms, *Decretorum libri XX* (Cologne, 1548). Aubrey was apparently using a copy owned by Dr Francis Bernard and misdated its publication to 1549 (BL MS Lansdowne 231, fol. 131r [= Aubrey, *Remaines*, 43–4, 96]). For Bernard and his library see *ODNB, s.n.*

[30] BL MS Lansdowne 231, fol. 123r (= Aubrey, *Remaines*, 44).

magical receipt which he believed had originated in Jewish culture. 'The Jewes', he wrote, 'have strange fancies concerning the Invisible beane', which when properly prepared rendered its bearer invisible. Aubrey distanced himself from any actual belief in this legend, quoting the traditional anti-Semitic tag 'the Jew Apella may believe it, but not I', yet carefully recorded an account of its testing which he had received from his correspondent Wylde Clarke.[31] Clarke had allegedly been approached by two or three Jewish merchants who had desired to make the experiment in his garden at Mile End:

> 'twas much after this manner: They took a Black Catt, and cutt off it's head, at a certaine aspect of the Planets, and buryed it in his garden by night with some Ceremonies, what I have forgot, and put a Beane in the braine of the Catt: but about a day or two after, a Cock came and scratch't it all up. Mr Clarke told me that they did believe it: and yet they were crafty, subtle merchants.[32]

Despite his disbelief, Aubrey thought it worth recording the attempted test and did so in a fashion reminiscent of his records of what now seem to be more orthodox scientific experiments; magic could reveal itself as natural philosophy, which meant that recording even absurd magical processes could bear fruit in surprising ways. Reminding himself of this, Aubrey approvingly misquoted Francis Bacon 'that the fables of the Poets are the Mysteries of the Philosophers'.[33] For him, the study of folk customs could be both an antiquarian project and a philosophical one.

Aubrey's treatment of religion in the *Remaines*, exemplified by his determination to locate the origins of Christian ritual in Greco-Roman religious practice, derived in part from the ideas of his friend and fellow Wiltshire native Thomas Hobbes. Explaining his approach, Aubrey observed that 'in the Infancy of Christian Religion it was expedient to

---

[31] 'Credat Iudaeus Apella, non ego' (Horace, *Satires*, I.v.100–1).

[32] BL MS Lansdowne 231, fol. 167r (= Aubrey, *Remaines*, 103). Clarke was evidently in London at the time of the experiment but was principally a merchant at Santa Cruz, Barbados, from whence he wrote letters to Aubrey as early as November 1678 (Bodleian MS Aubrey 12, fols. 80–1) and as late as July 1692 (Bodleian MS Aubrey 12, fols. 76–7). He was also the godson of Aubrey's friend Edmund Wylde and apparently a relative of Wylde's partner, Jane Smith (Kate Bennett, 'John Aubrey and the Rhapsodic Book', *Renaissance Studies* 28 [2014]: 327).

[33] BL MS Lansdowne 231, fol. 123r (= Aubrey, *Remaines*, 44). Aubrey was recalling passages such as that in the *Advancement of Learning* where Bacon had observed that anciently 'as men founde out any obseruation that they thought was good for life, they would gather it and expresse it in parable or Aphorisme, or fable' (Francis Bacon, *The Advancement of Learning*, ed. Michael Kiernan [Oxford, 2000], 162). For Bacon's use of fable see Rhodri Lewis, 'Francis Bacon, Allegory, and the Uses of Myth', *Review of English Studies* 61 (2010): 360–89.

plough (as they say) with the heifer of the Gentiles... had they donne otherwise, they could not have gain'd so many Proselytes or established their Doctrine so well, and in so short a time'.[34] The new converts, he continued, were unwilling to relinquish their idols, so that the early Christian priests 'were persuaded to turne the Image of Jupiter with his thunderbolt to Christus crucifixus, and Venus and Cupid into the Madonna and her Babe, which Mr. Th. Hobbes sayth was prudently donne. See his *Leviathan*.'[35] Aubrey was referring to chapter 45 of *Leviathan*, 'Of Daemonology, and other Reliques of the Religion of the Gentiles', a title which may have provided the inspiration for the title of the *Remaines*.[36] There Hobbes argued that the worship of images was a 'relic of Gentilism', authority for which could not be found in the Bible, and that this idolatry led to the making of many costly images which, upon their conversion to Christianity, were retained by the pagans, '[t]he cause whereof, was the immoderate esteem, and prices set upon the workmanship of them'. This was aided and abetted by the priests, who permitted their worship under the names of Christ, the Virgin, and the Apostles, to please their converts and in the hope that they themselves might be similarly honoured upon their decease.[37] Aubrey followed Hobbes in recognizing that Christian practices had been, of necessity, adapted from earlier pagan tradition.

While Aubrey was not a deist, much less an atheist, his historicization of religious ritual was part of a larger sceptical approach to Christian theology. While he described Jesus as 'Our Saviour' elsewhere in his manuscripts and proposed vaguely Trinitarian prayers for his model school in the *Idea of Education of Young Gentlemen*, he also remained sceptical of the Trinity as doctrine, a stance apparent from the relevant passage in the *Remaines*.[38] Aubrey commenced with a quotation from John Selden's *Table-Talk*:

> The 2[d] person is made of a piece of Bread by the Papist. The Third Person is made of his owne Frenzy, Malice, Ignorance & Folly by the Roundhead

---

[34] BL MS Lansdowne 231, fol. 101r (= Aubrey, *Remaines*, 6). The image was an echo of Judges 14:18, 'if ye had not plowed with my heifer...'

[35] BL MS Lansdowne 231, fol. 101r (= Aubrey, *Remaines*, 6).

[36] Thomas Hobbes, *Leviathan*, 3 vols., ed. Noel Malcolm (Oxford, 2012), iii. 1012–51.

[37] Hobbes, *Leviathan*, iii. 1044. See also Jeffrey R. Collins, *The Allegiance of Thomas Hobbes* (Oxford, 2005), and the debate between him and Aloysius Martinich, 'Interpreting the Religion of Thomas Hobbes: An Exchange: Hobbes's Erastianism and Interpretation' and Collins, 'Interpreting Thomas Hobbes in Competing Contexts', *Journal of the History of Ideas* 70 (2009): 143–80.

[38] BL MS Lansdowne 231, fols. 168v–170r (= Aubrey, *Remaines*, 105–6). For the prayers, which are doctrinally vague, see Bodleian Library MS Aubrey 10, fols. 128r–131r, and for 'Our Saviours Sermon on the Mount', see Bodleian Library MS Aubrey 10, fol. 45r.

(to all these the Spirit is intituled) One the Baker makes, the other the Cobler; and between these Two, I think the first Person is sufficiently abused.[39]

Aubrey did not comment directly on this passage, but moved into an investigation of visual representations of the Trinity, discussing icono-clasm and the argument from Daniel against it. More significant, however, was his quotation of 1 John 5:7–8 (the Johannine Comma) in the Greek of the *textus receptus*.[40] 'The last clause of this verse', he noted, 'is not found in ancient MSS copies. e.g. that in the Vatican Library, and the Tecla MS in St James Library and others: as it is not in an old MS in Magdalen Coll: Library in Oxford.'[41] In the margin against this passage is a reminder to 'peruse these MSS again, and see if the whole verse be there'.[42]

This particular crux, one of the principal biblical authorities for the doctrine of the Trinity, had attracted considerable attention in previous decades with the publication of the New Testaments of John Fell and John Mill and would later be publicly noted as a late addition by Richard Bentley during his inaugural lecture as Regius Professor of Divinity at Cambridge in 1717.[43] It was also considered by Aubrey's fellow Royal Society member Isaac Newton, who composed a detailed disproof of the Comma in his *Historical Account of Two Notable Corruptions of Scripture*.[44] Aubrey, by contrast, did not go so far as to indict the Trinity as false doctrine, but contented himself merely with noting the absence of one of its proof-texts from the manuscripts available to him. As such, he was by no means making a novel claim, but only stating what had been common knowledge since Erasmus first observed the absence of the Comma from

[39] BL MS Lansdowne 231, fol. 170r (= Aubrey, *Remaines*, 105). See John Selden, *Table-Talk*, ed. Richard Milward (London, 1689), 56.

[40] BL MS Lansdowne 231, fol. 168v (= Aubrey, *Remaines*, 105–6). He quotes only verse seven, 'For there are three that bear record in heaven, the Father, the Word, and the Holy Ghost: and these three are one' (1 John 5:7, KJV).

[41] BL MS Lansdowne 231, fol. 168v (= Aubrey, *Remaines*, 106). Surprisingly, this passage is quoted by the bibliographer Thomas Hartwell Horne in his discussion of the 1786 facsimile of the Codex Alexandrinus (*An Introduction to the Critical Study and Knowledge of the Holy Scriptures* [Philadelphia, 1836], ii. 13).

[42] BL MS Lansdowne 231, fol. 168v (= Aubrey, *Remaines*, 106).

[43] Kristine Louise Haugen, *Richard Bentley: Poetry and Enlightenment* (Cambridge, MA, 2011), 207. For this, and more general shifts in Trinitarian scholarship, see Haugen, 'Transformations of the Trinity Doctrine in English Scholarship', *Archiv für Religions-geschichte* 3 (2001): 149–68.

[44] First published in full in Isaac Newton, *Opera quae exstant omnia*, 5 vols., ed. Samuel Horsley (London, 1779–85), v. 495–550, for which see Scott Mandelbrote, 'Eighteenth-Century Reactions to Newton's Anti-Trinitarianism', in *Newton and Newtonianism: New Studies*, ed. J. E. Force and S. Hutton (Dordrecht, 2004), 93–112. For Newton's forays into ancient chronology and biblical exegesis more generally see Jed Z. Buchwald and Morde-chai Feingold, *Newton and the Origin of Civilization* (Princeton, NJ, 2013).

the Greek manuscript tradition in 1516.[45] What is surprising is Aubrey's interest here in biblical philology (not seen elsewhere in his surviving manuscripts), his active consultation of several significant exemplars of the Greek New Testament in England, and his willingness to discount what Anglican orthodoxy saw as a keystone of Trinitarian theology. He stood in a theological middle ground, willing to question concepts as basic as the Trinity but still invested in the essentials of a biblical worldview, crucially including a chronology which took the Flood to be modern civilization's starting point.

THE TRAUMA OF THE CIVIL WARS

This theological flexibility allowed Aubrey to analyse his own culture with a more critical eye than might otherwise have been possible. Just as with magic or folkways, he could locate the origin point of contemporary religious practice in the ancient world and so make an ever-stronger case for the systematic and widespread survival of an entire ancient belief system almost into the present day. This 'almost', however, represented a crucial and traumatic discontinuity. When drawing up the title page for the first section of the *Remaines*, Aubrey had headed it with a charged epigraph from the Roman historian Quintus Curtius: 'nothing is so efficacious for ruling the multitude as superstition'.[46] At some later point, however, he scored out this Hobbesian interpretation of ritual, replacing it with a very different, albeit equally powerful couplet from Ovid's *Fasti*: 'the rest of the tale I had learned long since in my boyish

---

[45] Erika Rummel, *Erasmus'* Annotations *on the New Testament: From Philologist to Theologian* (Toronto, 1986), 132–4.

[46] 'Nulla res efficacius multitudinem regit, quam superstitio' (BL MS Lansdowne 231, fol. 102r [= Aubrey, *Remaines*, 6]), quoting Quintus Curtius Rufus, *Historiae*, IV.x.7. Aubrey mistakenly attributed the tag to Livy, rather than Quintus Curtius, probably due to the presence of a similar passage in the former author. Livy, describing the reign of Numa Pompilius, wrote that 'omnium primum, rem ad multitudinem imperitam et illis saeculis rudem efficacissimam, deorum metum iniciendum ratus est'—'he thought the very first thing to do, as being the most efficacious with a populace which was ignorant and, in those early days, uncivilized, was to imbue them with the fear of Heaven' (Livy, *Historia*, I.xix.5). A note by Jan Gruter in Johann Friedrich Gronovius's edition of Livy glosses Numa's actions with a reference to the passage in Quintus Curtius, among others, and may be the source of Aubrey's confusion (see Livy, *Historiarum quod extat*, 3 vols., ed. Gronovius [Amsterdam, 1665], i. 41). Aubrey's own copy of this edition, heavily annotated, is lacking its first volume (Livy, *Historiarum quod extat*, 3 vols., ed. Gronovius [Amsterdam, 1678], Bodleian Library Ashmole D 23–4, signed on the title page of D 24, 'Musaeo Ashmoleano dedit V. C. Joannes Aubrey').

years, yet not on that account may I pass it over in silence'.[47] At the heart of the *Remaines* was an older man remembering the world of his childhood. Throughout the text there are passages which begin 'when I was a little boy (before the Civill warres)', 'when I was a Boy in North Wilts (before the late Civill-warres)', 'even to my remembrance when I was a youth', and similar expressions of personal distance and recollection.[48] These childhood memories could also expand to include older, familial ones. In the *Remaines* and elsewhere Aubrey often recalled things he had evidently heard from his grandfather Isaac Lyte, noting in one place that 'the Shop-keepers in my Grandfathers time used to reckon with Counters' or that 'when my grandfather went to schoole at Yatton-Keynell (neer Easton-Piers) Mr. Camden came to see the church, and particularly tooke notice of a little painted-glasse-windowe in the chancell'.[49] Aubrey's childhood and the stories of older family members anchored him in the recent past.

But that past was lost forever. It is no accident that Aubrey's recollections beginning 'when I was a Boy' were almost always paired with the heavy parenthesis 'before the Civill warres'. Again and again he pressed gingerly at the open wound left by the conflict, sometimes tiptoeing around the moment of loss, as when he wrote of carved representations of the Trinity, 'I have seen many of these before the rage & zeale of the Civil wars', or facing it head on as when he wrote of one location-specific tradition 'in the late warres this Howse was burned downe by the Soldiers: and the Custome of Supping is yet discontinued'.[50] The Civil Wars were a moment of stark discontinuity, in which houses were burned, traditions abandoned, and the whole mental and physical landscape of England profoundly disturbed. The only equivalent period of disruption in his larger narratives of European history was the 'comeing in of the Gothes', but even that is more often presented as a moment of transformation than of unremitting, bleak loss.[51] With this in mind, Aubrey's otherwise metaphorical statement that 'Printing and Gunpowder have frighted away Robin-good-fellow' acquires a darker, more literal meaning.[52] What on one level was a statement about the displacement of an older knowledge tradition by a newer one, becomes, on another level, a recognition of violent cultural loss.

---

[47] 'Cetera iam pridem didici puerilibus annis, non tamen idcirco praetereunda mihi' (BL MS Lansdowne 231, fol. 102r [= Aubrey, *Remaines*, 6]), quoting Ovid, *Fasti*, VI. 417–18.
[48] BL MS Lansdowne 231, fols. 109v, 111r, 178r, 205v, and *passim*.
[49] BL MS Lansdowne 231, fol. 178r (= Aubrey, *Remaines*, 124); *Brief Lives*, i. 146–7.
[50] BL MS Lansdowne 231, fols. 168v, 188r (= Aubrey, *Remaines*, 105, 138).
[51] BL MS Lansdowne 231, fol. 176v.
[52] BL MS Lansdowne 231, fol. 140v (= Aubrey, *Remaines*, 68).

The *Remaines*, then, was a work rooted in memory and trauma, especially the memory and trauma of childhood and youth. Aubrey believed he was capturing a vanishing tradition, and that if he did not record it the same fate would befall it as had befallen other 'matters of Antiquitie': 'as with the light after sun-sett—at which time, clear; by and by, comes the crepusculum; then, totall darknes'.[53] At the same time, however, he remained alert to the survival of these traditions, especially amongst marginal figures: women, children, and the poor. Aubrey noted that 'the Schoolboies in the West: still religiously observe St Nicholas day' and that 'little Children have a custome, when it raines to Sing, or charme away the Raine'.[54] His own childhood memories of tradition became associated with the traditions of children across time. Closely tied to this was a female oral tradition, exemplified for Aubrey by the songs and ballads, often historical in content, sung to him as a child by his nurse, Katherine Bushell.[55] Elsewhere in the *Remaines* he made the point more explicitly that female oral culture was an ancient repository of memory and tradition:

> in the old ignorant times, before woomen were Readers, the history was handed downe from mother to daughter, &c: and W. Malmesburiensis picks up his history from the time of Ven: Bede to his time out of old Songs . . . so my Nurse had the History from the Conquest downe to Carl. I. in Ballad.[56]

Old wives' tales might no longer be as 'ingeniose' as once they were, but they and the oral culture from which they derived had a long and by no means undistinguished history, reaching back to William of Malmesbury and, ultimately, to the ancient world. 'The old time' could be both a fragile memory and a living recollection.[57]

---

[53] Bodleian MS Aubrey 9, fol. 29r (= Aubrey, 'Hobbes', i. 18).

[54] BL MS Lansdowne 231, fols. 121r, 221v (= Aubrey, *Remaines*, 40, 180).

[55] See, for example, BL MS Lansdowne 231, fol. 143r (= Aubrey, *Remaines*, 70). The name of Aubrey's nurse survives in a marginal annotation at Bodleian MS Top. Gen. C. 25, fol. 200bv (for its context see Aubrey, *Three Prose Works*, 444–5).

[56] BL MS Lansdowne 231, fol. 141r (= Aubrey, *Remaines*, 68). Aubrey was, however, incorrect in thinking that Katherine Bushell's ballad inheritance was solely oral. Robert A. Schwegler identified 'the History from the Conquest' as the well-known *Wandering Jew's Chronicle*, first published about 1634, and the ballad of Fair Rosamund, which Aubrey mentions elsewhere, also had a print origin (Schwegler, 'Oral Tradition and Print: Domestic Performance in Renaissance England', *Journal of American Folklore* 93 [1980]: 435–7). For the complex publishing history of the *Wandering Jew's Chronicle* see the electronic archive edited by Giles Bergel, <http://wjc.bodleian.ox.ac.uk/index.html> (accessed 13 January 2016).

[57] BL MS Lansdowne 231, fol. 177r (= Aubrey, *Remaines*, 121). This point is discussed at length by Dragstra, 'Readers', 41–53.

HETERODOX ANTIQUITIES

Aubrey's manuscripts were read, added to, and copied by a wide circle of friends including John Evelyn, Anthony Wood, Thomas Gale, Edward Lhuyd, and others. The *Remaines* was exceptional even in this context, however, for two significant overlays of further material inserted into the manuscript in accordance with Aubrey's original design.[58] Leaving aside a series of undated and largely undecipherable pencil notes by John Evelyn, the first evidence of any study of the manuscript is probably that by John Ray, the naturalist, who may have seen it in late 1691 or early 1692. Ray passed it on to Balthasar Gottfried Cramer, a German scholar who was proposed to the Royal Society in 1690 and subsequently transcribed Aubrey's *Naturall Historie of Wiltshire* for the Society.[59] Cramer added a series of notes comparing the customs described by Aubrey with those in and around his native Anhalt-Zerbst in north-central Germany.[60] Cramer's annotations are informative but pedestrian and chiefly consist of 'so do we' sorts of comments. A characteristic example is his expansion upon Aubrey's gloss of two lines from Catullus: 'we have a Custome that when One sneezes every one els putts off his hatt, and bowes, and cries God bless ye Sir'.[61] Cramer added that, 'in Germanie 'tis counted to be very uncivilly done not to say at one's sneezing, God help thee, or salutem'.[62] However, Cramer lacked Aubrey's determination to record unprintable detail, which at times led him into elaborate dances around the point, as when he noted that

[58] The history of the *Remaines'* circulation is given by Buchanan-Brown in Aubrey, *Three Prose Works*, 402–7.

[59] He first appears on 20 January 1671, when he disputed on the subject 'De commodis paupertatis' for a doctorate in law from the University of Basel. In the published copy of his disputation he was described as 'Servestâ Anhaltinus', i.e., a native of the principality of Anhalt-Zerbst in north-central Germany (Cramer, *Disputatio juridica inauguralis de commodis paupertatis... Balthas. Gothofredus Cramerus...* [Basel, 1671]). For some years after 1690 he served as clerk of the Royal Society (cf. the material collected by Buchanan-Brown in Aubrey, *Three Prose Works*, 402–3), and in 1690–1 transcribed Aubrey's *Natural History* (Hunter, *Aubrey*, 89, and see the note at Bodleian MS Aubrey 2, fol. 124a proving the identity of its scribe).

[60] Buchanan-Brown (Aubrey, *Three Prose Works*, 402–3) thought that these notes were written by John Ray, presumably as transcriptions of material supplied by Cramer, but Hunter identified the handwriting with that, known to be in Cramer's hand, in Royal Society MS 92 (the fair copy of Aubrey's *Natural History*) and doubted that Ray had ever seen the *Remaines* (Hunter, *Aubrey*, 161).

[61] BL MS Lansdowne 231, fol. 168r (= Aubrey, *Remaines*, 103). The relevant passage is at Catullus 45.8–9, 'hoc ut dixit, Amor, sinistra, ut ante / dextra, sternuit approbationem' ('As he said this, Love on the left, as before on the right, sneezed goodwill').

[62] BL MS Lansdowne 231, fol. 168r (= Aubrey, *Remaines*, 104).

in Germany...about 50 or 60 yeares since, or not so long...in the
wintertime all the mayds of the Village met together, and brough[t] with
them along their spinning wheel, or distaff, and spun very late in the night,
where then the young men, were not far off, which now is quite abolished by
reason of the great exorbitances they committed.[63]

These exorbitances are not described. Nonetheless, Cramer's contributions are noteworthy as evidence not only of another scholar taking
(or being told to take) an interest in Aubrey's project, but also of that
scholar attempting to insert another modern European folk tradition into
Aubrey's narrative. England was no longer the sole end point of the
ancient tradition; Germany also had a place in its evolution.

At some stage subsequent to Cramer's annotations, the manuscript of
the *Remaines* went astray and, on 27 March 1694, Aubrey wrote to
Edward Lhuyd asking, plaintively, 'have you my MS of Remaines of
Gentilisme? I feare it is too light for the University.'[64] It was probably at
about this time that Aubrey scribbled on a letter from Lhuyd dated
9 January 1694 that 'my Gentilisme would not befitt to leave to the
Critiques of the University. I thinke it is in Mr Tanners custodie.'[65]
Lhuyd attempted to set Aubrey's mind to rest, confirming that the
manuscript was safe in his possession, and assuring him that it was 'very
curious' and that while 'we have not many at present in the University that
prosecute that study very far...[we] may well hope that such collections
will make more'.[66] Aubrey's worries over what might happen should the
'Critiques of the University' obtain his manuscript may have stemmed
from an awareness of its heterodox religious views; criticisms of subjects
such as the Trinity or Christian ritual were hardly fit material to leave in
unknown hands. Equally, however, he may have believed its folk content
made the *Remaines* unfit to be deposited at Oxford, as he was undoubtedly
aware of the larger distaste for folk tradition within the Anglican scholarly
establishment (where it was labelled papist superstition better abolished
than studied).

Another hint that Aubrey saw something potentially subversive in the
Remaines comes from his lending of the manuscript to John Toland, who
had it in his possession in October 1694.[67] Although not yet sent packing
from Oxford on account of his 'little religion', Toland was already
developing a reputation as a learned and dangerous freethinker, fresh

---

[63] BL MS Lansdowne 231, fol. 124r (= Aubrey, *Remaines*, 46).
[64] Bodleian MS. Ashmole 1814, fol. 109r.
[65] Bodleian MS. Aubrey 12, fol. 251.
[66] Bodleian MS. Aubrey 12, fol. 255r.
[67] Bodleian MS. Ashmole 1814, fol. 117r.

from the pedagogical benches of Friedrich Spanheim and Jean Le Clerc and eager to make his mark on British erudition.[68] If Aubrey had been looking for someone who would not cavil at, and might indeed sympathize with, his Hobbesian interpretation of religious custom, the young Toland was his man. Unfortunately, no evidence of Toland's engagement with the *Remaines* survives, although he did make use of the *Monumenta Britannica*—he and Aubrey also shared a fascination with Druids—and praised Aubrey in his subsequent writings on ancient Britain.[69] However, Aubrey's association with Toland seems to highlight an awareness—and perhaps acceptance—of the heterodoxy of his own endeavours.

Regardless of whether Aubrey believed the *Remaines* was heterodox or otherwise theologically unsafe, he appears to have wished it to be organized and published from an early date. Thomas Tanner, writing on 16 May 1693, had assured Aubrey that 'if we get [the *Remaines*] among us, we will quickly put it into a Method'.[70] The 'us' mentioned here were perhaps the circle surrounding men like Edmund Gibson, editor of the 1695 *Britannia*, and George Hickes, the Anglo-Saxonist, a possibility which is strengthened by the manuscript's subsequent deposition with White Kennett, a young clergyman in the circle of Gibson, Hickes, Tanner, and other nonjuring Oxford antiquaries and philologists.[71] As well as this connection, Kennett had probably also been recommended to Aubrey's notice as another assistant of Anthony Wood in the research for the *Athenae Oxonienses*.[72] In either case, Kennett was sitting on the *Remaines* by the winter of 1695–6, having seemingly promised to 'methodize' it in the wake of publishing his *Parochial Antiquities Attempted in the History of Ambrosden, Burchester, and Other Adjacent Parts of Oxford and Bucks*.[73] Aubrey wrote on 26 January and again on 12 November

[68] The oft-quoted character of Toland as 'a man of fine parts, great learning, and little religion' comes from an anonymous letter addressed to him and dated at Oxford, 4 May 1694, contemporaneous with his interactions with Aubrey (*A Collection of Several Pieces of Mr. John Toland, Now First Publish'd from his Original Manuscripts*, 2 vols. [London, 1726], ii. 295). For its wider context see Justin Champion, *Republican Learning: John Toland and the Crisis of Christian Culture, 1696–1722* (Manchester, 2003), 69–70.

[69] John Toland, 'The History of the Druids', in *Collection of Several Pieces*, i. 112.

[70] Bodleian MS. Aubrey 13, fol. 199r.   [71] *ODNB, s.n.*

[72] For Kennett see G. V. Bennett, *White Kennett, 1660–1728, Bishop of Peterborough: Study in the Political and Ecclesiastical History of the Early Eighteenth Century* (London, 1957); *ODNB, s.n.* Additional evidence of Wood's role as intermediary comes from a note in his diary for 26 April 1695 that he was at the Fleur de luce in the company of Aubrey, Kennett, Thomas Tanner, Nicholas Martin, and a Mr Colling (*The Life and Times of Anthony Wood, Antiquary, of Oxford, 1632–1695*, 5 vols., ed. Andrew Clark [Oxford, 1891–1900], iii. 483).

[73] White Kennett, *Parochial Antiquities Attempted in the History of Ambrosden, Burchester, and Other Adjacent Parts in the Counties of Oxford and Bucks* (Oxford, 1695).

1696 to Lhuyd, asking the latter to enquire of Kennett whether 'he haz donne anything as to my Remains of Gentilisme, or whether he will' and requesting that, if not, it be returned and the project turned over to his old friend Walter Charleton.[74] Charleton was in many ways a likelier Aristarchus for Aubrey than Kennett. He had long been a close friend and 'high admirer' of Hobbes and his own *Darknes of Atheism* (1652) owed much of its natural theology to the works of Hobbes, among others.[75] That Aubrey considered him at all suggests that he thought the Hobbesian cast of the *Remaines* was one of its key characteristics and wished to see it completed by someone of the same philosophical bent.

At Aubrey's death, however, the *Remaines* was still in Kennett's hands. At some time around 1695–7 Kennett had begun, not just to 'methodize' the *Remaines*, but to incorporate it in its entirety into a projected *History of Custom* upon which he had commenced research. This project was never completed, however, and survives only as a few folios of notes. Fragments from the *Remaines* did make their way into a manuscript revision of the *Parochial Antiquities* and Kennett's unpublished *Etymological Collections*, showing that it continued to be a part of the younger antiquary's working library, but it was not until the nineteenth century that substantial portions of the manuscript were published for the first time.[76]

The *Remaines* is a complex text, existing across generic and topical divisions. Superficially it is part of the larger trend in early modern scholarship which used classical religion and culture as lenses through which to understand the culturally other, but in Aubrey's case this was dramatically complicated by his choice to turn those lenses upon his own culture. His willingness to take a Hobbesian view of Christian religious practice confirmed the text's place within the increasingly sceptical narratives of religious development which had arisen alongside comparatism, but also established it within an existing tradition of sceptical English

---

[74] Bodleian MSS. Ashmole 1814, fol. 118r; Ashmole 1829, fol. 78r.

[75] Aubrey, 'Hobbes', i. 371; Walter Charleton, *The Darknes of Atheism Dispelled by the Light of Nature: A Physico-Theologicall Treatise* (London, 1652). For Charleton and his ideas see Eric Lewis, 'Walter Charleton and Early Modern Eclecticism', *Journal of the History of Ideas* 62 (2001): 651–64; *ODNB*, *s.n.*; Lindsay Sharp, 'Walter Charleton's Early Life, 1620–1659, and Relationship to Natural Philosophy in Mid-Seventeenth Century England', *Annals of Science* 30 (1973): 311–40. See also his notes towards an essay on the 'Fundamentals of Natural Religion', Bodleian MS Smith 13, fols. 89ff.

[76] For Kennett's notes on folklore see BL MSS Lansdowne 1033 and Lansdowne 1039, fols. 8–19, and for his engagement with the *Remaines* see Aubrey, *Three Prose Works*, 404–7. A brief discussion of Kennett's philological work appears in Javier Ruano-García, 'Towards an Understanding of Joseph Wright's Sources: White Kennett's *Parochial Antiquities* (1695) and the *English Dialect Dictionary*', in *Middle and Modern English Corpus Linguistics: A Multi-Dimensional Approach*, ed. Manfred Markus, Yoko Iyeiri, Reinhard Heuberger, and Emil Chamson (Amsterdam, 2012), 241–56.

scholarship, exemplified not just by Hobbes but by John Selden's *Table-Talk* and the anti-Trinitarian scholarship of polymaths from Richard Bentley to Isaac Newton. Finally, as well as being a work of antiquarian erudition the *Remaines* was a poignant testament to Aubrey's own sense of the traumatic cultural loss brought about by the Civil Wars. Like the *Brief Lives*, the *Remaines* was a personal as well as a general act of antiquarianism, a recovery of the details of Aubrey's own childhood and the lives of his parents and grandparents just as much as it was of older traditions and folkways.

Above all, it was a text asserting cultural continuities between the ancient past and the contemporary present. In the *Monumenta* Aubrey had tried to relate the seemingly distant and unfathomable world of Roman Britain to Restoration England by reading the landscape, literally mapping the ancient past onto the present in his map of southern Britain, and tracing the development of architecture from the even more distant Babel to the work of Inigo Jones and Christopher Wren. In the *Remaines* he followed the same practices and built analogical links between the fragmentary visions of Greek and Roman life in a dozen classical texts and the folk culture which he had seen around him since his youth to make yet another case for contemporary England's inextricable ties to the ancient past.

6

A New Philology

Toponyms and Comparative Linguistics in Aubrey's Late Works

At first glance a study of Aubrey's philology might seem like an oxymoron. Unlike many of his contemporaries he never edited a text, prepared a dictionary, or proposed a conjectural emendation. Nor did his studies of pre-Roman and Roman Britain fit easily into the intellectual frameworks of a generation of English philologists who were increasingly focused on the exotic, whether Greek, Arabic, or Anglo-Saxon. However, Aubrey was nonetheless a philologist. In his manuscript tracts *The Proportion of the Several Languages Ingredient of our English* and *Interpretation of Villare Anglicanum* and in his interactions with younger scholars he applied philological approaches to the same problem he had taken up in the *Remaines of Gentilisme*: the ethnic and cultural origins of seventeenth-century England. The fragmentary, scattered nature of this material has caused it to be largely overlooked, but when examined as a whole it reveals that Aubrey's final years were increasingly dominated by a fascination with the mutability of language and the ways in which that mutability could be interrogated to reveal the shifting nature of the ancient cultural landscape. These fascinations aligned him with an evolving tradition which began in Restoration Cambridge and reached its culmination in the work of Aubrey's friend and younger contemporary Edward Lhuyd, a tradition in which Aubrey played a central, though subsequently forgotten, role.

THOMAS GALE AND THE *ANTONINE ITINERARY*

On 6 December 1677 the Royal Society saw one antiquary, the traveller George Wheler, proposed as a member, and three more, Robert Plot,

Thomas Smith, and Thomas Gale admitted.[1] The last of these, Dr Gale, had already had a meteoric career as a fellow and tutor at Trinity College, Cambridge, followed by a brief stint as Regius Professor of Greek there before becoming High Master of St Paul's School in 1672, doctor of divinity at his alma mater in 1675, and prebend of St Paul's Cathedral in 1676.[2] Gale was steeped in Restoration-era classical scholarship and shared his contemporaries' fascination with Hellenistic Greek texts, particularly mythological and rhetorical works. By 1677 he had already published three volumes, each consisting of editions of multiple classical texts, including the imposing 1675 *Historiae poeticae scriptores antiqui*, which included his 'Dissertation on Mythological Writers', a substantial essay placing his work in the tradition of Scaliger and Selden, as well as 151 pages of explanatory notes and 18 genealogical tables illustrating the works edited.[3]

No letters between Gale and Aubrey survive—there may not have been any, if they simply met each other in London—but their collaborations can be reconstructed from the textual traces each left in the other's archive. If shared membership in the Royal Society was not enough, it seems likely that they must have known each other by the time Gale proposed Johan Heysig—a visiting Swedish scholar and friend of Aubrey's—for membership in the Royal Society on 23 November 1681.[4] This chronology dovetails closely with Gale's growing interest in medieval British texts; already in his 1678 edition of the *De mysteriis* of Iamblichus his notes include references to Gerald of Wales and the early history of post-classical Britain.[5] Subsequently this led him to a dramatic volte-face in his scholarship, leaving the world of Greek texts behind and editing two major folio editions of medieval chronicles, the *Historiae Anglicanae scriptores quinque* of 1687 and the *Historiae Britanniae, Saxonicae, Anglo-Danicae, Scriptores XV* of 1691.[6] At some point between the publication of these latter two volumes Gale gave Aubrey a manuscript list of his works, both published

---

[1] Thomas Birch, *The History of the Royal Society of London for Improving of Natural Knowledge...*, 4 vols. (London, 1756–7), iii. 359.

[2] For Gale see *ODNB*, *s.n.*, and D. C. Douglas, *English Scholars, 1660–1730*, 2nd edn. (London, 1951), 170–4.

[3] *Historiae poeticae scriptores antiqui...accessere breves notae & indices necessarii*, ed. Thomas Gale (Paris, 1675). The other two works were *Opuscula mythologica, ethica et physica* (Cambridge, 1671), which contained reprints of earlier editions with the occasional preface or improvement by Gale, and *Rhetores selecti* (Oxford, 1676), the centrepiece of which was an edition of the *De elocutione* of pseudo-Demetrius of Phalerum.

[4] Birch, *History*, iv. 104. See William Poole and Kelsey Jackson Williams, 'A Swede in Restoration Oxford: Gothic Patriots, Swedish Books, English Scholars', *Lias* 39 (2012): 19.

[5] Iamblichus, *De mysteriis liber*, ed. Thomas Gale (Oxford, 1678), 219.

[6] Thomas Gale, ed., *Historiae Anglicanae scriptores quinque* (Oxford, 1687) and *Historiae Britanniae, Saxonicae, Anglo-Danicae, Scriptores XV* (Oxford, 1691).

and in preparation, which shows the full extent of his ambitions.[7] From then on, aside from a projected edition of the *Naumachica* (a tenth-century CE Byzantine tract on naval warfare), Gale's projects were all British in focus, including new editions of the Venerable Bede and Matthew Paris, a collection of laws from Ethelbert to Edward I, a history of the reign of Edward II, a baronage of England in three parts, and an edition of the British section of the so-called *Antonine Itinerary*.[8]

Whether this change in focus is in any way indebted to Aubrey is unknown, but the two men certainly worked closely together on these topics during the 1680s and 1690s. Beginning in December 1692, Aubrey's letters began to be directed to Gale's London address, at least while Aubrey was resident in the city, with correspondence sent to him there from that date until as late as 31 July 1695 marked 'to be left with Doctor Gale'.[9] It may have been during this time of shared post, shared company, and perhaps a shared library, that a series of annotations were made by Aubrey in Gale's copy of the 1607 edition of Camden's *Britannia*.[10] Besides extensive annotations by Gale, largely concerning ancient British toponyms, there is a note on the recto of the flyleaf, unmistakeably in Aubrey's hand, reading 'A ms history of England in the possesion of James Earl of Abingdon. Anno.....Henrici III. a very great dearth of corn sold for...' This was evidently related both to Aubrey's interest in economic history, which manifested itself elsewhere in the *Stromata*, and to Gale's collection and publication of medieval histories and chronicles.[11]

More substantial, however, were Gale's footprints in Aubrey's works. Gale contributed extensive annotations to Aubrey's *Monumenta Britannica*, his *Perambulation of Surrey*, and his *Naturall Historie of Wiltshire*, as well as making a transcription, now lost, of the *Monumenta*.[12] His

---

[7] Aubrey, *Lives*, i. 8–11, ii. 766–7.

[8] Gale's heavily annotated copy of Matthew Paris, *Historia major*, ed. William Wats (London, 1640) is now Bodleian Gough Gen. Top. 232, but the other never-completed projects are known only from their mention in Aubrey, *Lives*, i. 8–11. For the *Antonine Itinerary* see p. 139.

[9] Bodleian MSS Aubrey 12, fols. 136–7, Wood F 45, fol. 208.

[10] William Camden, *Britannia*... (London, 1607), subsequently purchased by Richard Gough at the Gale sale and now Bodleian Gough Gen. Top. 51.

[11] James Bertie, Earl of Abingdon, the husband of Aubrey's cousin Eleanora Lee, took him in at various points after his bankruptcy, opened his manuscript collection to him, and desired transcripts of the *Remaines* and the *Monumenta* for his own use (Hunter, *Aubrey*, 88; George E. Cokayne *Complete Peerage*, 13 vols. in 14, ed. Vicary Gibbs [London, 1910–98], i. 45–6). The manuscript history mentioned by Aubrey has not been identified.

[12] For Gale's transcription of the *Monumenta*, see Chapter 2; for the several annotators of Aubrey's manuscripts see Hunter, *Aubrey*, 88. It is perhaps significant that the three works Gale annotated—*Surrey*, the *Naturall Historie*, and the *Monumenta*—were those of which Aubrey made fair copies between 1689 and 1692 (see Hunter, *Aubrey*, 87).

annotations were particularly heavy in the *Monumenta*, where he drew upon his already extensive studies of the *Antonine Itinerary* and Romano-British toponyms to correct and amplify Aubrey's manuscript. A characteristic example is his marginal gloss of Aubrey's equation of the Roman 'Avone' with Bristol, 'In Antoninus Avone is Bristow, Trajectus is the passe over Severn. Here hath happened a misplacing of these two names as it doeth often happen in Antonine.'[13] Elsewhere he was concerned with more fully contextualizing Aubrey's records of archaeological discoveries, noting against a passage on mosaic floors that '[t]hese pavements often found in Cityes. These pavements were often found in Bathes. These Pavements served for bounds, called termini tessellati [pavement borders].'[14] His notes were sufficiently expansive that the manuscript of the *Monumenta* which Aubrey envisaged, optimistically, as compositor-ready copy, stated that it was 'Illustrated with Notes of Thomas Gale, D.D and John Evelyn Esquier'.[15]

Gale's philological comments on British toponyms, which make up a large part of his annotations to the *Monumenta*, were derived directly from his own project to re-edit the British section of the *Antonine Itinerary*. The *Itinerary* was a text dating possibly to the third century CE which recorded stations and the distances between them along the main roads of the Roman Empire; as such it offered a unique snapshot of later imperial Britain complete with a geographical framework which, theoretically, allowed for the equation of classical toponyms with modern locations.[16] The only catch was that the surviving manuscripts were extremely corrupt in their readings, offering a tantalizing puzzle to any would-be editor. By Gale's time this had already been attempted more than once. Abraham Ortelius had edited the complete *Itinerary* in 1600 and the philologist and antiquary William Burton had prepared an English commentary on the British section of the *Itinerary* which was posthumously published in 1658.[17] By this latter date textual scholarship on the document was already sufficiently advanced for Burton to point to previous editions and corrections by Aldus Manutius, William Harrison, Josias Simler, and Jerome Surita.[18]

---

[13] Aubrey, *Monumenta*, i. 465.   [14] Aubrey, *Monumenta*, ii. 935.
[15] Aubrey, *Monumenta*, i. 3.
[16] Otto Cuntz, ed., *Itineraria Romana*, vol. 1: *Itineraria Antonini Augusti et Burdigalense* (Leipzig, 1929); A. L. F. Rivet and Kenneth Jackson, 'The British Section of the Antonine Itinerary', *Britannia* 1 (1970): 34–82.
[17] Abraham Ortelius, ed., *Itinerarium Antonini Augusti, et Burdigalense* (Cologne, 1600); William Burton, *A Commentary on Antoninus his Itinerary, or Journies of the Romane Empire, so far as it Concerneth Britain* (London, 1658).
[18] Burton, *Commentary on Antoninus*, *passim*.

When Gale began work on the *Itinerary* he was entering an already well-trodden field and could, perhaps, lament at the difficulty of making any new contribution to the study of an already exhaustively interrogated text. However, his edition, posthumously edited and published by his son Roger in 1709, nonetheless broke new ground.[19] As well as the *Itinerary*, Gale also included in his work the *Ravenna Cosmography*, an eighth-century CE list of place names from across Europe and Asia, based upon the 1688 edition by the Maurist scholar David-Placide Porcheron.[20] Once again, however, the *Cosmography*, which Gale knew in two variant forms deriving from Vatican and Bibliothèque Nationale de France manuscripts, presented significant textual problems on the most basic level. Gale attempted to systematically restore accurate readings across both texts, with a view towards recovering a detailed understanding of the toponyms of Roman and post-Roman Britain.[21]

PLACE NAMES AND THE LANGUAGE
OF ANCIENT BRITAIN

Gale's study of ancient toponyms was significant not just for the ways in which it informed his annotation of the *Monumenta Britannica*, but also for the blueprint it provided Aubrey when he subsequently came to attempt his own study of toponyms within the context of ancient linguistic change. Gale, focusing on recovering accurate manuscript readings, had dealt with linguistic change only incidentally, but both his work and that of Aubrey derived from a longer history of linguistic study. Earlier schools of thought had proposed a predetermined relationship between objects and meaning in the tradition of Plato's *Cratylus*, an understanding of which could allow the proper names of places, people, and things to be

---

[19] Thomas Gale, *Antonini iter Britanniarum commentariis illustratum . . . opus posthumum*, ed. Roger Gale (London, 1709).

[20] David-Placide Porcheron, ed., *Anonymi Ravennatis qui circa saeculum VII. vixit de geographia libri quinque* (Paris, 1688). Gale's edition included marginal directions to the equivalent pages in Porcheron's edition. See also Bodleian Gough Gen. Top. 81, a copy of Porcheron owned by William Stukeley which may have a Galian provenance and contains manuscript additions of variant place names.

[21] Subsequent generations of scholars were unimpressed. The biography of Gale in the *Biographia Britannica* caustically notes that 'this is the most exceptionable of Dr Gale's works: for, out of an affectation for saying something new, he hath displaced most of the ancient stations, without sufficient authority; and hath indulged himself a great deal too much in fancy and conjectures' (*Biographia Britannica* [London, 1747], iii. 2076).

read as a historical palimpsest.[22] Such theories had declined in favour, however, by the early seventeenth century, and by the end of the century there was a growing recognition of the relationships between languages and the ways in which toponyms could reflect the linguistic past of a place. In England, this form of linguistic and antiquarian enquiry had been popularized first by Camden and subsequently by the Gresham professor of astronomy, Edward Brerewood, whose 1614 *Enquiries touching the diversity of languages* articulated a theory of internal linguistic change which historicized the development of Greek and Latin as well as hinting at the possibility of larger, more dramatic linguistic changes which could provide an alternative narrative to the biblical confusion of tongues.[23]

When Aubrey composed his *Interpretation of Villare Anglicanum*, he built upon these gradual shifts in early modern linguistic theory and attempted to provide a comprehensive etymological dictionary of English, Scottish, and Irish toponyms and their origins, setting works like Gale's upon firm and systematic etymological foundations.[24] Aubrey had long been interested in Welsh and its relationship to modern English, first 'perusing' John David Rhys's Welsh grammar in the 1650s, and obtaining a Welsh–English word list from his London-based friend Meredith Lloyd in 1675.[25] In 1680 he even went so far as to ask the former Royal Society printer, Octavian Pulleyn, then in Rome, to search the Vatican Library for a manuscript allegedly by the late antique British historian Gildas, apparently in the hope that it could be used to shed light on linguistic issues.[26] This pattern of philological engagement culminated in a decision in the 1680s to comb Henry Spelman's catalogue of English toponyms, the *Villare Anglicanum*, for 'the small Remnant of British words, that have escaped the Deluge of the Saxon Conquest; and to interpret them by

[22] For this theory and the history of such studies in the period immediately before Aubrey, see Angus Vine, 'Etymology, Names and the Search for Origins: Deriving the Past in Early Modern England', *The Seventeenth Century* 21 (2006): 1–21.
[23] Edward Brerewood, *Enquiries Touching the Diversity of Languages*... (London, 1614); Vine, 'Etymology, Names and the Search for Origins', *passim*.
[24] The *Interpretation* is now Bodleian MS Aubrey 5. See also Gillian Fellows-Jensen, 'John Aubrey, Pioneer Onomast?', *Nomina* 23 (2000): 89–106.
[25] Bodleian MS Aubrey 5, fols. 4–5 (Lloyd's word list), 17v (Rhys). The grammar was John David Rhys, *Cambrobrytannicae Cymraecaeue linguae institutiones et rudimenta accuratè, & (quantùm fieri potuit) succinctè & compendiosè conscripta* (London, 1592), a copy of which Aubrey donated to the Royal Society Library on 15 December 1670 (John Buchanan-Brown, 'The Books Presented to the Royal Society By John Aubrey, F.R.S.', *Notes and Records of the Royal Society* 28 [1974]: 168, 181–2).
[26] See Pulleyn's letters to Aubrey, dated 15/25 May 1680 (Bodleian MS Aubrey 13, fol. 166r–v) and 2/12 November 1680 (Bodleian MS Aubrey 13, fol. 165r–v), and a subsequent note at Bodleian MS Aubrey 5, fol. 19av, which suggests that he planned to compare the language of the manuscript with modern Scottish and Irish.

the help of Dr Davies Welsh Dictionary' and the assistance of a Welsh-
speaking acquaintance, Mr Evans.[27] He later expanded this to include 'the
hard obsolete Saxon words' which lay behind other toponyms. By the time
he came to write the preface to the *Interpretation*, on 31 October 1687, he
envisaged an etymological dictionary of place names that would, if completed, cover every significant toponym in England.[28]

For Aubrey, linguistic traces—like the remnants of folklore in his
Remaines of Gentilisme—were indicators of previous cultural exchange or
colonization. Though he did not explicitly state the purpose of the
Interpretation, his ultimate aim seems to have been to use the etymologies
he intended to recover to shed light on pre-Saxon Britain. Unlike many of
his other antiquarian projects, the *Interpretation* gave surprisingly little
attention to the Roman presence in Britain, with Latin being marginalized
as a possible origin for toponyms, despite a repetition of his assertion that
'[t]he Romans were settled here, & mixt with the Britons . . . . hundred
yeares'.[29] Instead, Aubrey highlighted the role of 'British' as spoken in the
classical word, pleading for its historical importance within the framework
of learning,

> this ancient Language (that is now crept into Co[rners] and disesteemed) was
> heretofore the <u>current</u> Speech over a[ll] <u>Brittaine</u> & <u>Gaule</u>: from the <u>Orcades</u>
> and the northern Isles, to the <u>Appenine</u>-hills . . . and though it be out of
> fashion; is in it selfe, as Significant & copious as a[ny] of the modern
> languages, which the Learned that understand [it] doe assert.[30]

This concern with the ancient British language led Aubrey to discuss
more generally the development and interaction of languages in the British
Isles. He was under no illusions that etymologies could be straightforwardly derived, one from Welsh, or another from German, observing that:

> Graines of allowance are [to] be given to these Etymologies. There were (no
> doubt) severall Dialects in <u>Britaine</u>, as we see there are now [in] <u>England</u>:
> they did not speake alike all over this great Isle: just as the South,
> or North-Welchmen doe now; who also diff[er . . .] Besides a thousand
> yeares & (a foraigne language be[. . .]setled) will make a great alteration in

---

[27] Bodleian MS Aubrey 5, fol. 17r; Sir Henry Spelman, *Villare Anglicum, or, a View of
the Townes of England* (London, 1656; 2nd edn., 1678). The dictionary is John Davies,
Antiquae linguae Britannicae . . . (London, 1621; 2nd edn., 1632), but Mr Evans, described
as 'of the Bridge-house at London', has not been identified.
[28] For the interpretation of Saxon words, Aubrey intended to use Abraham Wheelocke's
Anglo-Saxon dictionary, presumably a manuscript copy, as it had been left incomplete at
the latter's death (*ODNB, s.n.*).
[29] Bodleian MS Aubrey 5, fol. 19ar. The ellipsis is Aubrey's.
[30] Bodleian MS Aubrey 5, fol. 17v.

pronunciation which will much disguise words, as we well know how names
of men & Places are so by the Vulgar.[31]

When Aubrey referred to 'British' he did not, then, equate the term
unproblematically with modern Welsh. Instead he recognized that, from
an ancient beginning of multiple dialects, the language had subsequently
evolved, not only by the intrusion of another language through conquest
(here he meant Anglo-Saxon, rather than Norman French), but also, more
subtly, by gradual internal change. This echoed Brerewood's discussion of
Byzantine Greek earlier in the century. It was certainly different from the
classical Greek dialects, Brerewood had concluded, but that difference
could not be attributed to foreign invasion or settlement, 'which is to me a
certaine argument, that it had no violent nor sodaine beginning... but
hath gotten into their language, by the ordinarie change, which time and
many common occasions... are wont to bring'.[32]

Aubrey, in attributing linguistic difference to a combination of gradual
change and foreign influence, was analysing his topic in line with the most
recent scholarship and it is unsurprising that he positioned himself as
engaged in the same activity as 'Buxhornius [who] has made... the
Interpretation of the names of severall Townes, and Rivers in France'.[33]
Aubrey was referring to the Dutch scholar Marcus Zuerius van Boxhorn's
1654 *Originum Gallicarum*.[34] In the *Originum* Boxhorn had argued for a
kinship between ancient British and Gaulish and for the status of Breton
and Welsh as their closest living descendants.[35] This was only one portion
of a larger project arguing for a single, 'Scythian' origin for all European
languages, but a crucial one, as Boxhorn believed the ancient Celtic
languages were amongst the earliest exemplars of his theorized 'Scythian'.
As such, he took pains in the *Originum* to argue against the Hebrew origin

[31] Bodleian MS Aubrey 5, fol. 17r. The edge of the page is illegible.
[32] Brerewood, *Enquiries*, 10.   [33] Bodleian MS Aubrey 5, fol. 17v.
[34] Marcus Zuerius van Boxhorn, *Originum Gallicarum liber* (Amsterdam, 1654).
Aubrey may have been introduced to Boxhorn's work by his friend Meredith Lloyd, who
wrote approvingly of it to the Welsh antiquary Robert Vaughan of Hengwrt as early as May
1655 (Prys Morgan, 'Boxhorn and the Welsh: Some Cambro-Dutch Contacts in the
Seventeenth Century', *Dutch Crossing* 24 [2000]: 188, citing NLW Peniarth MS 275,
fol. 7). However, his close friend Edmund Wylde had recommended Boxhorn to Edward
Lhuyd, which may instead suggest that Aubrey became acquainted with the *Originum* in
Wylde's library (Bodleian MS Aubrey 12, fol. 240r, letter from Lhuyd to Aubrey, 12
February 1687?).
[35] Boxhorn, *Originum, passim*; cf. also Kees Dekker, *Origins of Old Germanic Studies in
the Low Countries* (Leiden, 1999), 208–15; Prys Morgan, 'Boxhorn, Leibniz, and the
Welsh', *Studia Celtica* 8/9 (1973–4): 220–8; Morgan, 'Boxhorn and the Welsh',
183–190; Toon Van Hal, 'When Quotation Marks Matter: Rhellicanus and Boxhornius
on the Differences between the *lingua Gallica* and the *lingua Germanica*', *Historiographia
Linguistica* 38 (2011): 241–52.

for Welsh which had been proposed by Welsh scholars in the sixteenth century, asserting instead its relationship to the other Celtic languages.[36]

Aubrey accepted Boxhorn's theories, but only up to a point. In referring to the Dutch scholar, he questioned the validity of his linguistic knowledge, insisting that 'no body can doe [such a project] as it should be, but a Welshman, that is master of the French tongue' (why a Frenchman who was also fluent in Welsh was not an option is unclear).[37] More substantially, however, he differed from Boxhorn on the origins of ancient British. He agreed that those who derived Welsh from Hebrew 'forceth it too much, and drawe the thred beyond the Staple', but was more accepting of the similarities between Greek and Welsh.[38] Rather than seeing such concordances as evidence of a single proto-European language, he interpreted them by recourse to the theory of invasive language change:

> I am assured by severall learned Gentlemen of Wales, as Capt: Rob. Pugh è soc: Jesus, Sir Llewellin Jenkins (Secretary of Estate) & Mr Meredith Lloyd, that there are more Greeke words intermixt with the British, than there are Latin. I would have another Sample or Collection to be made of the Greeke words yet remaining in the Welsh: which would afford good Evidence (without being beholding to Historie) that there was a time, when the Greekes had Colonies here.[39]

In making this choice, Aubrey was falling back on earlier theories of linguistic change, particularly the historico-linguistic ideas of Samuel Bochart, who had proposed, on linguistic grounds, that the Phoenicians had had colonies in Britain.[40] In this case, rather than accepting that cultural exchange and internal decay could occur simultaneously, as he had done with the medieval evolution of the Celtic languages, Aubrey seems to have been shutting down the possibility of an internal decay which would allow for a genetic relationship between Welsh and Greek by emphasizing the probability that the Greek loanwords in Welsh were due solely to cultural exchange. His preference for the invasion hypothesis is confirmed by a brief excursus in support of Greek colonization: 'There are severall Persian words mixt with the German, which Shewes that there has

---

[36] Boxhorn, *Originum*, 89–102. In this context see also the discussion of Hebrew in relation to mystical theories of language at Rhodri Lewis, *Language, Mind and Nature: Artificial Languages in England from Bacon to Locke* (Cambridge, 2007), 110–28.

[37] Bodleian MS Aubrey 5, fol. 17v.

[38] Bodleian MS Aubrey 5, fol. 19ar. Aubrey was reacting specifically against Charles Edwards's *Hebraismorum Cambro-Britannicorum specimen honorandis antiquae Britannicae gentis primoribus . . .* (London, 1675).

[39] Bodleian MS Aubrey 5, fol. 19ar.

[40] Samuel Bochart, *Geographia sacra* (Caen, 1646). See Zur Shalev, *Sacred Words and Worlds: Geography, Religion, and Scholarship, 1550–1700* (Leiden, 2012), 180–90.

been an <u>Incursion</u> of them into those northern countryes; but no Historie tells us when: Time and Oblivion have obliterated it.'[41] This is an even more direct attack on Boxhorn, who had refuted the Frisian scholar Bernhardus Furmerius's assertion that Old Frisian (and, by analogy, German) displayed Persian elements.[42]

Aubrey emerges from this aware of the current linguistic theories, but essentially conservative in his outlook. While prepared to accept internal decay as a cause of linguistic change during recorded history, he rejected the idea that such decay could ultimately result in distinct languages and appears to have viewed languages as separate, autochthonous units, which might interact with each other but did not share a common genealogy beyond that caused by Babel.

The care with which Aubrey placed the ancient British language in a larger context might at first seem excessive, given that his work ventured so far beyond the remit of what was intended to be a study of British toponyms, but it would be more accurate to see this prologue as creating a framework within which these toponyms could be successfully interpreted. Aubrey was aware of the extent to which language could evolve, even over a comparatively short period, and recognized the necessity of understanding the development of the British languages through time in order to accurately interpret place names.

EDWARD LHUYD: COLLABORATION AND INHERITANCE

Aubrey prepared the preface of the *Interpretation* in 1687, but the work was still incomplete four years later when he wrote to his then-new acquaintance Edward Lhuyd, keeper of the recently founded Ashmolean Museum in Oxford, telling him that 'there is no body that I know, that is so fitt to goe through with that Designe as your selfe . . . the Taske will be extreme easy to you, and it will be delightfull to ingeniose persons to peruse'.[43]

---

[41] Bodleian MS Aubrey 5, fol. 19ar.

[42] Boxhorn, *Originum*, 87. For an overview of understandings of the relationships between Teutonic languages during the sixteenth and seventeenth centuries see Kees Dekker, *Origins of Old Germanic Studies*, esp. 212 (Boxhorn vs. Furmerius), as well as *Bonaventura Vulcanius, Works and Networks*, ed. Hélène Cazes (Leiden, 2010), and Toon Van Hal, 'A Man of Eight Hearts: Hadrianus Junius and Sixteenth-Century Plurilingualism', in *The Kaleidoscopic Scholarship of Hadrianus Junius (1511–1575): Northern Humanism at the Dawn of the Dutch Golden Age*, ed. Dirk van Miert (Leiden, 2011), 188–213.

[43] Bodleian MS Aubrey 5, fol. 2r.

How had Aubrey come to know the young Welsh scholar and what made him choose Lhuyd as the preferred continuator of his project?

Lhuyd was the illegitimate son of a failed gentry entrepreneur and had gone up to Jesus College, Oxford, in 1682. He quickly became associated with the Oxford Philosophical Society, then headed by Robert Plot, the first keeper of the Ashmolean Museum and an acquaintance of Aubrey's; in 1687 he was appointed Plot's assistant, a position he would hold until he succeeded him as keeper in 1691.[44] Despite their mutual association with Plot, Aubrey and Lhuyd appear to have first met in the house of Aubrey's longtime friend the gentlemanly virtuoso Edmund Wylde in Bloomsbury.[45] Wylde is an enigmatic figure, a 'rich philosopher' according to one contemporary account, who played Maecenas to some of the less financially stable individuals surrounding the Royal Society and 'delighted in nothing more than in showing his multifarious contrivances'.[46] Although it does not survive, he possessed a library known for its rare works on antiquarian and other subjects, which may have led him into acquaintance with the budding antiquary and natural philosopher Lhuyd.[47] Certainly Lhuyd subsequently recalled that it was Wylde who 'was the first that gave me any encouragement to study British Antiquities'.[48]

Lhuyd had already demonstrated his linguistic capabilities by the time Aubrey proposed that he take on the task of continuing the *Interpretation*. In May of 1690 he had penned a peculiar etymological document, apparently under the pseudonym of Meredyth Owen, and sent it to Plot.[49] This was in response to the publication in 1689 of George Hickes's *Institutiones grammaticae Anglo-Saxonicae et Moeso-Gothicae*.[50] Included in Hickes's treatise was the *Etymologicon Britannicum* of Edward Bernard, one of the senior oriental philologists then active in Oxford.[51] Bernard, in

---

[44] *ODNB, s.n.*

[45] Bodleian MS Aubrey 12, fol. 240r is a letter from Lhuyd to Aubrey dated 12 February (by internal evidence 1691), the first in the series of their correspondence, in which Lhuyd writes that, 'I remember when we talk'd last together at Mr. Wyldes.'

[46] Powell, *Aubrey*, 253–4.

[47] Traces of Wylde's library appear in Aubrey's manuscripts as notes and memoranda: 'Edmund Wyld Esq has it' (Bodleian MS Aubrey 10, fol. 25r), 'Edm: Wyld Esq has a copie' (Bodleian MS Top. Gen. c. 24, fol. 208r), or 'from the library of Edmund Wyld' (Bodleian Top. Gen. c. 25, fol. 8v).

[48] Bodleian MS Aubrey 12, fol. 250r.

[49] Bodleian MS Ashmole 1817b, fols. 405r–406v. A truncated version of this document, now significantly damaged, is given in R. T. Gunther, *Dr. Plot and the Correspondence of the Philosophical Society of Oxford* (Oxford, 1939), 329–32.

[50] George Hickes, *Institutiones grammaticae Anglo-Saxonicae et Moeso-Gothicae* (Oxford, 1689).

[51] Edward Bernard, 'Etymologicon Britannicum', in Hickes, *Institutiones grammaticae*, sigs. Qqr–Uuv. For Bernard see G. J. Toomer, *Eastern Wisedome and Learning: The Study of Arabic in Seventeenth-Century England* (Oxford, 1996), 299–305.

a virtuoso demonstration of multilingualism, had attempted to demonstrate the Russian, Slavic, Persian, and Armenian origins of English and
British (i.e., Welsh) words, a feat which Lhuyd believed was a bridge too
far. In his pseudonymous letter he criticized Bernard for his unnecessary
exoticism and instead gave a table of Welsh words with their Latin and
English cognates, as well as mentioning potential sources which might help
further investigations of the origins of the Celtic languages. At about the
same time he contributed a list of Welsh words parallel to northern English
dialect words to a new edition of John Ray's *Collection of English Words not
Generally Used*.[52] By 1691 Lhuyd already had a reputation as a scholar on
the make with a particular interest in the Celtic languages; in short, he was
the ideal person to continue the etymological project Aubrey had begun.

Much of their early correspondence focused on philological issues.
Aubrey, probably recollecting Lhuyd's earlier work on the etymological
origins of Welsh, mentioned to him in December 1691 that his friend the
natural philosopher, phonetician, and musician William Holder hoped
that 'somebody should runne over a good English Latin-Dictionary, and
make markes of all the radicall words of the Latin English and French. You
might pick-out some British words.'[53] Aubrey, continuing to heap unsoli-
cited projects on Lhuyd's shoulders, ended by hoping that 'some time or
other, pian piano [little by little], you may finish this piece of Curiosity'.[54]
This was in addition not only to his suggestion that Lhuyd take the lead
on the *Interpretation* but also to an even grander proposal that Lhuyd
might also attempt a similar project for France. Boxhorn, Aubrey wrote,
'hath been tampering at (and fumbled at it) Gaulish Etymologies' and
besides, if Lhuyd accomplished such a work, ''tis likely [the King of
France] might make you an honourable Present'.[55]

Aubrey evidently intended Lhuyd to be a collaborator in a larger project
to recover, not just the origins of toponyms, but the relationships of
the several languages in Britain. In a letter of February 1692 he wrote
excitedly that he had 'lately accidentally at the Coffee-house fall'n into the

---

[52] John Ray, *A Collection of English Words not Generally Used*, 2nd edn. (London, 1691),
sig. A6r.

[53] For Holder and his linguistic interests see David Abercrombie, 'William Holder and
Other 17th-Century Phoneticians', *Historiographia Linguistica* 20 (1993): 309–30, and
Joseph L. Subbiondo, 'William Holder's *Elements of Speech* (1669): A Study of Applied
English Phonetics and Speech Therapy', *Lingua* 46 (1978): 169–84. Holder had been the
first scholar to successfully teach the deaf Alexander Popham to speak. After a subsequent
relapse Popham was famously retaught by John Wallis and the so-called 'Popham Notebook', recording this second round of pedagogy, was rediscovered in 2008, cf. David Cram
and Jaap Maat, eds., *The Popham Notebook: John Wallis's Manual for Teaching Language to a
Boy Born Deaf* (Oxford, forthcoming 2016).

[54] Bodleian MS Ashmole 1814, fol. 98r.   [55] Bodleian MS Aubrey 5, fol. 2r.

acquaintance of an ingeniose young Cornish Gent'. This new informant told him of John Keigwin, the scholar of Cornish who would later meet Lhuyd and contribute to his work, and Aubrey sanguinely observed to Lhuyd that his coffee-house acquaintance would write to Keigwin and 'putt him upon making a Cornish Dictionary, in order to my desired Designe' for the *Interpretation*.[56] Aubrey returned to the subject of Keigwin in December of the same year, asking Lhuyd, now in possession of the manuscript of the *Interpretation*, to insert a paragraph discussing him, his manuscripts, and the possibility of his authorship of a Cornish dictionary, 'out of my note-booke, into my Villare'.[57] As with his other manuscripts, Aubrey was using the manuscript of the *Interpretation* both as a working text and as a series of notes and memoranda towards its completion.

In 1691 and 1692 Aubrey and Lhuyd corresponded on specific philological issues arising from the *Interpretation* project. In one letter Aubrey mentioned that he had been told that the name of 'the Whithway' in North Wales (i.e., Yr Wyddfa—better known as Snowdon) meant simply 'locus perspicuus', a high place.[58] Lhuyd responded systematically to the implicit question. First, he began, the word *wydhva* must be restored to its nominative case of *gwydhva*. This word could signify 'locus perspicuus' but 'the most natural signification . . . is a wyld place or Desart' or perhaps a 'woody place'. Yr Wyddfa, Lhuyd added, was 'the highest peak in the Forrest of Snowdon, & is certainly the most desert place that may be in a countrey inhabited; no place in the three Kingdomes being so high; or more steep & rockie'.[59] This was something more than simply an equation of a place name with a similar word; Lhuyd was using the landscape as a tool with which to understand language in the same way that Aubrey had used the landscape to recover ancient history in the *Monumenta Britannica*. This was the seed of Lhuyd's later attempt—in a letter to William Nicolson—to systematically describe Welsh place name elements and relate them back to the natural and human geographies of their locations. In that document the same etymology of *gwydhva* reappears together with more general observations such as that 'the most common way of naming Hills was by Metaphors from the Parts of the Body', while 'another Way of Denomination of Mountains was from Persons who had been once Proprietors of them'.[60]

Elsewhere, this geographically centred approach to understanding toponyms touched even more closely on the two men's shared interest in

---

[56] Bodleian MS Ashmole 1814, fol. 96r. For Keigwin see *ODNB*, *s.n.*
[57] Bodleian MS Ashmole 1814, fol. 101r. By 'Villare' Aubrey meant his *Interpretation of Villare Anglicanum*.
[58] Bodleian MS Aubrey 5, fol. 2r.
[59] Bodleian MS Aubrey 12, fol. 247r.   [60] BL Harleian MS 2289, fols. 158–9.

material antiquities. In 1691 Aubrey had asked Lhuyd, 'what is Crick? Is it not a contraction of Kerig' (i.e., stone, stony)?[61] At the time Lhuyd had responded that it seemed a 'very probable' conjecture, but did not pursue the matter for lack of evidence.[62] In August 1693, however, having returned to Oxford after a perambulation through Wales gathering material for his portion of the 1695 edition of Camden's *Britannia*, he wrote to Aubrey stating that

> you askd me formerly the meaning of Crig of Cric Howel; which question I could not then solve, but now I can assure you, that by Crick Howel is meant nothing else but Howels Barrow. I have seen at least 12 ancient Tumuli this journey in several places which are all of them call'd Crigau.[63]

In the same letter speculations by Aubrey's two philological collaborators finally met when Lhuyd commented that 'Gwŷg or y Wŷg signifies a Wood; and thence probably Wickham, etc. and so there may be something in that notion of Dr. Gales, (when we consider it narrowly) that some places that have <u>Wick</u> in their names, have been heretofore consecrated to the Druids.'[64] In both cases past and present landscapes were related to language to reveal the imprint of past cultures upon them.

It was at about this time that Aubrey added another small tract to the *Stromata*, his collection of works on the evolution of scripts, heraldry, architecture, clothing, and other aspects of the material past.[65] This was the *Proportion of the several Languages Ingredients of our English or, the Proportion of the Languages mix't in our present English*, the final tract in the *Stromata*, and probably also the last composed (it is dated 1692/3 on the title page). It was a series of tables identifying etymologies contained in John Rider's *Dictionary*, a popular school-text of the late sixteenth century, of a sort which Aubrey himself might have used as a child.[66] Aubrey went through the *Dictionary* methodically, noting the origins of words and keeping running tallies of those whose origins could be identified as English (i.e., Old English), French, Latin, Greek, British or Welsh, and Danish.[67]

The decision to place the *Proportion* within the *Stromata* probably came from Aubrey's sense of it as another investigation into the mutability of custom over the course of time. This is highlighted by his quotation from Horace's *Ars Poetica* on the title page of the *Proportion*: 'Many terms that

---

[61] Bodleian MS Aubrey 5, fol. 2r.   [62] Bodleian MS Aubrey 12, fol. 247r.
[63] Bodleian MS Aubrey 12, fol. 248r.   [64] Bodleian MS Aubrey 12, fol. 248r.
[65] See Chapter 3.
[66] For Rider, cf. *ODNB*, *s.n.* Aubrey used an edition of Rider edited and enlarged by Francis Holyoke, but which is unclear.
[67] Bodleian MS Top. Gen. c. 25, fol. 239rff.

have fallen out of use shall be born again, and those shall fall that are now
in repute, if Usage so will it, in whose hands lies the judgement, the right
and the rule of speech.'[68] Aubrey was thinking of language here in much
the same way as he thought of architecture in the *Architectonica*: it was
continuously changing and had its own distinct historical morphology.
Although the surviving parts of the *Proportion* are concerned only with the
linguistic origins of early modern English, Aubrey appears to have had
plans to collect obsolete words as well. After noting that Rider's *Dictionarie* claimed to omit 'Barbarous words' to encourage good style, he added
that he had read through Philemon Holland's translations of Livy and
Pliny in parallel with the Latin originals in search of 'the English words &
phrases, now obsolete: which amount to a page in folio close writt on both
sides; which is in the Museum at Oxford'.[69] This suggests a larger scope
for the *Proportion* than its surviving pages would otherwise indicate.[70]

What does survive is an attempt to quantify the influence of other
languages upon seventeenth-century English. Aubrey was aware that
many words then in use did not have Anglo-Saxon roots, commenting
that 'it appears, that the English Speech that we now use, *furtivis nudata
coloribus*, will shrink into a little roome'.[71] His conclusions from analysing Rider's *Dictionarie* were that, while authentically 'English' words were
in the majority (at 3,459), Latin (1,892) and French (1,002) were of
considerable importance, with Greek (208) and Welsh (13) being more
marginal.[72] Though he included a column for it, he recorded no Danish
words at all, noting only that 'Mr . . . Arnold a Danish Gent an acquaintance of mine who hath lived in England ever since 1659, tells me, we have
abundance of Danish words in our Language: but I suspect many of these
words are also Dutch.'[73] More exotically, and harking back to Edward
Bernard's *Etymologicon*, John Evelyn read the *Proportion* at some stage
after its completion and made a note therein on the congruence between
English and Persian.[74]

---

[68] Horace, *Ars Poetica*, ll. 70–2 ('Multa renascentur, quae jam cecidere, cadentque |
Quae nunc sunt in honore, vocabula, si volet usus, | Quem penes arbitrium est et jus et
norma loquendi').

[69] Bodleian MS Top. Gen. c. 25, fol. 238v.

[70] Livy, *The Romane Historie*, trans. Philemon Holland (London, 1600) and Pliny, *The
Historie of the World Commonly Called, the Naturall Historie*, trans. Philemon Holland
(London, 1601). Aubrey's word list is at Bodleian MS Aubrey 5, fols. 91r–92v.

[71] Bodleian MS Top. Gen. c. 25, fol. 238v. The quotation ('stripped of its stolen
colours') is from Horace, *Epistles*, I.iii.20.

[72] Bodleian MS Top. Gen. c. 25, fol. 241r.

[73] Bodleian MS Top. Gen. c. 25, fol. 240v. Mr Arnold (*recte* Arnoldt?) has not been
identified.

[74] Bodleian MS Top. Gen. c. 25, fol. 238v. Evelyn's knowledge of Persian, such as it
was, may have been the result of his acquaintance with Pietro Cesij, a Persian convert to

The *Proportion* bears an obvious resemblance to Lhuyd's journeyman work on Welsh and to William Holder's 1691 proposal for a study of English word origins.[75] It also speaks directly to Aubrey's concerns in the *Interpretation*. By trying to recover reliable statistics on the languages incorporated into contemporary English, Aubrey was attempting to test larger theories about cultural inheritances, engagements, or oppositions, which were predicated upon his linguistic essentialism and his conviction that linguistic change was more likely to be brought about by external interaction than by internal change. That he viewed the *Proportion* as an important part of his larger work is clear from a letter to Lhuyd of 10 May 1694 in which he remarked ruefully that 'it did cost me 4 months time, at halfe an houre every morning to doe it: fresh & fasting, but a Task unpleasant enough'. In the same letter he emphasized to Lhuyd that the *Proportion* was 'annexed' to the *Monumenta Britannica* and sent him both his 'English Pliny', the 1600 Holland translation which he had previously used as a source for obsolete words, and his copy of Rider's *Dictionary*, 'to let it appeare how I found out the proportion of the severall Languages of which our present English doth consist'. These two volumes were to be deposited in the Ashmolean as permanently available auxiliary material which could elucidate Aubrey's larger linguistic project.[76]

As the decade progressed, Aubrey increasingly relinquished the leading role to Lhuyd in what he viewed as their joint endeavour. From the elder scholar asking Lhuyd for specialist advice on toponyms, he became the assistant in turn, seeking out books and advising Lhuyd of new arrivals on the antiquarian scene who could be enlisted onto the project. One ongoing saga, which regularly reappears in the two men's letters, was Aubrey's attempt to convince Edmund Wylde that he ought to lend certain rare volumes to Lhuyd. As early as March 1693 Lhuyd mentioned to Aubrey that he had 'been long enquiring after' Claude Fauchet's *Recueil des antiquités gauloises et françoises* (1579), which had been recommended to him by Wylde, but, unable to locate another copy, he hoped that Wylde might consider lending his.[77] Aubrey's initial response was not calculated to encourage: 'Mr Wyld remembers him to you but will send no booke to anyone.'[78] Nonetheless, when Lhuyd subsequently expressed a wish to borrow an 'Armorican' (i.e., Breton) dictionary from Wylde's

---

Christianity, who also supplied materials for Evelyn's *History of the Three Late Famous Impostors* (Geoffrey Keynes, *John Evelyn: A Study in Bibliophily and a Bibliography of his Writings* [Cambridge, 1937], 194; Michael Fixler, 'A Note on John Evelyn's *History of the Three Late Famous Impostors*', *The Library*, 5th ser., 9 [1954]: 267–8).

[75] See Bodleian MS Ashmole 1814, fol. 98r.
[76] Bodleian MS Ashmole 1814, fol. 112r.
[77] Bodleian MS Aubrey 12, fol. 241r.   [78] Bodleian MS Ashmole 1814, fol. 90r.

collection, Aubrey did his best to wear their mutual friend down.[79] By August 1693 he thought he had 'almost prevailed', but the dictionary was still in Bloomsbury at Wylde's death and one of Aubrey's last letters, dated 19 March 1696, recorded the promise that he 'shall gett of Mr Wylds Gentlewomen the Armoric Dictionary for you'.[80]

By the autumn of 1695 Lhuyd's own plans had progressed to the point of publishing *A Design of a British Dictionary, Historical and Geographical*.[81] This was a fundraising advertisement on a far more ambitious scale than any request for subscriptions prior to printing. Lhuyd outlined a vast, tripartite work consisting of a historical and geographical dictionary of Britain, a linguistic essay entitled *Archaeologia Britannica*, and a natural history of the island. This would, he maintained, entail extensive travel and the first section would not be ready for at least five years, the next not until two years after that, and as for the natural history, 'I can set no time for its Publication, as not being able to guess how tedious it may prove.'[82] While this project went far beyond the remit of anything he had discussed with Aubrey, two of its subsections deserve further scrutiny.

The historical and geographical dictionary was to contain not just names of persons, but also 'of all Places in *Britain* mention'd by the *Greeks* and *Romans*; and of all Hundreds, Comots, Towns, Castles, Villages, and Seats of the Nobility and Gentry of chiefist Note now in *Wales*'. Moreover, these names were to be 'interpreted' with the ultimate goal of 'rectifying several Errors already committed in the Interpreting of the Names of Places in this Kingdom; and the preventing of many more in *Wales* and *Scotland*; as also in some Places of *England*, where the *British* Names, either entire or corrupt, are still preserv'd'. Nor, Lhuyd added, was there any need to apologise for such a plan, given the evident usefulness of such 'Etymological Observations' made by previous scholars including Bochart, Camden, Boxhorn, Vossius, and Ménage.[83] This section, described in more detail than any other part of Lhuyd's project, may

---

[79] In the *Archaeologia* Lhuyd reproduced the Breton grammar and vocabulary written by Julien Maunoir 'about 50 years since . . . and so scarce that 'twas my Fortune to meet but with only two Copies, and those in *Convents*' (Edward Lhuyd, *Archaeologia Britannica* [Oxford, 1707], sig. b2v), but both he and Aubrey referred to the text owned by Wylde as a dictionary, not a grammar or vocabulary. Given that Wylde is known to have possessed other extremely rare books, it is possible that the two men were discussing a copy of Jehan Lagadeuc's *Le Catholicon* (Tréguier, 1499), the first printed Breton dictionary.

[80] Bodleian MS Ashmole 1814, fol. 92r; MS Ashmole 1829, fol. 13r.

[81] Edward Lhuyd, *A Design of a British Dictionary* (Oxford, 1695).

[82] Lhuyd, *Design*, verso.

[83] Lhuyd, *Design*, recto. For the 'Etymological Observations' of these scholars and the crucial differences between their philologies and Lhuyd's, see David Cram, 'Edward Lhuyd's *Archaeologia Britannica*: Method and Madness in Early Modern Comparative Philology', *Welsh History Review* 25 (2010): 75–96.

have been narrower in scope, but its debt to Aubrey's *Interpretation* is clear. Lhuyd was proposing to carry through with the *Interpretation*, as Aubrey had asked him to do four years before, but to focus exclusively on place names of 'British' origin.

Lhuyd's dictionary was never compiled, but the second section of the overall project, the *Archaeologia Britannica*, was. In the *Design* Lhuyd had intimated that its first part would contain a 'Comparison of the Modern *Welsh* with other *European* Languages; more especially with the *Greek, Latin, Irish, Cornish*, and *Armorican*'.[84] In the published *Archaeologia* this had become a 'comparative etymology' which examined both the 'Changes or Alteration into various Dialects' of the Celtic languages and 'the Analogy they bear to those [languages] of our neighbouring Nations'.[85] This was supported by an extensive apparatus of vocabularies and grammars for the languages central to Lhuyd's argument. While undertaken on a far more detailed and systematic level, Lhuyd was working towards the same answers that Aubrey had sought in the *Proportion* and *Interpretation*: how were languages formed? What relations did they bear to each other? What could be inferred about historical linguistic, and, by extension, cultural, change from the composition of modern languages?

It has been remarked before that Lhuyd carried Aubrey's tradition of meticulously surveying ancient sites and locating them within local land-scapes into the next generation.[86] Likewise, his crucial role as keeper of the Ashmolean and, as such, receiver and preserver of Aubrey's material and textual archives has been observed.[87] In addition, however, his famous linguistic projects, which bore fruit in the *Archaeologia Britannica*, appear to have been closely related to and influenced by Aubrey's earlier studies and by the two men's correspondence on philological topics in the 1690s. Looking back through Aubrey's *Interpretation* to its roots in Thomas Gale's studies of the *Antonine Itinerary* and the *Ravenna Cosmography*, it becomes possible to chart an evolving culture of toponymic and etymological study of ancient Britain from the Cambridge classicists of the 1670s through to Lhuyd's monumental achievements in the early eighteenth century, with Aubrey occupying a crucial mediating position.

---

[84] Lhuyd, *Design*, recto.   [85] Lhuyd, *Archaeologia Britannica*, sig. Ar.
[86] For example in Nancy Edwards, 'Edward Lhuyd and the Origins of Early Medieval Celtic Archaeology', *Antiquaries Journal* 87 (2007): 165–96.
[87] Kate Bennett, 'John Aubrey's Collections and the Early-Modern Museum', *Bodleian Library Record*, 17 (2001): 213–45.

Conclusion

In the polymathic variety of Aubrey's antiquarian writings two desires stand out: to recover the links which bound seventeenth-century England to its ancient past, and to preserve present knowledge which would otherwise fade away. That first impulse, to recover and restore, had an illustrious pedigree dating back to—and before—William Camden's resolution in the preface to his *Britannia* that 'I would restore antiquity to Britaine, and Britain to his antiquity.'[1] Aubrey, who had at times conceived of his work as complementing or even supplementing the great restoration project undertaken by Camden, was participating in the same tradition: mapping, sketching, measuring, describing, collecting, and theorizing the forgotten past into being. In his determination to find connections to the ancient world in sources as diverse as standing stones, hill forts, burial mounds, folk customs, place names, and the landscape itself, he was recovering occluded links which he knew were there, links which would tie the quotidian society of the Restoration back to an almost mythical time of Druids, Homeric warriors, and Roman legions.

That urge to recover what was forgotten, the impulse behind texts such as the *Monumenta Britannica* and *Remaines of Gentilisme*, was one product of a volition which also resulted in Aubrey becoming acutely aware of what was being lost, every day and all around him. As a member of the Royal Society he sought out the papers of deceased scholars and attempted to rescue what he could before the pie-makers claimed them. As a biographer and practitioner of *historia literaria* he preserved the specificities of his contemporaries' lives, holding in his mind the dictum that 'Men thinke, because every body remembers a memorable Accident shortly after 'tis donne, 'twill never be forgotten, which for want of writing... at last is drowned in Oblivion.'[2] Even strolling through the crowded London streets he could suddenly and painfully be struck by the evanescence of things, such as when he came across a remnant of the

---

[1] William Camden, *Britain*, trans. Philemon Holland (London, 1610), sig. [leaf]4r.
[2] Bodleian MS Aubrey 9, fol. 29r (= Aubrey, 'Hobbes', i. 18).

sumptuous monument erected by Sir Kenelm Digby to his wife Venetia Stanley and later, or so Aubrey had believed, 'utterly destroyed by the great conflagration':

> About 1676, or 5, as I was walking through Newgate street, I sawe Dame Venetia's Bust standing at a Stall at the golden Crosse, a Brasiers shop; I perfectly remembred it; but the fire had gott-off the Guilding: but taking notice of it to one that was with me, I could never see it afterwards exposed to the street. They melted it downe. How these curiosities would be quite forgott, did not such idle fellowes as I am putt them downe![3]

Despite his self-deprecation, Aubrey passionately believed in the value of what he was doing. He 'perfectly remembred' much that was lost and more that soon would be; the violent discontinuity of the Civil Wars had ensured that, if nothing else. Moreover, he was convinced that while some people—people like his erstwhile collaborator Richard Blackburne—might find his records of seemingly trivial things unnecessary or unpleasant, 'a hundred yeere hence that minutenesse will be gratefull'.[4]

These twin goals of recording and preserving informed Aubrey's characteristic methodologies: minuteness and analogy. By minuteness Aubrey meant the recording of detail. That detail could be the physical and mental peculiarities of his biographical subjects, circumstantial accounts of the practice of folk traditions, or surveys and sketches of Roman camps. This, Aubrey believed, was the kind of data most easily lost and most worth preserving. Minuteness led to mensurability and to the naturalization of data into a framework where it could be examined and compared, as in the case of Gothic window styles in the *Chronologia Architectonica*: recording their minute variations led to the ability to distinguish one style from another and so, ultimately, to securely date hitherto undateable structures.

The dating of windows only became possible, however, because Aubrey adhered to the principles not just of minuteness but also analogy. This could be as simple as saying 'x is similar to y' or, more subtly, 'x is similar to y except in z', but Aubrey was well aware of the power inherent in what he described as 'comparative antiquitie'.[5] In the context of megaliths he described his comparative method in mathematical terms: he would 'restore a kind of Algebraical method, by comparing [those monuments] that I have seen one with another; and reducing them to a kind of

---

[3] Aubrey, *Lives*, i. 333.   [4] Bodleian MS Wood F 39, fol. 340r.
[5] See Alain Schnapp, *The Discovery of the Past*, trans. Ian Kinnes and Gillian Varndell (London, 1996), 191–2, for further discussion of this phrase.

Æquation'.[6] In other words, comparatism had the potential to generate new information simply from the examination of two things in tandem; when presented with a series of ancient monuments, some already well understood, others not, one could make sense of the obscure monuments through the lens of those already explicated. Aubrey was not alone in using comparative methods for antiquarian purposes, but where his contemporaries tended to apply such methods to issues of culture and religion, he was unusual in focusing them principally on physical artefacts and sites.[7] This focus in turn led him to realize the power of placing objects in a chronological series. His *Chronologiae*, especially the *Architectonica* and the *Graphica*, represent pioneering ways of thinking about objects in history, ways which utilized both minuteness and comparatism to develop a diachronic framework against which new discoveries could be compared and into which they could be slotted. Aubrey's awareness of difference and change, exemplified in his pained recollection of Venetia Stanley's bust, could be harnessed as a series of powerful tools for understanding the past.

These desires and methods both informed and were informed by what we might call Aubrey's 'worldview', the particular vision of history and cultural development which gradually emerges from a reading of his works. Building upon Robert Hooke's lectures on earthquakes, Athanasius Kircher's *Mundus Subterraneus*, and other works of natural philosophy, Aubrey had no compunctions stating that 'the world is much older, than is commonly supposed'.[8] An ancient earth did not necessarily mean pre-diluvian civilizations, much less pre-Adamites, however, and his human history began with the Ark and Babel.[9] In this latter view he was neither radical nor unduly conservative, but rather represented the main line of contemporary thought. Following on from this, he was a syncretist in ancient history, seeing links between Rome and Egypt, Greece and Britain, as all cultures had had a relatively recent origin in post-Babelic humanity. This comes through most clearly in texts like 'Of Mausolea', where a history of architecture could begin with Babel, and the *Remaines of Gentilisme*, where parallels to almost any religious custom or tradition could be found sometime or somewhere else, be it in ancient Egypt or rural Yorkshire.

---

[6] Aubrey, *Monumenta*, 32.
[7] Cf. Guy G. Stroumsa, *A New Science: The Discovery of Religion in the Age of Reason* (Cambridge, MA, and London, 2010).
[8] Bodleian MS Aubrey 1, fol. 100. See Hunter, *Aubrey*, 58–9, and William Poole, *The World Makers: Scientists of the Restoration and the Search for the Origins of the Earth* (Oxford, 2010), 111–12.
[9] See Philip Almond, 'Adam, Pre-Adamites, and Extra-Terrestrial Beings in Early Modern Europe', *Journal of Religious History* 30 (2006): 163–74.

Ancient Britain was a part of this post-Babelic civilization. In 'Of Mausolea' Aubrey compared the artificial mound at Silbury Hill in Wiltshire to the ruins of Babel and Chinese burial mounds, just as he compared megaliths to the tomb of Lars Porsenna. This ancient British culture was defined for him by its Druids and what he took to be their temples: the stone circles at Stonehenge, Avebury, and in many locations across Britain. In line with his comparatism elsewhere, Aubrey seems to have imagined this culture as being not unlike that of Homeric Greece, with its hierarchical society of priests and warriors ruled over by 'several Reguli, which often made wars upon one another'.[10] It could be known only through the traces it left in the landscape—ditches, mounds, standing stones, and other human interventions—and existed in a misty, timeless era after Babel but before the arrival of the Romans.

The incoming of the Romans represented a turning point for British antiquaries, not just because of the cultural capital they brought to remote Britannia, but because of the composition of what were some of the earliest textual accounts of Britain and its inhabitants. For early modern Scots their paradigmatic text was Tacitus's *Agricola* and much ink was spilt over the locations of places, the identities of tribes, and the success or lack thereof of Gnaeus Julius Agricola's invasion of the northerly parts of the island.[11] For English antiquaries of the same period, the text to study was Julius Caesar's *Commentaries*: Camden had put great emphasis on Caesar as a source for ancient Britain and early in his career Aubrey followed suit, happily identifying all manner of camps, hill forts, and burial mounds as places associated with the Roman leader's progress through southern England. As Aubrey's ideas developed, however, this gave way to a more historically aware sense of Roman Britain on his part, as later references to rebuilding projects by Theodosius in the fourth century CE show.[12] The Romans were not simply invaders, but 'settled here, & mixt with the Britons'.[13] Aubrey was echoing the genetic language of Camden, who had rhapsodized that the Romans, 'both planted themselves, and also begat children here . . . [a]nd meet it is we should beleeve, that the Britans and Romans in so many ages, by a blessed and joyfull mutuall ingrassing, as it were, have growen into one stocke and nation'.[14] For both men the

---

[10] Bodleian MS Aubrey 3, fol. 10r.
[11] See, for example, Robert Sibbald, *Miscellanea quaedam eruditae antiquitatis quae ad Borealem Britanniae majoris partem pertinent* (Edinburgh, 1710) and Alexander Gordon, *Itinerarium Septentrionale: or, a Journey thro' Most of the Counties of Scotland and Those in the North of England* (London, 1726).
[12] Aubrey, *Monumenta*, i. 437.   [13] Bodleian MS Aubrey 5, fol. 19ar.
[14] Camden, *Britain*, 87–8.

Romans mattered because they were Romans, but also because they were the ancestors of modern Britons.

Or were they? Aubrey was all too acutely aware of the great chasm between the ancient world and the modern, a chasm he knew with absolute conviction had been caused by barbarians like the Goths and the Saxons. The 'inundation of the Goths' was to Aubrey more a natural disaster than a human event, one which 'seemed to come to hasten time and precipitate the end of the world'.[15] Taste, architecture, even writing were destroyed or under threat and civilization was pushed to the verge of collapse. What followed, in Aubrey's eyes, was little better: the occupation of Britain by the Saxons. With them came ignorance, barbarism, and a breakdown of all social distinctions: 'their very Kings were but a sort of Farmers'.[16] Partly because of his self-identification with the Welsh, who he believed were descended from Romanized Britons, Aubrey had little patience for the Saxon interlopers and was particularly unimpressed by their alleged inability to build proper stone buildings. He went against the antiquarian fashion of the times, did not learn Anglo-Saxon (though he had at least some knowledge of Welsh, a far more unusual language to have), and resisted giving any role in the development of English civilization to what he believed was a culture of dim-witted, ale-soaked farmers.

For many seventeenth-century English antiquaries the period from the Norman Conquest to the Reformation lay at the centre of their research, but Aubrey touched upon the later Middle Ages only lightly, using its architecture in the *Chronologia Architectonica* and collecting medieval charters and monumental inscriptions in his county histories of Wiltshire and Surrey.[17] He was far more interested in the recent past, when humanism had spread into England from the continent, bringing with it new inventions, neo-classical architecture, the advancement of mathematics and natural philosophy, and a host of other topics which he addressed in the *Stromata*, the *Lives*, and elsewhere. This was the 'Old Time' of Aubrey's *Remaines*, when England existed between two worlds, the ancient, half-pagan vision of the folk customs he had collected, and the scintillating possibilities developed by scholars like the Elizabethan magus John Dee or his contemporary the mathematician Leonard Digges.[18] It was the rural Wiltshire world of his grandfather Isaac Lyte,

---

[15] Bodleian MS Top. Gen. c. 24, fol. 29r, quoting Jean-Louise Guez, Seigneur de Balzac, *The Roman: The Conversation of the Romans and Maecenas, in Three Excellent Discourses* (London, 1652), 92.

[16] Bodleian MS Aubrey 3, fol. 10v.

[17] See Bodleian MSS Aubrey 3–4 and Chapter 3.

[18] Aubrey, *Lives*, i. 114–19 (Dee), 730–2 (Digges).

which reappears over and over again in his writings, tinged with the melancholy of childhood loss, and which Aubrey knew had been cast beyond reach by the cultural discontinuity of the Civil Wars. Since then, 'the old Roman fashion is become the common Mode' and the modern world, Aubrey's world, had flowered fully into being: a neo-classical age of progress when coffee houses allowed men to be properly sociable for the first time and 'ingeniose' persons could pursue natural philosophy and antiquities in a (mostly) congenial environment.[19]

This grand historical narrative is, of course, an eccentric one and it is doubtful if Aubrey would have expressed himself quite so strongly had he been set the task of writing a general history of mankind. These were not the parts of a fully articulated theory, but rather assumptions, prejudices, and preconceptions which reappeared throughout his works, informing them almost without Aubrey himself being aware that they did so. These preconceptions defined his scholarship, ensuring that he focused on ancient Britons and Romans at the expense of Anglo-Saxons for example, but were also themselves defined by the nature of his work. His fascination with physical artefacts and sites led him to the poorly understood ancient landscape of England. Meanwhile his ear for, and sympathy with, a vanishing system of folk knowledge, combined with his steeping in classical literature, laid the foundations for the *Remaines*. Aubrey was a humanist scholar who experienced the world through phrases from Ovid and Horace, Cicero and Homer; living in a country only lightly touched by that culture, he mentally reshaped it through classical lenses until not only were the English descendants of the Romans but his own dreamt-of Wiltshire villa looked out upon Italian vistas.

Aubrey is often portrayed as being somehow unusual, though whether that is presented as innovation or eccentricity depends upon the critic. He certainly did not fit neatly into that English antiquarian tradition which focused on local history in the Camdenian style.[20] Although he attempted two county histories in the tradition of William Dugdale, William Burton, and Sampson Erdeswick, he found the gathering of old documents and the copying of texts not to his taste; 'I am tyred with transcribing', he wrote of reproducing a passage from Walter Charleton's *Chorea Gigantum*, '[in] this hot weather'.[21] Nor was he a grammar-making, text-editing philologist like the antiquaries who flourished in Oxford and Cambridge

[19] Bodleian MS Top. Gen. c. 25, fol. 169r. For the beneficial effects of coffee houses p. 111.

[20] For which see Jan Broadway, *'No historie so meete': Gentry Culture and the Development of Local History in Elizabethan and Early Stuart England* (Manchester and New York, 2006).

[21] Bodleian MS Aubrey 11, fol. 15v. See Hunter, *Aubrey*, 151–2.

during the salad days of Restoration scholarship.[22] His disdain for the
Anglo-Saxons could hardly lead him into the arms of George Hickes and
his Septentrionalists, but nor did his interests—or linguistic abilities—
extend to the esoteric deeps of Arabic and Hellenistic scholarship then
being plumbed by men such as Edward Pococke and Edward Bernard.
While he shared certain prejudices with Welsh antiquaries from the school
of Robert Vaughan of Hengwrt, he was no more like them than like
Hickes or Dugdale; he did not collect manuscripts, draw pedigrees, or
focus on the medieval Welsh world.

This inability to pigeonhole Aubrey and his activities within a comfort-
ably parochial English landscape has lain behind many of the claims that
he was an outlier of one sort or another. But in antiquarianism, as in other
branches of humanist scholarship, it is dangerous to limit the field of
enquiry to a single modern nation. If we are in search of a model which
Aubrey could have looked to, we need look no further than the Danish
polymath Ole Worm, whose *Danicorum monumentorum libri sex* (1643)
inspired the title of the *Monumenta Britannica*.[23] Worm's influence on
Aubrey is traceable through the regular citations which appear in the
latter's manuscripts and his methodological inheritance is writ large across
Aubrey's approach to sites and artefacts.[24] The two scholars shared practices of surveying, comparitism, attention to minuteness, and a willingness
to go beyond the written word as well as both turning their attention to
the ancient landscapes of their respective countries. The place which
Camden occupied in the intellectual genealogies of so many English
antiquaries was occupied in Aubrey's case by Worm.[25]

Seeking parallels amongst Aubrey's continental contemporaries is
equally fruitful. His philological interests echo those of the Dutch scholar

---

[22] See Mordechai Feingold, 'Oriental Studies', in *The History of the University of Oxford*,
vol. 4: *Seventeenth-Century Oxford*, ed. Nicholas Tyacke (Oxford, 1997), 449–503; Kristine
Haugen, *Richard Bentley: Poetry and Enlightenment* (Cambridge, MA, and London, 2011),
ch. 1; Gerald J. Toomer, *Eastern Wisedome and Learning: the Study of Arabic in Seventeenth-
Century England* (Oxford, 1996).

[23] Bodleian MS Wood F 39, fol. 340r.

[24] For citations to Worm's *Monumenta* see, for example, Bodleian MSS Aubrey 3, fol.
85r, Aubrey 11, fol. 13v, Top. Gen. c. 24, fols. 132v, 271v, 276r, and Top. Gen. c. 25, fols.
74r–77v. Aubrey also knew Worm's record of his own collections, the *Museum Wormianum, seu historia rerum rariorum* (Leiden, 1655), which he cited at Bodleian MS Top. Gen.
c. 24, fol. 276r.

[25] Jan Broadway has recently argued that Aubrey was not alone in this approach, but
that a number of otherwise little-known English antiquaries engaged in excavation and
study reminiscent of the *Monumenta Britannica* in or around the 1650s (Broadway,
'"Ocular Exploration, and Subterraneous Enquiry": Developing Archaeological Fieldwork
in the Mid-Seventeenth Century', *Antiquaries Journal* 92 [2012]: 353–69). Although this
was undoubtedly the case, they seem still to have been a minority.

Marcus Zuerius van Boxhorn, who was also well received by Welsh antiquaries of Aubrey's acquaintance.[26] His biographical writings partook of a number of continental traditions: *historia literaria*, collections of sayings by famous men, and intimate biography along the lines of Gassendi's *Life of Peiresc*. His *Chronologia Graphica* was composed almost simultaneously with Jean Mabillon's better-known *De re diplomatica*.[27] More than anyone, though, Aubrey resembles Olof Rudbeck. The comparison is a strange one to modern eyes, given that Aubrey has been consistently identified as a 'pioneer' or 'precursor' of modern archaeology, while Rudbeck is seen simply as an interesting, but mad, curiosity, a scholarly dead end and cautionary tale. The two scholars had much in common, however. Each wrote his magnum opus on the prehistory of their respective countries, each developed radical new methods for understanding non-textual artefacts and sites, each drew upon a mixture of archaeological, oral, and textual sources, and each built towering scholarly frameworks to justify essentially nationalist assumptions about the past. Aubrey becomes less an eccentric and more a participant in the mainstream of northern European scholarship once he is situated alongside the likes of Worm and Boxhorn, Mabillon and Rudbeck.

A better understanding of Aubrey and his continental contemporaries sheds a different light on the stories told about antiquarianism's evolution. In 1950 Arnaldo Momigliano drew a memorable pen-portrait of the changes which came about during the eighteenth century, when antiquarianism 'was fostered by gentlemen rather than by schoolmasters', men who 'preferred travel to the emendation of texts and altogether subordinated literary texts to coins, statues, vases and inscriptions'.[28] This and subsequent expansions on the same theme have articulated a gradual shift from text-based to artefact-based antiquarianism, one that ended with the development of modern history and archaeology. But there are good reasons for questioning the universal validity of such a narrative, firmly located as it is in classical antiquarianism, especially as practised in Italy and elsewhere in southern Europe. Aubrey and the Danish, Swedish, Dutch, and French scholars working on what Peter Burke has described as the 'third antiquity', that of the barbarians, were forced by necessity to approach their topic differently.[29] As Alain Schnapp has shown, even

---

[26] Prys Morgan, 'Boxhorn and the Welsh: Some Cambro-Dutch Contacts in the Seventeenth Century', *Dutch Crossing* 24 (2000): 183–90.

[27] Cf. Poole, *Aubrey*, 90.

[28] Arnaldo Momigliano, 'Ancient History and the Antiquarian', *Journal of the Warburg and Courtauld Institutes* 13 (1950): 285–315.

[29] Peter Burke, 'Images as Evidence in Seventeenth-Century Europe', *Journal of the History of Ideas* 64 (2003): 283.

before the Reformation German scholars such as Nicolaus Marschalk were excavating burial mounds and sketching megaliths.[30] Aubrey was doing something novel by attempting a systematic national survey of sites, but the idea of recovering history from non-textual materials was not new in northern European antiquarianism. If anything, Aubrey was more innovative in his late turn towards philology, inaugurating a tradition combining it with the study of sites which Edward Lhuyd would go on to develop further. Aubrey's antiquarian scholarship serves as a case study in the many varieties of antiquarianism possible in early modern Europe and of the different ways in which their foci and methodologies evolved. By questioning the idea of any single antiquarian tradition across Europe, it is possible to recover a multitude of traditions, and to identify the particular one in which Aubrey took part. This was, above all, an attempt to make sense of a near-textless, non-classical ancient past through a variety of artefacts and sites, while nonetheless inevitably returning to the classical world as inspiration, analogy, and ideal, all the time feverishly working to preserve an ephemeral and fast-disappearing present.

---

[30] Schnapp, *Discovery of the Past*, 142–5.

Bibliography

Unless stated otherwise, all references to classical texts are to their editions in the Loeb Classical Library (not included in this bibliography).

PRIMARY SOURCES

1. Manuscripts and Annotated Books

Bodleian Library, Oxford

8° A 7 Art. Aubrey's copy of Martino Martini, *Bellum Tartaricum* (1654).

Ashmole 1555. Aubrey's copy of John Selden, *Jani Anglorum facies altera* (1610).

Ashmole 1561. Aubrey's copy of Thomas May, *Virgil's Georgicks Englished* (1628).

Ashmole 1572. Aubrey's copy of Thomas Smith, *Syntagma de Druidum moribus ac institutis* (1664).

Ashmole 1722. Aubrey's copy of Robert Plot, *Natural History of Oxford-Shire* (1677).

Ashmole 1814. Correspondence of Edward Lhuyd.

Ashmole 1817a. Correspondence of Edward Lhuyd.

Ashmole 1817b. Correspondence of Edward Lhuyd.

Ashmole 1829. Correspondence of Edward Lhuyd.

Ashmole A 35. Aubrey's copy of Virgil, *Opera* (1632).

Ashmole C 10. Aubrey's copy of Nicolaus Steno, *Prodromus to a Dissertation Concerning Solids* (1671).

Ashmole D 23–4. Aubrey's copy of the latter two volumes of Livy, *Historiarum ab urbe condita*, ed. J. F. Gronovius (1678).

Ashmole F 22. Aubrey's copy of Henricus Regius, *Philosophia naturalis* (1654).

Aubrey 1–2. John Aubrey, 'The Naturall Historie of Wiltshire'.

Aubrey 3. John Aubrey, 'An Essay towards the Description of the North Division of Wiltshire'.

Aubrey 4. John Aubrey, 'A Perambulation of Surrey anno Domini 1673'.

Aubrey 5. John Aubrey, 'An Interpretation of Villare Anglicanum'.

Aubrey 6–8. John Aubrey, 'Brief Lives'.

Aubrey 9. John Aubrey, 'The Life of Mr. Thomas Hobbes of Malmesbury'.

Aubrey 10. John Aubrey, 'An Idea of Education of Young Gentlemen'.

Aubrey 11. John Aubrey, 'An Extract or Summary of the Lemmata of *Stone-heng restored to the Danes* by Walter Charlton'.

Aubrey 12–13. Correspondence of John Aubrey.

Aubrey 17. John Aubrey, 'Designatio de Easton-Piers in Com: Wilts. Per me (heu!) infortunatum Johannem Awbrey R.S. Socium . . . Anno Domini 1669'.

Ballard 14. Correspondence, chiefly of Sir William Dugdale and Anthony Wood.

Gough Gen. Top. 14. Transcript by Richard Gough of extracts from Aubrey's *Monumenta Britannica*.

Gough Gen. Top. 22. Thomas Gale's copy of Matthew Paris, *Historia major* (1640).

Gough Gen. Top. 51. Thomas Gale's copy of William Camden, *Britannia* (1607).

Gough Gen. Top. 81. William Stukeley's copy of the Ravenna Cosmography, ed. David-Placide Porcheron (1688).

Smith 13. Miscellaneous papers of Walter Charleton.

T 1.11 Jur. Seld. John Selden's copy of Ole Worm, *Monumenta Danica* (1643).

Tanner 25. Collection of correspondence, compiled by Thomas Tanner.

Tanner 456a. Correspondence of Anthony Wood.

Top. Gen. c. 24–5. John Aubrey, 'Monumenta Britannica'.

Wood 434. Anthony Wood's copy of Richard Blackburne and John Aubrey, *Thomae Hobbes vita* (1681).

Wood 657 (6). Anthony Wood's copy of Thomas Hobbes, *Life of Mr. Thomas Hobbes of Malmesbury* (1680).

Wood 658. Anthony Wood's copy of John Pits, *Relationum historicarum de rebus Anglicis* (1619).

Wood 780. Anthony Wood's copy of Aubrey, *Proposals for Printing Monumenta Britannica* (1693).

Wood F 39. Correspondence of Anthony Wood and John Aubrey.

Wood F 45. Correspondence of Anthony Wood.

Wood F 51. Correspondence of Anthony Wood.

British Library, London

Additional 78660. Transcript by John Hutchins of extracts from Aubrey's *Monumenta Britannica*.

Harleian 2289. Heraldic, genealogical, and historical notes in the hand of Hugh Thomas.

Landowne 231. John Aubrey, 'Remaines of Gentilisme'.

Lansdowne 1033. White Kennett, 'Etymological Collections of English Words and Provincial Expressions'.

Lansdowne 1039. Miscellaneous collections by White Kennett.

Royal Society, London

92. John Aubrey, 'Memoires of Naturall Remarques in the county of Wilts'.

Wiltshire Archaeological & Natural Historical Society Library, Devizes

889. Transcript by William Stukeley of extracts from Aubrey's *Monumenta Britannica*.

890. Transcript by Edward Meredith of extracts from Aubrey's *Monumenta Britannica*.

Worcester College Library, Oxford

5.4. Mathematical notes and extracts by John Aubrey.

2. Printed Books

Adam of Bremen. *History of the Archbishops of Hamburg-Bremen*, trans. Francis J. Tschan. New York: Columbia University Press, 1959.

Alciati, Andrea. *Paradoxorum ad Pratum libri VI...* Basel: Apud And. Cratandrum, 1523.

Aubrey, John. *Proposals for Printing Monumenta Britannica.* [London]: n.p., [1693].

Aubrey, John. *The Natural History and Antiquities of the County of Surrey,* 5 vols. London: Printed for E. Curll, 1718–19.

Aubrey, John. *Remaines of Gentilisme and Judaisme,* ed. James Britten. London: Published for the Folk-Lore Society by W. Satchell, Peyton, and Co., 1881.

Aubrey, John. The Life of Mr. Thomas Hobbes, of Malmesburie, in *'Brief Lives', Chiefly of Contemporaries, Set Down by John Aubrey, Between the Years 1669 & 1696,* 2 vols., ed. Andrew Clark. Oxford: At the Clarendon Press, 1898, i. 321–403.

Aubrey, John. *Three Prose Works: Miscellanies, Remaines of Gentilisme and Judaisme, Observations.* ed. John Buchanan-Brown. Fontwell, Sussex: Centaur Press, 1972.

Aubrey, John. *Monumenta Britannica, or, a Miscellany of British Antiquities,* 2 vols., ed. John Fowles and Rodney Legg. Sherborne, Dorset: Dorset Publishing Co., 1980–2.

Aubrey, John. *Brief Lives with An Apparatus for the Lives of our English Mathematical Writers,* 2 vols., ed. Kate Bennett. Oxford: Oxford University Press, 2015.

Avity, Pierre d', Sieur de Montmartin. *The Estates, Empires, & Principallities of the World.* London: Printed by Adam Islip for Mathewe Lownes and John Bill, 1615.

Bacon, Francis. *The Advancement of Learning,* ed. Michael Kiernan. Oxford: Oxford University Press, 2000.

Bacon, Francis. *Instauratio Magna, Part II: Novum Organum and Associated Texts.* ed. Graham Rees. Oxford: Oxford University Press, 2004.

Bacon, Francis. *Instauratio Magna, Part III,* ed. Graham Rees with Maria Wakely. Oxford: Oxford University Press, 2007.

Balzac, Jean-Louise Guez, Seigneur de. *The Roman: The Conversation of the Romans and Maecenas, in Three Excellent Discourses.* London: Printed by T. N. for J. Holden, 1652.

Bartholin, Thomas. *Epistolarum medicinalium à Doctis vel ad Doctos scriptarum,* 3 vols. Copenhagen: Typis Matthiae Godicchenii, 1663–7.

Bartholin, Thomas. *Antiquitatum Danicarum de causis contemptae a Danis adhuc gentilibus mortis libri tres ex vetustus codicibus & monumentis hactenus ineditis congesti.* Copenhagen: Literis Joh. Phil. Bockenhoffer, 1689.

Benjamin of Tudela. *Itinerarium Benjaminis,* trans. and ed. Constantijn L'Empereur. Leiden: Ex officina Elzeviriana, 1633.

Bernard, Edward. Etymologicon Britannicum, in George Hickes, *Institutiones grammaticae Anglo-Saxonicae et Moeso-Gothicae.* Oxford: E Theatro Sheldoniano, 1689. sigs. Qqr-Uuv.

Bernard, Edward. *Orbis eruditi literatura à Charactere Samaritico deducta.* Oxford: Apud Theatrum, 1689.

Biographia Britannica, 6 vols. in 8. London: Printed for W. Innys, 1747–66.

Birch, Thomas. *The History of the Royal Society of London for Improving of Natural Knowledge*, 4 vols. London: Printed for A. Millar in the Strand, 1756–7.

Blackburne, Richard and John Aubrey. *Thomae Hobbes Angli Malmesburiensis philosophi vita*. Carolopoli: Apud Eleutherium Anglicum [*sic*], 1681.

Blount, Sir Thomas Pope. *Censura celebriorum authorum: sive tractatus in quo varia virorum doctorum de clarissimis cujusque seculi scriptoribus judicia traduntur*... London: Impensis Richardi Chiswel, 1690.

Bochart, Samuel. *Geographia sacra*. Caen: Typis Petri Cardonelli, 1646.

Boece, Hector. *Scotorum historiae a prima gentis origine*. Paris: Iodoci Badii Ascensii typis, 1527.

Boece, Hector. *The Chronicles of Scotland*, ed. R. W. Chambers and Edith C. Batho, 2 vols. Edinburgh and London: Printed for the [Scottish Text] Society by W. Blackwood & Sons, Ltd., 1938–41.

Bolton, Edmund Mary. *Nero Caesar, or Monarchie Depraved*. London: Printed by Thomas Snodham and Bernard Alsop for Thomas Walkley, 1624.

Bosio, Antonio. *Roma sotteranea*. Rome: Appresso Guglielmo Facciotti, 1632.

Bourne, Henry. *Antiquitates Vulgares; or the Antiquities of the Common People. Giving an Account of Several of Their Opinions and Ceremonies With Proper Reflections Upon Each of Them; Shewing Which May be Retain'd, and Which Ought to be Laid Aside*. Newcastle: Printed by J. White for the author, 1725.

Boxhorn, Marcus Zuerius van. *Originum Gallicarum liber*. Amsterdam: Apud Joannem Janssonium, 1654.

Boyle, Robert. *Essays of the Strange Subtilty Great Efficacy Determinate Nature of Effluviums... To Which is Added The Prodromus to a Dissertation... By Nicholas Steno*. London: Printed by W. G. for M. Pitt..., 1673.

Brerewood, Edward. *Enquiries Touching the Diversity of Languages*... London: Printed for Iohn Bill, 1614.

Browne, Edward. *An Account of Several Travels Through a Great Part of Germany*. London: Printed for Benj. Tooke, 1677.

Browne, Sir Thomas. *Pseudodoxia epidemica*. London: Printed by T. H. for E. Dod, 1646.

Browne, Sir Thomas. *Hydriotaphia, Urne-buriall, or, A Discourse of the Sepulchrall Urnes Lately Found in Norfolk. Together With The Garden of Cyrus*... London: Printed for Hen. Brome, 1658.

Browne, Sir Thomas. *Certain Miscellany Tracts*. London: Printed for Charles Mearne, 1683.

Budé, Guillaume. *De asse et partibus*. Paris: Venundantur in aedibus Ascensianis, 1516.

Burchard of Worms, *Decretorum libri XX*. Cologne: Ex officina Melchioris Noueslani, 1548.

Burton, William. *A Commentary on Antoninus his Itinerary, or Journies of the Romane Empire, so far as it Concerneth Britain*. London: Printed by Tho. Roycroft, and are to be sold by Henry Twyford... and T. Twyford, 1658.

Calderwood, David. *The History of the Kirk of Scotland*, 8 vols., ed. Thomas Thomson. Edinburgh: Printed for the Wodrow Society, 1842–9.

Camden, William. *Britannia*. London: Impensis Georgii Bishop & Ioannis Norton, 1607.

Camden, William. *Britain*, trans. Philemon Holland. London: Impensis Georgii Bishop & Ioannis Norton, 1610.

Camden, William. *Camden's Britannia*. ed. Edmund Gibson et al. London: Printed by F. Collins, 1695.

Carew, Thomas, and Inigo Jones. *Coelum Britanicum: a Masque at White-Hall in the Banquetting-House, on Shrove-Tuesday-night, the 18. of February, 1633*. London: Printed for Thomas Walkley, 1634.

Casaubon, Meric. *A Treatise of Use and Custome*. London: Printed by I. L., 1638.

Celtis, Conrad. De origine, situ, moribus & institutis Norimbergae, in *Quatuor libri amorum secundum quatuor latera Germaniæ feliciter incipiunt*. Nuremberg: n.p., 1502. sigs. miii^r–pvii^v.

Charleton, Walter. *The Darknes of Atheism Dispelled By the Light of Nature: a Physico-Theologicall Treatise*. London: Printed by J. F. for William Lee, 1652.

Charleton, Walter. *Chorea Gigantum, or, the Most Famous Antiquity of Great-Britan, Vulgarly Called Stone-Heng, Standing on Salisbury Plain, Restored to the Danes*. London: Printed for Henry Herringman, 1663.

Chishull, Edmund. *Travels in Turkey and Back to England*. London: Printed by W. Bowyer, 1747.

Cramer, Balthasar Gottfried. *Disputatio juridica inauguralis de commodis paupertatis... Balthas. Gothofredus Cramerus...* Basel: Decker, 1671.

Cudworth, Ralph. *Discourse Concerning the True Notion of the Lords Supper*. London: Printed for Richard Cotes, 1642.

Cunningham, James. *An Essay upon the Inscription of Macduff's Cross in Fyfe*. Edinburgh: Printed by William Adams Junior, 1678.

Davies, John. *Antiquae linguae Britannicae...* London: Impress. in aedibus R. Young, 1621.

Della Valle, Pietro. *Viaggi di Pietro della Valle il Pellegrino...*, 4 vols. Rome: Appresso Vitale Mascardi, 1650–63.

Desgodetz, Antoine Babuty. *Les edifices antiques de Rome*. Paris: Chez Jean Baptiste Coignard, 1682.

Dolet, Étienne. *Commentariorum linguae Latinae tomus primus*. Lyons: Apud Seb. Gryphium, 1536.

Drake, Francis. *Eboracum, or, the History and Antiquities of the City of York*. London: Printed by William Bowyer for the author, 1736.

Drayton, Michael. *Poly-Olbion*. London: Printed for M. Lownes [et al.], 1612.

Dryden, John. *The Works of John Dryden*, 20 vols., general eds. Edward Niles Hooker and H. T. Swedenberg. Berkeley, CA, and London: University of California Press, 1956–2000.

Dugdale, William. *History of Imbanking and Drayning...* London: Printed by Alice Warren, 1662.

Dwnn, Lewys. *Heraldic Visitations of Wales and Part of the Marches.* 2 vols., ed. Sir Samuel Rush Meyrick. Llandovery: W. Rees, 1846.

Edwards, Charles. *Hebraismorum Cambro-Britannicorum specimen honorandis antiquae Britannicae gentis primoribus...* London: n.p., 1675.

Estienne, Robert. *Dictionarium, seu Latinae linguae thesaurus.* Paris: Ex officina Roberti Stephani, 1531.

Evelyn, John. *The Diary of John Evelyn,* 6 vols., ed. E. S. de Beer. Oxford: Clarendon Press, 1955.

Fabricius, Johann Albert. *Bibliographia antiquaria,* 2nd edn. Hamburg and Leipzig: Impensis Christiani Liebezeit, 1716.

Flavio, Biondo. *Italia illustrata,* mult. vols., ed. and trans. Jeffrey A. White. Cambridge, MA: Harvard University Press, 2005–.

Foy-Vaillant, Jean. *Seleucidarum imperium, sive historia regum Syriae.* Paris: Excudebat Ludovicus Billaine, 1681.

Fréart de Chambray, Roland. *A Parallel of the Antient Architecture With the Modern,* trans. John Evelyn. London: Printed by Tho. Roycroft, 1664.

Fulman, William. *Academiae Oxoniensis notitia.* Oxford: Typis W.H. impensis R. Davis, 1665.

Gale, Theophilus. *Court of the Gentiles,* 2 vols. Oxford: Printed by Hen: Hall for Tho: Gilbert, 1669–70.

Gale, Thomas. *Antonini iter Britanniarum commentariis illustratum... opus posthumum,* ed. Roger Gale. London: Impensis M. Atkins, 1709.

Gale, Thomas, ed. *Opuscula mythologica, ethica et physica.* Cambridge: Ex officina J. Hayes, 1671.

Gale, Thomas, ed. *Historiae poeticae scriptores antiqui... accessere breves notae & indices necessarii.* Paris: Typis F. Muguet, Prostant apud R. Scott, bibliopolam Londinensem, 1675.

Gale, Thomas, ed. *Rhetores selecti.* Oxford: E Theatro Sheldoniano, 1676.

Gale, Thomas, ed. *Historiae Anglicanae scriptores quinque.* Oxford: E Theatro Sheldoniano, 1687.

Gale, Thomas, ed. *Historiae Britanniae, Saxonicae, Anglo-Danicae, Scriptores XV.* Oxford: E Theatro Sheldoniano, 1691.

Gassendi, Pierre. *The Mirrour of True Nobility & Gentility: Being the Life of the Renowned Nicolaus Claudius Fabricius, Lord of Pieresk,* trans. W. Rand. London: Printed by J. Streater for Humphrey Moseley, 1657.

Gassendi, Pierre. Philosophiae Epicuri syntagma, in *Opera omnia,* 6 vols. Lyons: Sumpt. Laurentii Anisson & Joannis Baptistae Devenet, 1658. iii. 27–36.

Geoffrey of Monmouth, *Historia Regum Britanniae: The First Variant Version: A Critical Edition,* ed. Neil Wright. Woodbridge: D. S. Brewer, 1988.

Gibbon, Edward. *The History of the Decline and Fall of the Roman Empire,* 3 vols., ed. David Womersley. London: Penguin, 1994.

Gibson, Edmund, ed. *Chronicon Saxonicum.* Oxford: E Theatro Sheldoniano, 1692.

Gordon, Alexander. *Itinerarium Septentrionale: or, a Journey thro' Most of the Counties of Scotland and Those in the North of England.* London: Printed for F. Gyles [et al.], 1726.

Gouldman, Francis. *A Copious Dictionary in Three Parts*. London: Printed by John Field, 1664.

Greaves, John. *Pyramidographia or a Description of the Pyramids in Ægypt*. London: Printed for George Badger, 1646.

Halley, Edmond. Discourse Tending to Prove at What Time and Place, Julius Cesar Made his First Descent upon Britain. *Philosophical Transactions* 16 (1686–92): 495–501.

Hardouin, Jean. *Ad censuram scriptorum veterum prolegomena*. London: Sumptibus P. Vaillant, 1766.

Hickes, George. *Institutiones grammaticae Anglo-Saxonicae et Moeso-Gothicae*. Oxford: E Theatro Sheldoniano, 1689.

Hobbes, Thomas. *The Life of Mr. Thomas Hobbes of Malmesbury, Written By Himself in a Latine Poem, and Now Translated into English*. London: Printed for A. C., 1680.

Hobbes, Thomas. *Leviathan*, 3 vols., ed. Noel Malcolm. Oxford: Oxford University Press, 2012.

Homer. *Homeri poemata duo, Ilias et Odyssea, sive Ulyssea*, 2 vols. Geneva: Excudebat Paulus Stephanus, 1604.

Hooke, Robert. Lecture and Discourses of Earthquakes and Subterraneous Eruptions, in *Posthumous Works*. London: Printed by Sam. Smith and Benj. Walford, 1705, 277–450.

Hooke, Robert. *Diary of Robert Hooke, M.A., M.D., F.R.S., 1672–1680*, ed. Henry W. Robinson and Walter Adams. London: Taylor & Francis, 1935.

Hopton, Arthur. *A Concordancy of Yeares . . .* London: Printed for the Company of Stationers, 1612.

Horsley, John. *Britannia Romana: or the Roman Antiquities of Britain*. London: Printed for John Osborn and Thomas Longman, 1732.

Hyde, Thomas. *Catalogus impressorum librorum Bibliothecae Bodleianae in Academia Oxoniensi*. Oxford: E theatro Sheldoniano, 1674.

Iamblichus. *De mysteriis liber*, ed. Thomas Gale. Oxford: E Theatro Sheldoniano, 1678.

Itineraria Romana, volumen prius: Itineraria Antonini Augusti et Burdigalense, ed. Otto Cuntz. Leipzig: In aedibus B. G. Teubneri, 1929.

Jones, Inigo. *The Most Notable Antiquity of Great Britain, Vulgarly Called Stone-Heng on Salisbury Plain Restored*. London: Printed by James Flesher, 1655.

Junius, Hadrianus. *Emblemata*. Antwerp: Ex officina Christophori Plantini, 1565.

Kennett, White. *Parochial Antiquities Attempted in the History of Ambrosden, Burchester, and Other Adjacent Parts in the Counties of Oxford and Bucks*. Oxford: Printed at the Theater, 1695.

Kircher, Athanasius. *Oedipus Aegyptiacus*, 3 vols. Rome: Ex typographia Vitalis Mascardi, 1652.

Kircher, Athanasius. *Mundus subterraneus*, 2 vols. Amsterdam: Apud Joannem Janssonium & Elizeum Weyerstraten, 1665.

Kircher, Athanasius. *Turris Babel*. Amsterdam: Ex officina Janssonio-Waesbergiana, 1679.

Lactantius. *Divinae institutiones*, ed. J.-P. Migne. Paris: Garnier, 1844.

Lagadeuc, Jehan. *Le Catholicon*. Tréguier: Jehan Calvez, 1499.

Leland, John. *The Laboryouse Journey [and] Serche of Johan Leylande, for Englandes Antiquitees*. London: Printed by S. Mierdman for John Bale, 1549.

Lhuyd, Edward. *A Design of a British Dictionary*. Oxford: n.p., 1695.

Lhuyd, Edward. *Archaeologia Britannica*. Oxford: Printed at the Theater, 1707.

Lhuyd, Edward. *Life and Letters of Edward Lhuyd*, ed. R. T. Gunther. Oxford: Oxford University Press, 1945.

Liceti, Fortunio. *De lucernis antiquorum reconditis libb. sex*. Udine: Ex typographia Nicolai Schiratti, 1652.

Livy. *The Romane Historie*, trans. Philemon Holland. London: Printed by Adam Islip, 1600.

Livy. *Historiarum quod extat*, 3 vols., ed. Johann Friedrich Gronovius. Amsterdam: Apud Ludovicum & Danielem Elzevirios, 1665.

Livy. *Historiarum quod extat*, 3 vols., ed. Johann Friedrich Gronovius. Amsterdam: Apud Danielem Elsevirium, 1678.

Mabillon, Jean. *De re diplomatica*. Paris: Sumptibus Ludovici Billaine, 1681.

Maffei, Raffaello. *Commentariorum rerum urbanorum libri XXXVIII*. Rome: Per Ioannem Besicken Alemanum, 1506.

Maggi, Girolamo. *De tintinnabulis liber postumus*, ed. Franciscus Sweertius. Amsterdam: Sumptibus Andreae Frisii, 1664.

Martini, Martino. *Bellum Tartaricum, or the Conquest of China by the Tartars*. London: Printed for John Crook, 1654.

Mercurius Pragmaticus, 53 numbers. London: n.p., 1647~9.

Middleton, Conyers. *A Letter From Rome, Showing an Exact Conformity Between Popery and Paganism: or, the Religion of the Present Romans Derived From That of Their Heathen Ancestors*, 3rd edn. London: Printed for William Innys and Richard Manby, 1733.

Milton, John. *The History of Britain . . .* London: Printed by J. M. for James Allestry, 1670.

Nebrija, Antonio de. *Relectio nona de accentu latino aut latinitate donato quam habuit Salma[n]tice*. Seville: Ex impressione hispalensi, 1513.

New Proposals For Printing By Subscription Camden's Britannia. English. n.p.: n.p., 1693.

Newton, Isaac. *Opera quae exstant omnia*, 5 vols., ed. Samuel Horsley. London: Excudebat Joannes Nichols, 1779–85.

Olofsson, Erik. *Historia Suecorum Gothorumque*, ed. Johan Loccenius. Stockholm: Ex officina J. Janssonii, 1654.

Ortelius, Abraham, ed. *Itinerarium Antonini Augusti, et Burdigalense*. Cologne: In officina Birckmannica sumptibus Arnoldi Mylij, 1600.

Panciroli, Guido. *The History of Many Memorable Things Lost, Which Were in Use Among the Ancients*, 2 vols. London: Printed for John Nicholson, 1715.

Paris, Matthew. *Historia major*, ed. William Watts. London: R. Hodgkinson, 1639–40.

Pererius, Benedictus. *Commentariorum disputationum in Genesim Tomi Quatuor*. Mainz: Sumptibus Atonii Hierati, 1612.

Pits, John. *Relationum historicarum de rebus Anglicis*. Paris: Apud Rolinum Thiorry et Sebastianum Cramoisy, 1619.

Pliny. *The Historie of the World Commonly Called, the Naturall Historie*, trans. Philemon Holland. London: Printed by Adam Islip, 1601.

Plot, Robert. *The Natural History of Oxford-Shire: Being an Essay Toward the Natural History of England*. Oxford: Printed at the Theater, 1677.

Plot, Robert. A Discourse Concerning the Sepulchral Lamps of the Ancients, Shewing the Possibility of Their Being Made Divers Waies. *Philosophical Transactions* 14 (1684): 806–11.

Polybius. *The History of Polybius the Megalopolitan . . . Also the Manner of the Romane Encamping . . .*, trans. Edward Grimeston. London: Printed by N. Okes, 1634.

Porcheron, David-Placide, ed. *Anonymi Ravennatis qui circa saeculum VII. vixit de geographia libri quinque*. Paris: Apud Simonem Langronne, 1688.

Pratt, Roger. *The Architecture of Sir Roger Pratt*, ed. R. T. Gunther. Oxford: Printed by John Johnson for the author at the University Press, 1928.

Proposals for Printing by Subscription Cambden's Britannia, English. [London]: n.p., [1693].

Purchas, Samuel. *Purchas his Pilgrimage*. London: Printed by William Stansby for Henrie Fetherstone, 1613.

Ray, John. *A Collection of English Words not Generally Used*, 2nd edn. London: Printed by Christopher Wilkinson, 1691.

Regius, Henricus. *Philosophia naturalis*, 2nd edn. Amsterdam: Apud Ludovicum Elzevirium, 1654.

Reyher, Samuel. *Mathesis Mosaica, sive loca Pentateuchi mathematica mathematicè explicata*. Kiel: Typis Joachimi Reumanni, 1679.

Rhys, John David. *Cambrobrytannicae Cymraecaeue linguae institutiones et rudimenta accuratè, & (quantùm fieri potuit) succinctè & compendiosè conscripta*. London: Excudebat Thomas Orwinus, 1592.

Rickman, Thomas. *An Attempt to Discriminate the Styles of Architecture in England, From the Conquest to the Reformation*, 3rd edn. London: Longman, Hurst, Rees, Orme, & Co., 1825.

Rosinus, Johannes. *Romanarum antiquitatum libri decem*. Lyons: n.p., 1585.

Rudbeck, Olof. *Atland Eller Manhem . . . Atlantica sive Manheim*, 4 vols. Uppsala: Excudit Henricus Curio, 1679–1702.

Rudbeck, Olof. *Bref af Olof Rudbeck d.ä. rörande Uppsalas universitet*, 4 vols., ed. Claes Annerstedt. Uppsala: Akademiska Boktryckeriet, 1893–1905.

Sammes, Aylett. *Britannia antiqua illustrata*. London: Printed by Tho. Roycroft, for the author, 1676.

Savile, Sir Henry. A view of certaine militar matters, for the better vnderstanding of the ancient Roman stories, in *The End of Nero and Beginning of Galba: Fower Bookes of the Histories of Cornelius Tacitus . . .* Oxford: By Ioseph Barnes, 1591. sep. pag. 49–75.

Savile, Sir Henry. *Commentarius de militia Romana*, trans. Marquard Freher. Heidelberg: Typis Voegelianis, 1601.

Scaliger, Joseph Justus. *Ausonianarum lectionum libri duo*. Lyons: Apud Ant. Gryphium, 1574.

Scaliger, Joseph Justus. *Prima Scaligerana: nusquam antehac edita*. Groningen: Apud Petrum Smithaeum, 1669.

Scheffer, Johann. *Upsalia cujus occasione plurima in religione, sacris, festis . . . illustrantur*. Uppsala: Excudit H. Curio, 1666.

Schellius, Rabodus Hermannus, ed. *Hygini gromatici, et Polybii Megalopolitani, de castris Romanis, quae exstant*. Amsterdam: Apud Judocum Pluymer, 1660.

Selden, John. *Jani Anglorum facies altera*. London: Impens. auctor. typis T. S., 1610.

Selden, John. *Analecton Anglobritannicon libri duo*. Frankfurt: Prodeunt ex Officina Paltheniana, 1615.

Selden, John. *De diis Syris syntagmata II*. London: Bibliopolarum corpori excudebat Guilielmus Stansbeius, 1617.

Selden, John. *The Reverse or Back-Face of the English Janus*, trans. Adam Littleton. London: Printed for Thomas Basset, and Richard Chiswell, 1682.

Selden, John. *Table-Talk*, ed. Richard Milward. London: Printed for E. Smith, 1689.

Semedo, Alvaro. *The History of That Great and Renowned Monarchy of China*, trans. Thomas Henshaw. London: Printed by E. Tyler for Iohn Crook, 1655.

Sherburne, Edward. *The Sphere of Marcus Manilius Made an English Poem With Annotations and an Astronomical Appendix*. London: Printed for Nathanael Brooke, 1675.

Sibbald, Robert. *Miscellanea quaedam eruditae antiquitatis quae ad Borealem Britanniae majoris partem pertinent*. Edinburgh: Impensis authoris excudebat M. Andreas Symson, 1710.

Smith, Thomas. *Syntagma de Druidum Moribus ac Institutis*. London: Excudebat Thomas Roycroft, 1664.

Spanheim, Friedrich. *Introductio ad historiam et antiquitates sacras*. Leiden: Ex officina Adriani Severini, 1675.

Spelman, Sir Henry. *Villare Anglicum, or, a View of the Townes of England*. London: Printed by R. Hodgkinsonne, 1656.

Spelman, Sir Henry. *Glossarium Archaiologicum*. London: Excudebat Tho. Braddyll, 1664.

Spon, Jacques. *Miscellanea eruditae antiquitatis*. Lyons: Sumptibus auctoris, 1685.

Steno, Nicolaus. *De solido intra solidum naturaliter contento dissertationis prodromus*. Florence: Ex typographia sub signo stellae, 1669.

Steno, Nicolaus. *The Prodromus to a Dissertation Concerning Solids Naturally Contained Within Solids*, trans. H[enry] O[ldenburg]. London: Printed by J. Winter, 1671.

Stopford, Joshua. *Pagano-Papismus; or, an Exact Parallel Between Rome-Pagan and Rome-Christian in Their Doctrines and Ceremonies*. London: Printed by A. Maxwell, 1675.

Tavernier, Jean-Baptiste. *The Six Voyages of John Baptista Tavernier*. London: Printed by William Godbid, for Robert Littlebury, 1677.

Theocritus. *The Idylliums of Theocritus*, trans. Thomas Creech. Oxford: Printed by L. Lichfield, 1684.

Thesaurus linguae Romanae & Britannicae tam accurate congestus. London: [by Henry Denham], 1578.

Toland, John. *A Collection of Several Pieces of Mr. John Toland, Now First Publish'd From His Original Manuscripts*, 2 vols. London: Printed for J. Peele, 1726.

Verelius, Olof. *Manuductio compendiosa ad runographiam Scandicam antiquam, recte intelligendam*. Uppsala: Excudit Henricus Curio, 1675.

Verelius, Olof, ed. *Hervarar Saga på Gammal Gotska med Olai Vereli uttolkning och notis*. Uppsala: Excudet Henricus Curio, 1672.

Vergil, Polydore. *On Discovery*, ed. Brian P. Copenhaver. Cambridge, MA: Harvard University Press, 2002.

Virgil. *Virgil's Georgicks*, trans. Thomas May. London: Printed for Tho. Walkley, 1628.

Virgil. *Opera ... Pauli Manutii annotationes brevissimae in margine adscriptae*. Cambridge: Ex academiae celeberrimae typographeo, 1632.

Vulcanius, Bonaventura. *De literis et lingua Getarum, sive Gothorum*. Leiden: Ex officina Plantiniana, 1597.

Wallis, John. *The Popham Notebook: John Wallis's Manual for Teaching Language to a Boy Born Deaf*, ed. David Cram and Jaap Maat. Oxford: Oxford University Press, forthcoming 2016.

Warburton, William. *Letters From a Late Eminent Prelate to One of His Friends*. Kidderminster: Printed by George Gower, for T. Cadell and W. Davies, [1793?].

Webb, John. *A Vindication of Stone-Heng Restored*. London: Printed by R. Davenport, 1665.

White, Gilbert. *Natural History and Antiquities of Selborne ...* London: Printed by T. Bensley, 1789.

Wilkins, John. *Mathematicall Magick, or, the Wonders That May be Performed By Mechanicall Geometry*. London: Printed by M. F. for Sa. Gellibrand, 1648.

Wolf, Friedrich August. *Prolegomena to Homer*, trans. and ed. Anthony Grafton, Glenn W. Most, and James E. G. Zetzel. Princeton, NJ: Princeton University Press, 1985.

Wood, Anthony. *Historia et antiquitates Universitatis Oxoniensis*, 2 vols. Oxford: E Theatro Sheldoniano, 1674.

Wood, Anthony. *Athenae Oxonienses*, 2 vols. London: Printed for Tho. Bennet, 1691–2.

Wood, Anthony. *The Life and Times of Anthony Wood, Antiquary, of Oxford, 1632–1695, Described By Himself*, 5 vols., ed. Andrew Clark. Oxford: Printed for the Oxford Historical Society, at the Clarendon Press, 1891–1900.

Wood, Anthony. *The Life of Anthony Wood in His Own Words*, ed. Nicolas K. Kiessling. Oxford: Bodleian Library, 2009.

Wood, Robert. *The Ruins of Palmyra, Otherwise Tedmor, in the Desart*. London: n.p., 1753.

Wood, Robert. *The Ruins of Balbec, otherwise Heliopolis in Coelosyria*. London: n.p., 1757.

Worm, Ole. *Danicorum Monumentorum Libri Sex.* Copenhagen: Apud J. Moltkenium, 1643.

Worm, Ole. *Museum Wormianum, seu historia rerum rariorum.* Leiden: Apud Iohannem Elsevirium, 1655.

Worm, Ole. *Breve fra og til Ole Worm*, 3 vols., ed. H. D. Schepelern. Copenhagen: Munksgaard, 1965–8.

Worm, Ole. *Olai Wormii et ad eum doctorum virorum epistolae*, 2 vols. Copenhagen: n.p., 1751.

Worthington, John. *The Diary and Correspondence of Dr. John Worthington, Master of Jesus College, Cambridge*, 2 vols. in 3, ed. James Crossley and Richard Copley Christie. Manchester: Printed for the Chetham Society, 1847–86.

Wren, Christopher. *Wren's 'Tracts' on Architecture and Other Writings*, ed. Lydia M. Soo. Cambridge: Cambridge University Press, 1998.

SECONDARY SOURCES

Abercrombie, David. William Holder and Other 17th-Century Phoneticians. *Historiographia Linguistica* 20 (1993): 309–30.

Almond, Philip. Adam, Pre-Adamites, and Extra-Terrestrial Beings in Early Modern Europe. *Journal of Religious History* 30 (2006): 163–74.

Anderson, Christy. *Inigo Jones and the Classical Tradition.* Cambridge: Cambridge University Press, 2007.

Aston, Margaret. English Ruins and English History: The Dissolution and the Sense of the Past. *Journal of the Warburg and Courtauld Institutes* 36 (1973): 231–55.

Atkinson, Catherine. *Inventing Inventors in Renaissance Europe: Polydore Vergil's De inventoribus rerum.* Tübingen: Mohr Siebeck, 2007.

Aude, A. F. *Bibliographie critique et raisonné des Ana Français et étrangers.* Paris: H. Daragon, 1910.

Bath, Michael. Philostratus Comes to Scotland: A New Source for the Pictures at Pinkie. *Journal of the Northern Renaissance* 5 (2013), online at <http://www.northernrenaissance.org/philostratus-comes-to-scotland-a-new-source-for-the-pictures-at-pinkie/> (accessed 13 January 2016).

Bennett, G. V. *White Kennett, 1660–1728, Bishop of Peterborough: Study in the Political and Ecclesiastical History of the Early Eighteenth Century.* London: Published for the Church Historical Society by the S.P.C.K., 1957.

Bennett, J. A. W. The Beginnings of Runic Studies in England. *Saga-Book of the Viking Society* 13 (1946–53): 269–83.

Bennett, Kate. John Aubrey's Collections and the Early-Modern Museum. *Bodleian Library Record* 17 (2001): 213–45.

Bennett, Kate. John Aubrey, Hint-Keeper: Life-Writing and the Encouragement of Natural Philosophy in the pre-Newtonian Seventeenth Century. *The Seventeenth Century* 22 (2007): 358–80.

Bennett, Kate. John Aubrey and the 'Lives of our English Mathematical Writers', in *The Oxford Handbook of the History of Mathematics*, ed. Eleanor Robson and Jacqueline Stedall. Oxford: Oxford University Press, 2009, 329–52.

Bennett, Kate. John Aubrey and the Printed Book. *Huntington Library Quarterly* 76 (2013): 393–411.

Bennett, Kate. John Aubrey and the Rhapsodic Book. *Renaissance Studies* 28 (2014): 317–32.

Bold, John. *John Webb: Architectural Theory and Practice in the Seventeenth Century.* Oxford: Clarendon Press, 1989.

Borst, Arno. *Der Turmbau von Babel: Geschichte der Meinungen über Ursprung und Vielfalt der Sprachen und Völker*, 4 vols. in 6. Stuttgart: A. Hiersemann, 1957–63.

Boucher, Bruce. *Andrea Palladio: The Architect in his Time*, rev. edn. New York: Abbeville Press, 1998.

Broadway, Jan. *William Dugdale and the Significance of County History in Early Stuart England.* Stratford-upon-Avon: Dugdale Society, 1999.

Broadway, Jan. '*No Historie so meete*': *Gentry Culture and the Development of Local History in Elizabethan and Early Stuart England.* Manchester: Manchester University Press, 2006.

Broadway, Jan. 'Ocular Exploration, and Subterraneous Enquiry': Developing Archaeological Fieldwork in the Mid-Seventeenth Century. *Antiquaries Journal* 92 (2012): 353–69.

Buchanan-Brown, John. The Books Presented to the Royal Society by John Aubrey, F.R.S. *Notes and Records of the Royal Society of London* 28 (1974): 167–93.

Buchwald, Jed Z., and Mordechai Feingold. *Newton and the Origin of Civilization.* Princeton, NJ: Princeton University Press, 2013.

Burke, Peter. Images as Evidence in Seventeenth-Century Europe. *Journal of the History of Ideas* 64 (2003): 273–96.

Capp, Bernard. *England's Culture Wars: Puritan Reformation and its Enemies in the Interregnum, 1649–1660.* Oxford: Oxford University Press, 2012.

A Catalogue of Curious and Valuable MSS. in Hengwrt Library, A.D. 1658. *Cambrian Register* 3 (1818): 302–3.

Cazes, Hélène, ed. *Bonaventura Vulcanius, Works and Networks.* Leiden: Brill, 2010.

Champion, Justin. *Republican Learning: John Toland and the Crisis of Christian Culture, 1696–1722.* Manchester: Manchester University Press, 2003.

Cokayne, George E. *Complete Baronetage*, 6 vols. Exeter: Pollard, 1900–9.

Cokayne, George E. *The Complete Peerage of England, Scotland, Ireland, Great Britain and the United Kingdom*, 13 vols. in 14, ed. Vicary Gibbs et al. London: St Catherine Press, 1910–98.

Collins, Jeffrey R. *The Allegiance of Thomas Hobbes.* Oxford: Oxford University Press, 2005.

Collins, Jeffrey R. Interpreting Thomas Hobbes in Competing Contexts. *Journal of the History of Ideas* 70 (2009): 165–80.

Colvin, H. M. Aubrey's *Chronologia Architectonica*, in *Concerning Architecture: Essays on Architectural Writers and Writing Presented to Nikolaus Pevsner*, ed. John Summerson. London: Allen Lane, 1968, 1–12.

Constantine, David. *In the Footsteps of the Gods: Travellers to Greece and the Quest for the Hellenic Ideal.* 1984; repr. London: Tauris Parke Paperbacks, 2011.

Cram, David. Edward Lhuyd's *Archaeologia Britannica*: Method and Madness in Early Modern Comparative Philology. *Welsh History Review* 25 (2010): 75–96.

Cranston, Maurice. John Locke and John Aubrey. *Notes and Queries* 195 (1950): 552–4.

Cranston, Maurice. John Locke and John Aubrey. *Notes and Queries* 197 (1952): 383–4.

Crowley, D. A., ed. *Victoria County History of Wiltshire,* vol. 12: *Ramsbury Hundred, Selkley Hundred, Borough of Marlborough.* Oxford: Published for the Institute of Historical Research by Oxford University Press, 1983.

Darley, Gillian. *John Evelyn: Living For Ingenuity.* New Haven, CT, and London: Yale University Press, 2006.

Dekker, Kees. *Origins of Old Germanic Studies in the Low Countries.* Leiden: Brill, 1999.

Dekker, Kees. The Runes in Bonaventura Vulcanius *De literis & lingua getarum sive Gothorum* (1597): Provenance and Origins, in *Bonaventura Vulcanius, Works and Networks,* ed. Hélène Cazes. Leiden: Brill, 2010, 411–53.

Dewhurst, Kenneth. *Dr. Thomas Sydenham (1624–1689): His Life and Original Writings.* London: Wellcome Historical Medical Library, 1966.

Dictionary of Welsh Biography Down to 1940. London: Honourable Society of Cymmrodorion, 1959.

Douglas, D. C. *English Scholars,* 2nd edn. London: Eyre & Spottiswoode, 1951.

Dragstra, Henk. 'Before woomen were Readers': How John Aubrey Wrote Female Oral History, in *Oral Traditions and Gender in Early Modern Literary Texts,* ed. Mary Ellen Lamb and Karen Bamford. Aldershot: Ashgate, 2008, 41–53.

Drake, Ellen Tan. *Restless Genius: Robert Hooke and His Earthly Thoughts.* Oxford: Oxford University Press, 1996.

Du Prey, Pierre de la Ruffinière. *Hawksmoor's London Churches: Architecture and Theology.* Chicago: University of Chicago Press, 2000.

Edwards, Nancy. Edward Lhuyd and the Origins of Early Medieval Celtic Archaeology. *Antiquaries Journal* 87 (2007): 165–96.

Eerde, Katherine S. van. *John Ogilby and the Taste of His Times.* Folkestone: Dawson, 1976.

Ekman, Ernst. Gothic Patriotism and Olof Rudbeck. *Journal of Modern History* 34 (1962): 52–63.

Ellenius, Allan. Johannes Schefferus and Swedish Antiquity. *Journal of the Warburg and Courtauld Institutes* 20 (1957): 59–74.

Eriksson, Gunnar. *The Atlantic Vision: Olaus Rudbeck and Baroque Science.* Canton, MA: Science History Publications, 1994.

Eriksson, Gunnar. *Rudbeck 1630–1702: Liv, lärdom och dröm i barockens Sverige.* Stockholm: Atlantis, 2002.

Feingold, Mordechai. Oriental Studies, in *The History of the University of Oxford,* vol. 4: *Seventeenth-Century Oxford,* ed. Nicholas Tyacke. Oxford: Oxford University Press, 1997, 449–503.

Fellows-Jensen, Gillian. John Aubrey, Pioneer Onomast? *Nomina* 23 (2000): 89–106.

Fixler, Michael. A Note on John Evelyn's *History of the Three Late Famous Impostors*. *The Library*, 5th ser., 9 (1954): 267–8.

Foster, Joseph. *Alumni Oxonienses: The Members of the University of Oxford, 1500–1714*, 4 vols. Oxford: Parker, 1891–2.

Friedman, Alice. 'John Evelyn and English Architecture', in *John Evelyn's 'Elysium Britannicum' and European Gardening*, ed. Joachim Wolschke-Bulmahn and Therese O'Malley. Washington, DC: Dumbarton Oaks Research Library and Collection, 1998, 153–70.

Fulton, John F. *A Bibliography of the Honourable Robert Boyle, Fellow of the Royal Society*, 2nd edn. Oxford: Clarendon Press, 1961.

Geysbeek, P. G. Witsen. *Algemeen Noodwendig Woordenboek der Zamenleving*, 7 vols. Amsterdam: Bij Gebroeders Diederichs, 1836–61.

Grafton, Anthony. Prolegomena to Friedrich August Wolf. *Journal of the Warburg and Courtauld Institutes* 44 (1981): 101–29.

Grafton, Anthony. The World of the Polyhistors: Humanism and Encylcopedism. *Central European History* 18 (1985): 31–47.

Grafton, Anthony. *Defenders of the Text: The Traditions of Scholarship in an Age of Science, 1450–1800*. Cambridge, MA: Harvard University Press, 1991.

Grafton, Anthony. *The Footnote: A Curious History*. Cambridge, MA, and London: Harvard University Press, 1999.

Grafton, Anthony. Jean Hardouin: The Antiquary as Pariah. *Journal of the Warburg and Courtauld Institutes* 62 (1999): 241–67.

Grafton, Anthony. *What Was History? The Art of History in Early Modern Europe*. Cambridge: Cambridge University Press, 2007.

Grafton, Anthony. *Worlds Made by Words: Scholarship and Community in the Modern West*. Cambridge, MA, and London: Harvard University Press, 2009.

Grell, Chantal. Le vertige du pyrrhonisme: Hardouin face à l'histoire, in *The Return of Scepticism: From Hobbes and Descartes to Bayle*, ed. Gianni Paganini. Dordrecht: Kluwer Academic Publishers, 2003, 363–74.

Grell, Ole Peter. In Search of True Knowledge: Ole Worm (1588–1654) and the New Philosophy, in *Making Knowledge in Early Modern Europe: Practices, Objects, and Texts, 1400–1800*, ed. Pamela H. Smith and Benjamin Schmidt. Chicago and London: Chicago University Press, 2007, 214–32.

Gros, Pierre. *Palladio e l'antico*. Venice: Centro internazionale di studi di architettura Andrea Palladio, 2006.

Gunther, R. T. The Library of John Aubrey. *Bodleian Quarterly Record* 6 (1931): 230–6.

Gunther, R. T. *Dr. Plot and the Correspondence of the Philosophical Society of Oxford*. Oxford: Printed for the subscribers, 1939.

Hafstein, Valdimar Tr. Bodies of Knowledge: Ole Worm and Collecting in Late Renaissance Scandinavia. *Ethnologia Europaea* 33 (2003): 5–19.

Handa, Rumiko. Coelum Britannicum: Inigo Jones and Symbolic Geometry, in *Nexus IV: Architecture and Mathematics*, ed. José Francisco Rodrigues and Kim Williams. Turin: Kim Williams Books, 2002, 109–24.

Handa, Rumiko. Authorship of *The Most Notable Antiquity* (1655): Inigo Jones and Early Printed Books. *Papers of the Bibliographical Society of America* 100 (2006): 357–77.

Hansson, Craig Ashley. *The English Virtuoso: Art, Medicine and Antiquarianism in the Age of Empiricism*. Chicago and London: University of Chicago Press, 2009.

Hansson, Stina. The Lament of the Swedish Language: Sweden's Gothic Renaissance. *Renaissance Studies* 23 (2009): 151–60.

Hart, Vaughan. *Inigo Jones: The Architect of Kings*. New Haven, CT, and London: Yale University Press, 2011.

Hart, Vaughan, and Richard Tucker. 'Immaginacy set free': Aristotelian Ethics and Inigo Jones's Banqueting House at Whitehall. *RES: Anthropology and Aesthetics* 39 (2001): 151–67.

Haugen, Kristine Louise. Transformations of the Trinity Doctrine in English Scholarship. *Archiv für Religionsgeschichte* 3 (2001): 149–68.

Haugen, Kristine Louise. *Richard Bentley: Poetry and Enlightenment*. Cambridge, MA, and London: Harvard University Press, 2011.

Henderson, Felicity. Unpublished Material from the Memorandum Book of Robert Hooke, Guildhall Library MS 1758. *Notes and Records of the Royal Society* 61 (2007): 129–75.

Henning, Basil Duke. *The History of Parliament: The House of Commons, 1660–1690*, 3 vols. London: Published for the History of Parliament Trust, 1983.

Herendeen, Wyman H. *William Camden: A Life in Context*. Woodbridge: Boydell, 2007.

Herklotz, Ingo. *Cassiano Dal Pozzo und die Archäologie des 17. Jahrhunderts*. Munich: Hirmer, 1999.

Herklotz, Ingo. *La Roma degli antiquari: cultura e erudizione tra Cinquecento e Settecento*. Rome: De Luca Editori d'Arte, 2012.

Herrmann, Wolfgang. Antoine Desgodets and the Académie Royale d'Architecture. *The Art Bulletin* 40 (1958): 23–53.

Hirschi, Caspar. *The Origins of Nationalism: An Alternative History from Ancient Rome to Early Modern Germany*. Cambridge: Cambridge University Press, 2012.

Hodgson, Norma, and Cyprian Blagden. *The Notebook of Thomas Bennet and Henry Clements (1686–1719) With Some Aspects of Book Trade Practice*. Oxford: Oxford University Press, 1956.

Horne, Thomas Hartwell. *An Introduction to the Critical Study and Knowledge of the Holy Scriptures*, 2 vols. Philadelphia, PA: Desilver, Thomas, & Co., 1836.

Horsfall Turner, Olivia. 'The Windows of this Church are of several Fashions': Architectural Form and Historical Method in John Aubrey's 'Chronologia Architectonica'. *Architectural History* 54 (2011): 171–93.

Hunter, Michael. The Royal Society and the Origins of British Archaeology. *Antiquity* 65 (1971): 113–21, 187–92.

Hunter, Michael. *John Aubrey and the Realm of Learning*. London: Duckworth, 1975.

Hunter, Michael. *Establishing the New Science*. Woodbridge: Boydell Press, 1989.

Hutton, C. A. The Travels of 'Palmyra' Wood in 1750–51. *Journal of Hellenistic Studies* 47 (1927): 102–28.

Hutton, Ronald. *Blood and Mistletoe: The History of the Druids in Britain.* New Haven, CT, and London: Yale University Press, 2009.

Jackson Williams, Kelsey. Training the Virtuoso: John Aubrey's Education and Early Life. *The Seventeenth Century* 27 (2012): 157–82.

Jackson Williams, Kelsey. Canon before Canon, Literature before Literature: Thomas Pope Blount and the Scope of Early Modern Learning. *Huntington Library Quarterly* 77 (2014): 177–99.

Jackson Williams, Kelsey. Thomas Gray and the Goths: Philology, Poetry, and the Uses of the Norse Past in Eighteenth-Century England. *Review of English Studies* 65 (2014): 694–710.

Jardine, Lisa. *On a Grander Scale: The Outstanding Career of Sir Christopher Wren.* London: HarperCollins, 2003.

Kerrigan, John. *Archipelagic English: Literature, History, and Politics, 1603–1707.* Oxford: Oxford University Press, 2008.

Keynes, Geoffrey. *John Evelyn: A Study in Bibliophily and a Bibliography of his Writings.* Cambridge: Cambridge University Press, 1937.

Kidd, Colin. *British Identities before Nationalism: Ethnicity and Nationhood in the Atlantic World, 1600–1800.* Cambridge: Cambridge University Press, 1999.

Korshin, Paul J. The Development of Intellectual Biography in the Eighteenth Century. *Journal of English and Germanic Philology* 73 (1974): 518–22.

Kristeller, Paul Oskar, ed. *Iter Italicum: A Finding List of Uncatalogued or Incompletely Catalogued Humanistic Manuscripts of the Renaissance in Italian and Other Libraries*, 6 vols. London: Warburg Institute, 1963–96.

Lanciani, Rodolfo. *Pagan and Christian Rome.* Boston, MA, and New York: Houghton, Mifflin & Co., 1896.

Levy, F. J. The Making of Camden's *Britannia. Bibliothèque d'Humanisme et Renaissance* 26 (1964): 70–97.

Lewis, Eric. Walter Charleton and Early Modern Eclecticism. *Journal of the History of Ideas* 62 (2001): 651–64.

Lewis, Rhodri. The Efforts of the Aubrey Correspondence Group to Revise John Wilkins's *Essay* (1668) and their Context. *Historiographia Linguistica* 28 (2001): 331–64.

Lewis, Rhodri. A Babel Off Broad Street: Artificial Language Planning in 1650s Oxford. *History of Universities* 20 (2005): 108–45.

Lewis, Rhodri. *Language, Mind and Nature: Artificial Languages in England from Bacon to Locke.* Cambridge: Cambridge University Press, 2007.

Lewis, Rhodri. Francis Bacon, Allegory, and the Uses of Myth. *Review of English Studies* 61 (2010): 360–89.

Lewis, Rhodri. William Petty's Anthropology: Religion, Colonialism, and the Problem of Human Diversity. *Huntington Library Quarterly* 74 (2011): 261–88.

Ljungqkvist, John, Per Frölund, Hans Göthberg, and Daniel Löwenborg. Gamla Uppsala: Structural Development of a Centre in Middle Sweden. *Archäoligisches Korrespondenzblatt* 41 (2011): 571–85.

Loomis, Laura Hibbard. Geoffrey of Monmouth and Stonehenge. *Proceedings of the Modern Language Association* 45 (1930): 400–15.

Love, Harold. Sir William Petty, the London Coffee Houses, and the Restoration 'Leonine'. *The Seventeenth Century* 22 (2007): 381–94.

Loveman, Kate. *Reading Fictions, 1660–1740: Deception in English Literary and Political Culture*. Aldershot: Ashgate, 2008.

McCormick, Ted. *William Petty and the Ambitions of Political Arithmetic*. Oxford: Oxford University Press, 2009.

McKeon, Michael. 'Biography, Fiction, and the Emergence of "Identity" in Eighteenth-Century Britain', in *Writing Lives: Biography and Textuality, Identity and Representation in Early Modern England*, ed. Kevin Sharpe and Steven N. Zwicker. Oxford: Oxford University Press, 2008, 339–55.

Madan, Falconer, Richard William Hunt, H. H. E. Craster, and P. D. Record. *A Summary Catalogue of Western Manuscripts in the Bodleian Library at Oxford*, 7 vols. in 8. Oxford: Clarendon Press, 1895–1953.

Mandelbrote, Scott. 'Eighteenth-Century Reactions to Newton's Anti-Trinitarianism', in *Newton and Newtonianism: New Studies*, ed. J. E. Force and S. Hutton. Dordrecht: Kluwer Academic, 2004, 93–112.

Marchand, Suzanne. *Down from Olympus: Archaeology and Philhellenism in Germany, 1750–1970*. Princeton, NJ: Princeton University Press, 1996.

Martinich, Aloysius. Interpreting the Religion of Thomas Hobbes: An Exchange: Hobbes's Erastianism and Interpretation. *Journal of the History of Ideas* 70 (2009): 143–63.

Mendyk, Stanley. *'Speculum Britanniae': Regional Study, Antiquarianism, and Science in Britain to 1700*. Toronto: University of Toronto Press, 1989.

Meynell, G. G. *Materials for a Biography of Dr. Thomas Sydenham (1624–1689): A New Survey of Public and Private Archives*. Folkestone: Winterdown Books, 1988.

Miles, David, Simon Palmer, Gary Lock, Chris Gosden, and Anne Marie Cromarty. *Uffington White Horse and Its Landscape: Investigations at White Horse Hill, Uffington, 1989–95, and Tower Hill, Ashbury, 1993–4*. Oxford: Published for Oxford Archaeology by Oxford University School of Archaeology, 2003.

Miller, Peter. *Peiresc's Europe: Learning and Virtue in the Seventeenth Century*. New Haven, CT, and London: Yale University Press, 2000.

Miller, Peter. Major Trends in European Antiquarianism, Petrarch to Peiresc, in *The Oxford History of Historical Writing*, vol. 3: *1400–1800*, ed. Jose Rabasa et al. Oxford: Oxford University Press, 2012, 244–60.

Miller, Peter, ed. *Momigliano and Antiquarianism: Foundations of the Modern Cultural Sciences*. Toronto: University of Toronto Press, 2007.

Miller, Peter, and François Louis, eds. *Antiquarianism and Intellectual Life in Europe and China, 1500–1800*. Ann Arbor, MI: University of Michigan Press, 2012.

Momigliano, Arnaldo. Ancient History and the Antiquarian. *Journal of the Warburg and Courtauld Institutes* 13 (1950): 285–315.

Momigliano, Arnaldo. Gibbon's Contribution to Historical Method. *Historia* 2 (1954): 450–63.

Momigliano, Arnaldo. The Rise of Antiquarian Research, in *Classical Foundations of Modern Historiography*. Berkeley, CA: University of California Press, 1990, 54–79.

Morgan, Prys. Boxhorn, Leibniz, and the Welsh. *Studia Celtica* 8/9 (1973–4): 220–8.

Morgan, Prys. From Death to a View: The Hunt for the Welsh Past in the Romantic Period, in *The Invention of Tradition*, ed. Eric Hobsbawm and Terence Ranger. Cambridge: Cambridge University Press, 1983, 43–100.

Morgan, Prys. Boxhorn and the Welsh: Some Cambro-Dutch Contacts in the Seventeenth Century. *Dutch Crossing* 24 (2000): 183–90.

Orgel, Stephen, and Roy Strong. *Inigo Jones: The Theater of the Stuart Court*, 2 vols. Berkeley, CA: University of California Press, 1973.

Oryshkevich, Irina. Through a Netherlandish Looking-Glass: Philips van Winghe and Jean l'Heureux in the Catacombs. *Fragmenta* 5 (2011): 101–20.

Oxford Dictionary of National Biography, 60 vols., ed. H. C. G. Matthew and Brian Harrison. Oxford: Oxford University Press, 2004.

Oxford English Dictionary, 2nd edn., 20 vols., ed. J. A. Simpson and E. S. C. Weiner. Oxford: Clarendon Press, 1989.

Page, R. I., William Nicolson, F.R.S., and the Runes of the Bewcastle Cross. *Notes and Records of the Royal Society of London* 14 (1960): 184–90.

Parker, Geoffrey. *Global Crisis: War, Climate Change and Catastrophe in the Seventeenth Century*. New Haven, CT: Yale University Press, 2013.

Parry, Graham. *The Trophies of Time: English Antiquarians of the Seventeenth Century*. Oxford: Oxford University Press, 1995.

Piggott, Stuart. *Ruins in a Landscape: Essays in Antiquarianism*. Edinburgh: Edinburgh University Press, 1976.

Piggott, Stuart. *William Stukeley: An Eighteenth-Century Antiquary* (Oxford: Clarendon Press, 1950).

Piggott, Stuart. *William Stukeley: An Eighteenth-Century Antiquary*. rev. edn. London: Thames & Hudson, 1985.

Piggott, Stuart. *Ancient Britons and the Antiquarian Imagination: Ideas from the Renaissance to the Regency*. London: Thames & Hudson, 1989.

Platt, Colin. *The Great Rebuildings of Tudor and Stuart England: Revolutions in Architectural Taste*. London and Bristol, PA: UCL Press, 1994.

Poole, William. *John Aubrey and the Advancement of Learning*. Oxford: Bodleian Library, 2010.

Poole, William. *The World Makers: Scientists of the Restoration and the Search for the Origins of the Earth*. Oxford: Peter Lang, 2010.

Poole, William. John Aubrey, the Two George Ents, and the 'Paduan' *Laureae Apollinari*. *Bodleian Library Record* 27 (2014), 88–104.

Poole, William. An Early-Modern New College Dynasty: George, Thomas, and Bruno Ryves. *New College Notes*, online at <https://www.new.ox.ac.uk/sites/default/files/4NCN1%20Ryves'%20notes.pdf> (accessed 28 January 2015).

Poole, William. Property of a Late Warden, 1613 with Some More on the Ryves Family. *New College Notes*, online at <https://www.new.ox.ac.uk/sites/default/

files/5NCN7%20Poole%20on%20Ryves%20addenda.pdf> (accessed 28 January 2015).

Poole, William, and Kelsey Jackson Williams. A Swede in Restoration Oxford: Gothic Patriots, Swedish Books, English Scholars. *Lias* 39 (2012): 1–67.

Powell, Anthony. *John Aubrey and His Friends*, new and rev. edn. London: Heinemann, 1963.

Randsborg, Klavs. Ole Worm: An Essay on the Modernization of Antiquity. *Acta Archaeologica* 65 (1994): 135–69.

Rivet, A. L. F., and Kenneth Jackson. The British Section of the Antonine Itinerary. *Britannia* 1 (1970): 34–82.

Rockett, William. Historical Topography and British History in Camden's *Britannia*. *Renaissance and Reformation* 26 (1990): 71–80.

Ruano-García, Javier. Towards an Understanding of Joseph Wright's Sources: White Kennett's *Parochial Antiquities* (1695) and the *English Dialect Dictionary*, in *Middle and Modern English Corpus Linguistics: A Multi-Dimensional Approach*, ed. Manfred Markus, Yoko Iyeiri, Reinhard Heuberger, and Emil Chamson. Amsterdam: John Benjamins Pub. Co., 2012, 241–56.

Rummel, Erika. *Erasmus' Annotations on the New Testament: From Philologist to Theologian*. Toronto: University of Toronto Press, 1986.

Scala, Gail Ewald. An Index of Proper Names in Thomas Birch's *The History of the Royal Society. Notes and Records of the Royal Society of London* 28 (1974): 263–329.

Schepelern, H. D. Museum Wormianum: dets forudsætninger og tilblivelse. Københavns Universitet Doctoral Thesis, 1971.

Schnapp, Alain. *The Discovery of the Past: The Origins of Archaeology*, trans. Ian Kinnes and Gillian Varndell. London: British Museum Press, 1996.

Schwegler, Robert A. Oral Tradition and Print: Domestic Performance in Renaissance England. *Journal of American Folklore* 93 (1980): 435–41.

Seaton, Ethel. *Literary Relations of England and Scandinavia in the Seventeenth Century*. Oxford: Clarendon Press, 1935.

Shalev, Zur. *Sacred Words and Worlds: Geography, Religion, and Scholarship, 1550–1700*. Leiden: Brill, 2012.

Sharp, Lindsay. Walter Charleton's Early Life, 1620–1659, and Relationship to Natural Philosophy in Mid-Seventeenth Century England. *Annals of Science* 30 (1973): 311–40.

Sharpe, Richard. The English Bibliographical Tradition from Kirkestede to Tanner, in *Britannia Latina*, ed. C. S. F. Burnett and C. N. J. Mann. London: Warburg Institute, 2005, 86–128.

Silcox-Crowe, Nigel. Sir Roger Pratt, 1620–1685: The Ingenious Gentleman Architect, in *The Architectural Outsiders*, ed. Roderick Brown. London: Waterstone, 1985, 1–20.

Soo, Lydia M. Reconstructing Antiquity: Wren and His Circle and the Study of Natural History, Antiquarianism, and Architecture at the Royal Society. Princeton University PhD Thesis, 1989.

Stroumsa, Guy G. *A New Science: The Discovery of Religion in the Age of Reason*. Cambridge, MA, and London: Harvard University Press, 2010.

Subbiondo, Joseph L. William Holder's *Elements of Speech* (1669): A Study of Applied English Phonetics and Speech Therapy. *Lingua* 46 (1978): 169–84.

Sullivan, J. P. *Martial, the Unexpected Classic: A Literary and Historical Study.* Cambridge: Cambridge University Press, 1991.

Sweet, Rosemary. *Antiquaries: the Discovery of the Past in Eighteenth-Century Britain.* London: Hambledon and London, 2004.

Tait, A. A. Inigo Jones's 'Stone-Heng'. *Burlington Magazine* 120 (1978): 155–9.

Thrush, Andrew, ed. *The History of Parliament: The House of Commons, 1604–1629,* 6 vols. Cambridge: Published for the History of Parliament Trust by Cambridge University Press, 2010.

Toomer, Gerald J. *Eastern Wisedome and Learning: the Study of Arabic in Seventeenth-Century England.* Oxford: Clarendon Press, 1996.

Toomer, Gerald J. *John Selden: A Life in Scholarship,* 2 vols. Oxford: Oxford University Press, 2009.

Ucko, Peter J., Michael Hunter, Alan J. Clark, and Andrew David. *Avebury Reconsidered: From the 1660s to the 1900s.* London: Unwin Hyman, 1991.

Van Hal, Toon. A Man of Eight Hearts: Hadrianus Junius and Sixteenth-Century Plurilingualism, in *The Kaleidoscopic Scholarship of Hadrianus Junius (1511–1575): Northern Humanism at the Dawn of the Dutch Golden Age,* ed. Dirk van Miert. Leiden: Brill, 2011, 188–213.

Van Hal, Toon. When Quotation Marks Matter: Rhellicanus and Boxhornius on the Differences between the *lingua Gallica* and the *lingua Germanica. Historiographia Linguistica* 38 (2011): 241–52.

Venn, John, and J. A. Venn. *Alumni Cantabrigienses,* 2 pts. in 10 vols. Cambridge: Cambridge University Press, 1922–54.

Vidal-Naquet, Pierre. Hérodote et l'Atlantide: Entre les Grecs et les Juifs: Réflexions sur l'historiographie du siècle des lumières. *Quaderni di Storia* 16 (1982): 3–76.

Vidal-Naquet, Pierre, and Janet Lloyd. Atlantis and the Nations. *Critical Inquiry* 18 (1992): 300–26.

Vine, Angus. Etymology, Names and the Search for Origins: Deriving the Past in Early Modern England. *The Seventeenth Century* 21 (2006): 1–21.

Vine, Angus. *In Defiance of Time: Antiquarian Writing in Early Modern England.* Oxford: Oxford University Press, 2010.

Walsham, Alexandra. Recording Superstitions in Early Modern Britain: The Origins of Folklore. *Past and Present* 51 (2008): 178–206.

Walsham, Alexandra. *The Reformation of the Landscape: Religion, Identity, and Memory in Early Modern Britain and Ireland.* Oxford: Oxford University Press, 2011.

Williams, Richard. *Montgomeryshire Worthies,* 2nd edn. Newtown: Phillips & Son, 1894.

Wood, Christopher S. *Forgery, Replica, Fiction: Temporalities of German Renaissance Art.* Chicago: University of Chicago Press, 2008.

Woolf, Daniel. *The Social Circulation of the Past: English Historical Culture, 1500–1730.* Oxford: Oxford University Press, 2003.

Worsley, Giles. *Inigo Jones and the European Classicist Tradition*. New Haven, CT: Yale University Press, 2006.

Wragge-Morley, Alexander. Restitution, Description, and Knowledge in English Architecture and Natural Philosophy, 1650–1750. *Architecture Research Quarterly* 14 (2010): 247–54.

Zwicker, Steven N. Considering the Ancients: Dryden and the Uses of Biography, in *Writing Lives: Biography and Textuality, Identity and Representation in Early Modern England*, ed. Kevin Sharpe and Steven N. Zwicker. Oxford: Oxford University Press, 2008, 105–24.

Index